IRON MAN

IRON MAN

My Journey Through Heaven and Hell
with Black Sabbath

TONY IOMMI

With T. J. Lammers

DA CAPO PRESS
A Member of the Perseus Books Group

Picture Credits
Courtesy of the author: 1–15, 17–20, 23–30, 32–34
© Kees Baars: 16
© Ross Halfin: 21, 22, 35, 36
© Jas Sansi: 31

Cataloging-in-Publication data for this book is available from the Library of Congress.

First Da Capo Press edition 2011
First Da Capo Press paperback edition 2012
Reprinted by arrangement with Simon & Schuster UK
ISBN 978-0-306-81955-1 (hardcover)
ISBN 978-0-306-82054-0 (hardcover e-book)
ISBN 978-0-306-82145-5 (paperback)
ISBN 978-0-306-82231-5 (paperback e-book)
Library of Congress Control Number: 2011937165

Published by Da Capo Press
A Member of the Perseus Books Group
www.dacapopress.com

Da Capo Press books are available at special discounts for bulk purchases in the U.S. by
corporations, institutions, and other organizations. For more information, please contact the
Special Markets Department at the Perseus Books Group, 2300 Chestnut Street, Suite 200,
Philadelphia, PA 19103, or call (800) 810-4145, ext. 5000, or e-mail
special.markets@perseusbooks.com.

10 9 8 7 6 5 4 3 2 1

I dedicate this book to Maria; my wife and soulmate.

*My daughter Toni, for being the best daughter
any man could ever have.*

My late Mom and Dad, for giving me life.

Contents

Contents

Introduction:

The Sound of Heavy Metal

It was 1965, I was seventeen years old, and it was my very last day on the job. I'd done all sorts of things since leaving school at fifteen. I worked as a plumber for three or four days. Then I packed that in. I worked as a treadmiller, making rings with a screw that you put around rubber pipes to close them up, but that cut up my hands. I got a job in a music shop, because I was a guitarist and played in local bands, but they accused me of stealing. I didn't do it, but to hell with them: they had me cleaning the storeroom all day anyway. I was working as a welder at a sheet-metal factory when I got my big break: my new band, The Birds & The Bees, were booked for a tour of Europe. I hadn't actually played live with The Birds & The Bees, mind you; I'd just auditioned after my previous band, The Rockin' Chevrolets, had hoofed out their rhythm guitarist and subsequently broken up. The Rockin' Chevrolets had been my first break. We wore matching red lamé suits and played old rock 'n' roll like Chuck Berry and Buddy Holly. We were popular around my hometown of Birmingham, and played regular gigs. I even got my first serious girlfriend out of that band, Margareth Meredith, the sister of the original guitarist.

The Rockin' Chevrolets were fun, but playing in Europe with

The Birds & The Bees, that was a real professional turn. So I went home for lunch on Friday, my last day as a welder, and said to my mum: 'I'm not going back. I'm finished with that job.'

But she insisted: 'Iommis don't quit. You want to go back and finish the day off, finish it proper!'

So I did. I went back to work. There was a lady next to me on the line who bent pieces of metal on a machine, then sent the pieces down to me to weld together. That was my job. But the woman didn't come in that day, so they put me on her machine. It was a big guillotine press with a wobbly foot pedal. You'd pull a sheet of metal in and put your foot on the pedal and, bang, a giant industrial press would slam down and bend the metal.

I'd never used the thing before, but things went all right until I lost concentration for a moment, maybe dreaming about being on stage in Europe and, bang, the press slammed straight down on my right hand. I pulled my hand back as a reflex and the bloody press pulled the ends off my two middle fingers. I looked down and the bones were sticking out. Then I just saw blood going everywhere.

They took me to hospital, sat me down, put my hand in a bag and forgot about me. I thought I'd bleed to death. When someone thoughtfully brought my fingertips to hospital (in a matchbox) the doctors tried to graft them back on. But it was too late: they'd turned black. So instead they took skin from one of my arms and grafted it on to the tips of my wounded fingers. They fiddled around a bit more to try to ensure the skin graft would take, and that was it: rock 'n' roll history was made.

Or that's what some people say, anyway. They credit the loss of my fingers with the deeper, down-tuned sound of Black Sabbath, which in turn became the template for most of the heavy music created since. I admit, it hurt like hell to play guitar straight on the bones of my severed fingers, and I had to reinvent my style of playing to accommodate the pain. In the process, Black Sabbath started to sound like no band before it – or since, really. But creating heavy metal because of my fingers? Well, that's too bloody much.

After all, there's a lot more to the story than that.

1

The birth of a Cub

Of course, I wasn't born into heavy metal. As a matter of fact, in my first years I preferred ice cream – because at the time my parents lived over my grandfather's ice cream shop: Iommi's Ices. My grandfather and his wife, who I called Papa and Nan, had moved from Italy to England, looking for a better future by opening an ice cream business over here. It was probably a little factory, but to me it was huge, all these big stainless steel barrels in which the ice cream was being churned. It was great. I could just go in and help myself. I've never tasted anything that good since.

I was born on Thursday 19 February 1948 in Heathfield Road Hospital, just outside Birmingham city centre, the only child of Anthony Frank and Sylvie Maria Iommi, née Valenti. My mother had been in hospital for two months with toxaemia before I appeared; was this a sign of things to come she might have felt! Mum was born in Palermo, in Italy, one of three children, to a family of vineyard owners. I never knew my mum's mother. Her father used to come to the house once a week, but when you're young you don't hang around sitting there with the old folks, so I never knew him that well.

Papa on the other hand was very good natured and generous

and as well as giving money to help the local kids he'd always hand me half a crown when I came to see him. And some ice cream. And salami. And pasta. So you can imagine I loved visiting him. He was also very religious. He went to church all the time and he sent flowers and supplies over there every week.

I think my nan was from Brazil. My father was born here. He had five brothers and two sisters. My parents were Catholic, but I've only seen them go to church once or twice. It's strange that my dad wasn't as religious as his father, but he was probably like me. I hardly ever go to church either. I wouldn't even know what to do there. I actually do believe in a God, but I don't go to church to press the point.

My parents worked in a shop that Papa had given them as a wedding present, in Cardigan Street in Birmingham's Italian quarter. As well as the ice-cream factory, Papa owned other shops and he used to have a fleet of mobile baking machines. They'd go into town, set up and sell baked potatoes and chestnuts, whatever was in season. My dad was also a carpenter and a very good one at that; he made all our furniture.

When I was about five or six we moved away from ice-cream heaven to a place in Bennetts Road, in an area called Washwood Heath, which is part of Saltley, which in turn is a part of Birmingham. We had a tiny living room with a staircase going up to the bedroom. One of my earliest memories is of my mother carrying me down these steep stairs. She slipped and I went flying and, of course, landed on my head. That's probably why I am like I am . . .

I was always playing with my lead soldiers. I had a set of those and little tanks and so on. As a carpenter my dad was away a lot, building Cheltenham Racecourse. Whenever he came back home he'd bring me something, like a vehicle, adding to the collection.

When I was a kid I was always frightened of things, so I'd get under the blanket and shine a little light. Like a lot of kids do. My daughter was the same. Just like me, she couldn't sleep without the light on, and we'd have to keep her bedroom door open. Like father, like daughter.

One of the reasons I grew a moustache in later years was because of what happened to me in Bennetts Road one day. There was a guy up the road who used to collect great big spiders. I don't mind them now, but I was very much afraid of them then. I was eight or nine at the time. This guy was called Bobby Nuisance, which is the right name for him, and he chased me with one of his spiders once. I was shitting myself and running down this gravel road when I tripped, so all the gravel went into my face and along my lip. The scar is still there now. The kids even started calling me Scarface, so I got a terrible complex about that.

I did have another scar there as well, because not long after the spider thing somebody threw a firework, one of those sparklers, and it went straight up my face. Over the years the scars disappeared, but the one on my lip still stuck out when I was young, so as soon as I could I grew a moustache.

Still living in Bennetts Road I joined the Cubs. It's like the Scouts. The idea was that you'd go on trips, but my parents didn't want me to go away. They were very protective of me. Also these trips cost money and we didn't have that; they earned a pittance in those days. I did wear a Cubs uniform: little shorts and the little thing over the socks, a cap and a tie. So I looked like a younger version of Angus Young.

With scars.

2

It's the Italian thing

I did get some emotional scars as well. I know Dad didn't want me, I was an accident. I even heard him say this in one of his screaming moods: 'I never wanted you anyway!'

And there was a lot of screaming, because my parents used to fight a lot. He'd lose his temper and Mum'd lose hers, because with him the Italian thing would come out and she was very wild anyway and she'd go potty. They'd grab each other's hair and really seriously fight. When we lived in Bennetts Road I actually saw my mother hit Dad with a bottle and him grabbing her hand trying to defend himself. It was bloody awful, but the next day they'd be talking away like nothing had happened. Really peculiar.

I remember them fighting with the next-door neighbours as well. Mum was in the backyard and there was a wooden fence between us and the neighbours. Apparently one of them said something bad about our family and mother went into a rage. I looked out of my bedroom window and I saw her hanging over the fence hitting the neighbour lady over the head with a broom. And then Dad got involved and so did the woman's husband and it was a fight over the fence until the fence came down. I saw them screaming and shouting and hitting each other and I just stood there, looking out of my first-floor window, crying.

If I did anything wrong I would cop the brunt of it as well. I was frightened to do anything, always afraid of getting beaten up. But that's how it was in those days. It happened with a lot of families, people fighting and getting hit. It probably still is that way. Dad and me didn't get on that well when I was young. I was the kid who was never going to do any good. It was always: 'Oh, you haven't got a job like so-and-so has got. He is going to be an accountant and what are you going to do?'

I was belittled by him all the time, and then Mum joined in as well: 'Yeah, he's got to get a bloody job or he's out!'

It is one of the reasons I wanted to be successful, if only to show them.

Growing up and getting older, there came a point where I would not accept getting clipped around the earhole any more. One time I was on the couch and Dad was hitting me, and I grabbed his hands and stopped him. He went mad, almost to the point of crying: 'You don't do that to me!'

That was awful. But he never hit me again.

I must have been nine or ten when I saw my grandfather die. He was at home, very ill, when he went unconscious. He was in bed and my job was to watch him to see if he came round. I'd sit there, mopping his face, and Dad would pop in now and again. But I was alone with him when he got the 'death rattle'. He made this choking, gurgling sound and then he died. I felt really sad but it was also frightening. I saw the family coming in and out and they all seemed a bit afraid as well.

I've seen one or two people die since then. About twenty-five years ago this old lady, very well dressed and very well spoken, lived across the road from me. She went by a nickname, Bud; even her daughter called her that. I went over there once a week to see her and then she'd say: 'Oh, you know, let's have a brandy.'

One day her daughter came rushing over to my house, scream-ing: 'Quick, come over, come over!'

I went over and found Bud passed out on the floor. I lifted her up a bit, took her in my arms and I shouted: 'Call an ambulance!'

Her daughter ran off, and at that moment Bud died, right there in my arms. It was the same thing: the choking, gurgling sound and . . . bang. As soon as that happened, it brought me immedi-ately back to my grandfather.

I sat there with her until the ambulance showed up. After that I could smell her perfume everywhere and I could never smell that perfume again. For me it had turned into the smell of death.

3

The shop on Park Lane

When I was about ten we moved to Park Lane in Aston. It was an awful, gang-infested, rough part of Birmingham. My parents bought a sweet shop there, but soon they also sold fruit and vegetables, firewood, canned foods, all sorts of stuff. We'd get people knocking on our door in the middle of the night: 'Can we buy some cigarettes?'

With a shop like that, you basically never closed.

The shop had everything people needed, but it also turned into a meeting place. Some of the neighbours would always be on the step, gossiping away: 'Have you seen so-and-so down the road, ooh, she's wearing a new ...'

Et cetera. Sometimes they wouldn't even buy anything and stand there for hours, talking. And Mum would be behind the counter, listening.

My mother ran the shop, because Dad worked at the Midlands County Dairy, loading the trucks with milk. He needed to do that to supplement the family income, but I also think he did it because there he was around people he liked. Later on he bought a second shop in Victoria Road, also in Aston, where he started selling fruit and vegetables.

My parents liked Aston, but I didn't. I hated living in the shop because it was damp and cold. It was only a two-bedroom house, with the lounge downstairs, a kitchen and then, outside in the backyard, the toilet. You couldn't bring friends there, because our living room doubled as the stockroom: it was filled with beans and peas and all the tinned stuff. That's how we lived. You were surrounded by bloody boxes and shit all the time.

In our neighbourhood we were the first to have a telephone, a great luxury in those days, but where the thing was all depended on whether we'd had a delivery. It was either down here on top of a box, or if we'd had a lot of supplies it would be up there somewhere.

'Where's the phone?'

'Oh, it's up there.'

It was just a very small room. We had a couch and a telly, and behind this it was all beans and tins of fruit and everything.

And the phone.

Somewhere.

I did have my own room until I was forced to share it with Frankie. He was a lodger, but my parents treated him like a son. It was very strange to me when he first came into the house, because they said: 'Well, this is going to be your new . . . brother. Frankie is going to be like a brother to you.'

It was really peculiar. It was like somebody was coming in and taking over, because they gave him more attention than me and I resented that. I must have been about eleven at the time and he was about three or four years older. I liked him because he used to buy me stuff, but at the same time I didn't because I had to share my room with him. He lived with us for years and years. And it was me who finally got rid of him.

At the time I was maybe seventeen, but I knew more about girls than Frankie did, because he just stayed at home all the time. When he came with me to one of my gigs, I introduced him to this girl. I didn't expect him to get carried away like he did, but he was completely taken over with her. To him, finally meeting somebody was like . . . 'Ahhh!'

Dad wasn't pleased. He said: 'She's the wrong type of woman!'

But Frankie started staying over at her house and then, of course, Dad would really get the needle about him. As I basically stirred it all up by introducing them to each other, I got the blame. Half of me thought, great, we'll be able to get rid of him now, and the other half felt sorry for him.

Eventually he moved in with her. Maybe Dad went a little too far and Frankie left on bad terms. He didn't stay in touch with my family. He went and that was it.

Never seen him since.

4

The school of hard knocks

I went to the Birchfield Road School, a 'secondary modern school' as it was called. You went there from about the age of ten onwards, until you were fifteen years old, and then you left. The school was about four miles from our house. There was a bus that went there, but it was often full. And it cost a penny, so I saved that by walking.

I met my oldest friend, Albert, at that school. And Ozzy, who was a year behind us. Albert lived close to Birchfield Road. I regularly went over to his place for lunch and of course he came down to my house occasionally. That was about the extent of my social life in those early years, because I didn't go out that much. My parents wouldn't allow it. They were fairly strict and overprotective, and they were convinced I was going to do something wrong if I did go out: 'Don't you go bringing any trouble back here!'

So I was stuck in my room most of the time. And to this day it doesn't bother me to be alone. I like to be with people but it doesn't bother me if I'm not.

My parents did have some cause for concern. Our shop looked out on three or four 'terraced houses' – which means they were all stuck together – across the road, but next to those was a big space full of nothing but rubble. Whether it was a Second World War bomb that had caused that I don't know; it might just have been a house that had been knocked down, but we called it the 'bombed buildings'. It was that area where the gangs congregated. You could be walking down the road and get the shit kicked out of you or even stabbed by these gangs. And if you walked a lot, like I did, you were a prime target. So I started exercising, doing weights and stuff, because I wanted to be able to protect myself. I started going to judo and karate and finally I got into boxing. I did it initially because I didn't want to be picked on, but I really got into it.

At school Albert and me had our own little gang, just the two of us. We had these leather jackets with the words 'The Commanchies' written on the back. That was us: The Commanchies. The school tried to stop us wearing those jackets, but I didn't have any other clothes. Not that I would have wanted to wear it anyway, but my parents simply couldn't afford to buy me a bloody school uniform. All I had was a pair of jeans and that leather jacket.

With me working out and Albert being a big guy as well, we became cocks of the walk at school. Nobody messed with us, because they knew that we'd beat them up. Even the older kids left us alone. That school was totally functioning on violence. People had been stabbed there and I even carried a knife for a bit. It's not that I liked violence; it's just how you lived in those days. At school, if you didn't get one in first someone would get you. That's why I ended up fighting all the bloody time.

Where we had the shop there was the Aston gang, and they wanted me to join. I was around twelve or thirteen at the time. I went over to their bombed building site a couple of times, but I just didn't associate with the gang in the end. A couple of them nicked things from our shop, so it didn't make sense to hook up with them. I even caught one of these gang members thieving in the shop one day and I ran out to clobber him. He only lived a couple of doors away. He ran into his house and here I was, kicking his front door trying to get in. That's how you handled these people, with violence. Because you couldn't talk to them.

The gang could have turned on me, but it wasn't that bad because I lived in their area. All they were on about anyway was fighting this other gang from another neighbourhood close by. Because of where I lived, this other gang looked on me as belonging to the Aston gang; I wasn't part of it, but on the other hand I sort of was.

A few years later I had to walk through this other neighbourhood to get to work. I used to pass this one guy who was the leader of this gang. In the morning he'd be normal, but coming back at night, when he had all his mates around him, he'd be a different kettle of fish. The trick was to get through before anybody came out and saw you; it was like the cannonball run. One night I didn't make it and got the beating of a lifetime. You had either to defend yourself or join them, and I didn't want to join them.

I thought my thing would be something to do with boxing; I would probably become a bouncer in a club or something. And I used to get these dreams where I'd be on stage looking out at the crowds. I never quite knew what it was; I always thought it might be fighting, doing some contact sport in front of an audience. Of course, eventually I lived it and saw it and I realised, these are those dreams I was having. But it's playing the guitar!

As I had no interest in school, my grades weren't particularly good. Whenever they called my parents into school, my mother would come home afterwards and scold me: 'Oh, it's disgusting, disgraceful. What have you been up to now?'

I wasn't too bothered about what the teachers and the headmaster thought of me, but I was concerned about how my parents would react. They hated it if you got in trouble. They would worry about what the neighbours would think. People talked. In the shop it would be: 'Ooh, have you heard what happened to so-and-so down the road? Ooh, the police were around there at their house the other day . . .'

It was all gossip. Outside their own road they didn't know what was going on, but they would know everything about each other. So if your grades were bad, everybody would know about it.

At school they used to separate Albert and me because we were a nuisance. We'd either be flicking something at somebody or talking or whatever, so we were often ejected from class. You'd have to stand outside the classroom until the lessons finished, and if they sent us both out they'd have me stand in one place and Albert somewhere else. If the headmaster came around and saw you, you could get caned. Or you had to stay over late, an hour after school, which seemed like an eternity.

The headmaster either caned you on your hand or he made you bend over and he'd cane you on the backside with a stick or a slipper. One of the teachers even used a big compass. Of course kids put books down their trousers, so they'd check you first. It was called 'six of the best', which meant six strokes with this cane. They were nice enough to give you a choice: 'Where do you want it, on your backside or on your hand?'

The teachers who would administer this punishment had to log it in the black book. Every time you got caught again, they'd look in the book: 'You were around here only two days ago!'

I don't remember many of the teachers. Mr Low taught music. I didn't really learn anything from him, because at school the idea of 'music' was playing the recorder. That's all we had, playing those bloody things. And there was Mr Williams, the maths teacher. Funny I should remember him because it was the one lesson I was never in. I hated maths and I used to get bored shitless, so I'd get sent out. Sometimes I wouldn't even do anything, I'd walk in and it was straight away: 'Out!'

Mad, really. But that's what happened and that's the way they did it.

5

Out of The Shadows, into the limelight

Dad and all his brothers played the accordion, so they were quite a musical family. What I really wanted was a set of drums. I obviously had no room to put them in and certainly wouldn't be able to play them in the house, so it was the accordion or nothing. I started playing it when I was about ten years old. I still have a picture of me as a kid in our backyard, holding my bloody accordion.

We had a gramophone at home, or a 'radiogram', as it was called. It was a unit with a record player on it, and two speakers. And I used to have a little radio. Because I was in my room a lot, it was either listen to that or what do I do? Can't go and sit in the lounge, because we don't have one. I'd listen to the Top 20 or Radio Luxembourg. That's where my love of music originated, sitting in my room and listening to great instrumental guitar bands like The Shadows on my little radio. It made me want to play the guitar as well. I really loved that sound, it was instrumental stuff and I knew: this is what I want to do. So eventually my mother bought me a guitar. She was very good that way. She worked hard and saved up for it. Being left-handed, you were limited to what you could get, certainly in those days: 'A left-handed guitar, what's that?'

There was this electric Watkins Rapier that I saw in a catalogue. It cost something like £20, and Mum paid it off in weekly instalments. My left-handed Watkins had two pick-ups and a couple of little chrome selector switches that you'd push, and it came with a little Watkins Westminster amp. I stole one of the speakers from our radiogram and put it in that amp, which didn't go down very well. But it hardly mattered, because my parents didn't play music that much anyway.

So there I was, with my first little kit, playing away in my room. I'd listen to the Top 20 and wait for The Shadows to come on to tape them with a microphone on this old reel to reel, so I could try and learn their songs. Later I'd get the album and learn the songs from playing that over and over. I've always liked going back to The Shadows, as I like melodies and tunes. And I've always tried to make my guitar-playing melodic, as music is all about melody. Me trying to do that comes from those very early days. That stayed with me; it has always been a part of my songwriting.

I liked The Beatles, but The Shadows and Cliff Richard were more based on the rock 'n' roll stuff than The Beatles, so they were more my thing. Of course I liked Elvis as well, but not as much as Cliff and The Shadows. They were it for me. Cliff was bigger in England than Elvis was, and that might have had something to do with it. I've met Cliff a few times, but I never said to him: 'Oh, I was a big fan of yours.'

After school I'd sit upstairs and play my guitar for a couple of hours. I really took to the guitar and practised as much as I could, but bands weren't immediately knocking on the door asking me to join. That's why my first venture was with Albert. He was going to be the singer and I would take care of the music. He couldn't sing, but he thought he could. His house was rather posh: it had two living rooms. We'd be in the front room with me and my amp playing away and him singing, and you'd always hear his dad shouting from the other room: 'Shut that bloody row up! Can't you go somewhere else?'

We only knew one song, which we played over and over: 'Jezebel' by Frankie Laine. We must have been twelve or thirteen years old then, and Albert used to wail: 'If ever the devil was born, without a pair of horns, it was you, Jezebel, it was you.'

So that's really what started it all.

After that I hooked up with this piano player and his drummer. They were a lot older than me and they asked me if I'd play with them in this pub. I couldn't really play very well, but they thought I was great. I only did that a couple of times. I was incredibly nervous sitting in with these guys, but it was just something I would do then.

'Blimey, a gig! In a pub!'

I wasn't even old enough to be in a pub, but those were the first gigs I ever did.

Ron and Joan Woodward lived a couple of doors away from our shop. Ron visited us a lot. Him and Dad would be chatting and smoking away just about every night. He spent more time at our house than at his, and he became like another adopted son. He was probably ten or fifteen years older than me, but somehow I became friends with him. I talked him into buying a bass guitar. He started to learn to play it and we actually did a couple of little gigs. And everybody was going: 'Well, he's a bit old, isn't he?'

I'd just say: 'He's my mate and he wants to be in the band.'

That's how it was then; your mate would be in your band.

'Can he play?'

'Oh no, he can't play but he's my mate!'

We had a rhythm guitarist and a drummer playing with us. We rehearsed about three times a week at this youth club. It was great. From piddling around by yourself in your room to playing music with other people was a fantastic experience. Nigel, the rhythm guitarist, was a bit cocky. One day he was singing and the mic suddenly stuck to him, because it wasn't earthed. He went rolling around on the floor and got a bad electric shock. Because nobody liked him, we all thought, it serves you right. But in the end we did unplug him, so he survived. As a matter of fact, he was right as rain afterwards, better than ever in fact. It was like it had done him good. But he didn't last that long, and neither did that band.

I couldn't wait to leave school. I didn't like it, and I don't think it liked me very much either. Everybody left school at fifteen, unless you stayed on and went to a college. Fifteen and that was it, you were out. And so was I. It was a great relief. I started looking for a job and I applied myself to playing the guitar even more.

Because I practised all the time, I was getting much better than people like Ron Woodward, so I joined this other band which I thought was very good, The Rockin' Chevrolets. It must have been around 1964 so I was sixteen or so. To my mind they were really professional. They could play all The Shadows' songs perfectly and, because a couple of the guys were older than me, they also did a lot of rock 'n' roll. I'd never been a big fan of Chuck Berry, Gene Vincent or Buddy Holly, but I now got into that music as well.

The singer, Neil Morris, was the oldest guy in the band. There was a chap on bass called Dave Whaddley, the drummer was called Pat Pegg and the rhythm guitar player was Alan Meredith. That's when I met Alan's sister, Margareth. We were engaged to be married, actually. Our relationship would last a lot longer than The Chevrolets did.

I don't remember how I got into this band. I probably saw an advert in a music shop window. That was your life; you'd hang around a music shop or you'd go to see another band playing and you'd meet people through that.

My parents were wary of me playing with this band in pubs. I even had to be home at a certain time, but after a little while they were okay with it, also because I brought some money in. The

Rockin' Chevrolets made things easier for me as well by meeting Mum first. They came down and she made them bacon sandwiches. As she did in later years with Black Sabbath, the same thing: she'd always ask them if they wanted something to eat. Always. That's the sort of mother she was.

The Rockin' Chevrolets started getting a lot of work. We all had the same red lamé suits, so we wore those at every gig. I didn't really have any money to spend on a suit, but you had to look the part. At the weekend we played in pubs. One pub was in a bad part of Birmingham and every bloody time we played there'd be a fight. We provided the soundtrack to their fighting. We also played the odd wedding, or we'd end up in a bloody social club playing to people twice our age who would go: 'Ooh, you're too loud!'

Because things were getting more serious, I wanted a better guitar. Burns was one of the few companies that made left-handed guitars, so I bought me one of those, a Burns Trisonic. It had a control on it with the 'trisonic sound', whatever that was. I only played it until I eventually found a left-handed Fender Stratocaster. And I had a Selmer amp, with an echo in it.

The Rockin' Chevrolets broke up because they kicked out Alan Meredith. My next big band was going to be The Birds & The Bees. I auditioned for them and got the job. They were professional, worked a lot and were even due to go to Europe. I decided to really go for it, quit my job and become a professional musician. I was working as a welder in a factory at the time. I went to work on the Friday morning, my last day at the job, and at lunchtime I told Mum I wasn't going back for the afternoon shift. But she told me I had to, and to finish the job properly.

So I did. I went back to work.

And then my whole world fell apart.

6

Why don't you just give
me the finger?

So, as I said, it was my very last day at work. There was this lady who bent pieces of metal on a machine, and I then welded them together. Because she didn't come in that day, they put me on her machine; otherwise I'd have been standing around with nothing to do. I had never worked it, so I didn't know how to go about it. It was a big guillotine press with a foot pedal. You pulled this sheet in and put your foot down on the pedal and then this thing came down with a bang and bent the metal.

Things went all right in the morning. After I came back from my lunch break, I pushed the pedal and the press came straight down on my right hand. As I pulled my hand back as a reflex I pulled the ends of my fingers off. Stretch your hand out then line up your index finger and your little finger and draw a line between the tops of them: it's the bits sticking out from the two fingers in the middle that got chopped off. The bones were sticking out of them. I just couldn't believe it. There was blood everywhere. I was so much in shock it didn't even hurt at first.

They took me to hospital, and instead of doing something to

stop the bleeding they put my hand in a bag. It quickly filled up and I thought, when am I going to get some help, I'm bleeding to death here!

A little later somebody brought the missing bits to the hospital, in a matchbox. They were all black, completely ruined, so they couldn't put them back on. Eventually they cut skin from my arm and put it over the tips of my injured fingers. The nails had come straight off. They put a bit of beard back in one of them so that the nail would grow, they skin-grafted it and that was it.

Then I just sat at home moping. I thought, that's it, it's over with! I couldn't believe my luck. I had just joined a great band, it was my very last day at work and I was crippled for life. The manager of the factory came to see me a few times, an older, balding man with a thin moustache called Brian. He saw that I was really depressed, so one day he gave me this EP and said: 'Put this on.'

I was going: 'No, I don't really want to.'

Having to listen to music was certainly not going to cheer me up at that point.

He said: 'Well, I think you should, because I'll tell you a story. This guy plays guitar and he only plays with two fingers.'

It was the great Belgian-born gypsy jazz guitarist Django Reinhardt and, bloody hell, it was brilliant! I thought, if he's done it I can have a go at it as well. It was absolutely great of Brian to be thoughtful enough to buy me this. Without him I don't know what would have happened. Once I heard that music, I was determined to do something about it instead of sitting there moping.

I still had bandages on my fingers and so I tried playing with just my index finger and my little finger. It was very frustrating, because once you've played well it's hard to go backwards. Probably the easiest thing would have been to flip the guitar upside down and learn to play right-handed instead of left-handed. I wish I had in hindsight, but I thought, well, I've been playing for a few years already, it's going to take me another few years to learn it that way. That seemed like a very long time, so I was determined to keep playing left-handed. I persevered with two bandaged-up fingers, even though the doctors said: 'The best thing for you to do is to pack up, really. Get another job, do something else.'

But I thought, bloody hell, there has got to be something I can do.

After thinking things through for a while, I wondered whether I could make a cap to fit over my fingers. I got a Fairy Liquid bottle, melted it down, shaped it into a ball and waited until it cooled down. I then made a hole in it with a soldering iron until it sort of fitted over the finger. I shaped it a bit more with a knife and then I got some sandpaper and sat there for hours sandpapering it down to make it into a kind of thimble. I put it on one of my fingers and tried to play the guitar with it, but it didn't feel right. Because it was plastic it kept slipping off the string and I could barely touch it, it was so painful. So I tried to think of something I could put over it. I tried a piece of cloth, but of course it tore. I used different pieces of leather, which also didn't work. Then I found this old jacket of mine and cut a piece of leather off it. It was old leather, so it was a bit tougher. I cut it into a shape so that it would fit over the thimble and glued it on, left it to dry and then I tried it and I thought, bloody hell, I can actually touch the string with this now! I sanded down the leather a bit too, but then I had to rub it on to a hard surface to make it shiny so it wouldn't grip too much. It had to be just right so you could move it up and down the string.

Even with the thimbles on it hurt. If you look at my middle index finger, you will see a little bump on the end of it. Just underneath it is the bone. I have to be careful because sometimes if the thimbles come off and if I push hard on a string, the skin on the tips of my fingers just splits right open. The first ones I made fell off all the time. And it is trouble then; one of the roadies crawling about the stage, going: 'Where the hell has that gone?'

So when I go on stage I put surgical tape around my fingers, dab a little bit of Superglue on that and then I push the things on. And at the end of the day I have to pull them off again.

I've only lost the thimbles a couple of times. I virtually live with the bloody things when I'm on tour. I keep them with me all the time. I've always got a spare set and my guitar tech has one as well.

Going through customs with these things is another story. I have the thimbles in a box and they search your bag and go: 'Ah well, what's this? Drugs?'

And then, shock, it's fingers. I've had to explain it to customs on several occasions. And they go: 'Whoah.'

Putting my fake fingers away in disgust.

Nowadays the people at the hospital make the thimble for my ring finger. They actually make me a prosthetic limb, a complete arm, and all I use is two of its fingertips that I cut off it. I asked: 'Why don't you just do me a finger?'

'No, it's easier for us to give you a whole arm.'

So you can imagine what the dustman thinks when he finds an arm in the bin. The thimbles I cut off it look like real fingers; there's no leather on the ring finger one, I can play with the material it's made of. They are too soft sometimes, so I leave them out in the air for a while to harden, or I put a bit of Superglue on them to give them the right feel again. Otherwise they grip the string too much. It's a process that takes ages.

The home-made thimbles used to wear down, but these days the casing lasts; it's only the leather that wears out. Each thimble probably lasts a month, maybe half a tour, and when they start wearing out I have to go through the whole thing again. I still use the same piece of jacket I started with all those forty-odd years ago. There isn't much of it left now, but it should last another few years.

It's primitive, but it works. You've either got to pack it in, or you've got to fight and work with it. It takes a lot of work. Making them is one stage, but trying to play with them is another. Because you have no feeling. You're aware of this lump on your fingers, so you really have to practise at it to get it to work for you.

Part of my sound comes from learning to play primarily with my two good fingers, the index and the little finger. I'll lay chords like that and then I put vibrato on them. I use the chopped off fingers mostly for soloing. When I bend strings I bend them with my index finger and I learned to bend them with my little finger. I can only bend them with the other fingers to a lesser extent. Before the accident I didn't use the little finger at all, so I had to learn to use it. I'm limited because even with the thimbles there are certain chords I will never be able to play. Where I used to play a full chord before the accident, I often can't do them now, so I compensate by making it sound fuller. For instance, I'll hit the E chord and the E note and put vibrato on it to make it sound bigger, so it's making up for that full sound that I would be able to play if I still had full use of all the fingers. That's how I developed a style of playing that suits my physical limitations. It's an unorthodox style but it works for me.

7

A career hanging off an
extra thin string

Since I had my accident, I've had to rethink the whole thing, from the thimbles to how I play to the guitar itself. I can't pick up any guitar and start playing it; it has to have the right strings and has to have the right weight of strings. I had all these problems from day one. And it was worse then, because at the time there were no companies making light gauge strings. There were no companies you could find to work on a guitar either, so I had to do it all myself.

I was still playing a Fender Stratocaster at the time. I took that guitar apart countless times, trying to make it comfortable, filing the frets down, getting the strings to the right height. As opposed to normal people who still have the ends of their fingers, I can't feel how hard I'm pressing down on my string very well. I tend to really press hard, because if I don't the string will just flick off. I needed very thin strings, because bending thick strings was too hard for me.

The lightest gauge strings you had at the time were eleven or twelve; they were heavy because it was still in the style of the

popular *Play in a Day* guitar tutor Bert Weedon's thick strings.
That's what everybody had. They only made one set of strings, one
certain gauge. I was the first to come up with the idea of making
light strings, simply because I had to find a way to make the guitar
easier for me to play. The heavy strings would just rip the leather
off, I wouldn't have the strength in my fingers to bend the strings,
and it would hurt. The people in the music shops would say: 'You
can't get any lighter. These are it.'

And I would say: 'Well, are there any other strings that are thin-
ner?'

'No, apart from banjo strings.'

'Give me some of those then.'

I used the two lightest banjo strings as the B and the high E
strings on my guitar, which meant I could drop down the gauge
on the remaining guitar strings to make them lighter. This way I
managed to get rid of the thick low E string, using an A string
instead. And that worked for me. Out of necessity I had invented
the light gauge strings, combining banjo and guitar strings.

It was trial and error tuning the guitar, because if you tune an A
down to E, the string tends to rattle on the frets. It was an art
tuning it, and it was an art playing it.

Later on, when we had our first album out and the band was
doing well, I went to guitar string companies trying to persuade
them to make the lighter gauge strings. Their way of thinking was
incredibly conservative: 'Oh, you can't do that. They'll never work!
They would never be harmonically right.'

I said: 'Rubbish! It does! And I should know, because I use
them!'

And then they'd say: 'Nobody's ever going to buy them! Why
would anybody want that?'

They were all in such agreement about this that even I started
thinking: maybe they don't, maybe it's just me who wants them
because it makes me able to play and bend the strings. Eventually

the people at Picato Strings in Wales said: 'Yeah, we'll give this a go.'

This was in 1970, maybe 1971. They made the first set of light gauge strings for me. They worked, they were great and I used them for many years. Of course, then all the other companies jumped on the bandwagon, guitarists all over the world started using them and light gauge strings became popular. But to this day people still say: 'You won't get a full sound.'

I've even worked with producers who have told me that I'll need to use a set of thick strings to get a big sound.

My response to that is simple: 'I've never used a set of thick strings and I do have a big sound.'

8

Meeting Bill Ward and The Rest

After chopping my fingers off, it took at least six months for the worst of the pain to wear off and to get going again. I always felt uncomfortable about it and I always hid my hand. The same with playing: I used to hate anybody seeing it.

'What is that on your fingers?'

I later heard that some people actually thought it looked cool. There was a guitar teacher in New York who taught people how to play my things, and he had a pair of thimbles made. There was nothing wrong with his fingers, but he was convinced that these helped you to play.

My return to playing in a band came when I met Bill Ward. He was in The Rest and they all came around to our shop. They were trying to talk to me about joining them while people were coming in to be served. I said: 'Yeah, we'll have a go.'

They sounded really professional because they had two Vox AC 30 amplifiers. I also had an AC 30, so when you looked at it, three AC 30s, three Fenders – bloody hell, it must be a great band!

This was around 1966 or 1967. We had Bill Ward on drums, Vic Radford on guitar and Michael Pountney on bass. Singer

Chris Smith came later because Bill used to sing in the early days of The Rest and he did a good job of it, too.

At that time we had no money. Bill used to go around picking up all these bits of drumsticks that the drummers of other bands had played with and broken. He couldn't afford to buy any new ones, so he got used to playing with these half-sticks. Vic Radford had also chopped his finger off. I think he caught his middle index finger in a door and topped it off. Him losing his finger was a great help to me, because I had never met anybody else who had done that. I thought, bloody hell, both in the same band! He even tried one of my thimbles, but it's something you really have to get used to. It's just another world, it's a totally different style of playing, and you've just got to change all the rules. And that's what I did.

I didn't follow any rules at all. I made my own.

We did a lot of covers: some Shadows, some Beatles, maybe some Stones, more or less Top 20 stuff. You had to play that poppy stuff, or else you wouldn't get a gig. The Rest was quite popular; we started making a bit of a name, just locally. We'd play at the Midland Red Club, which was in the Midland Red Bus Depot. It was a social club where all the people who worked there would go. They had a band there every week. We used to play alternate weeks, and John Bonham was usually in the other band that played there. He'd last about five minutes in this band because he was too loud and they'd fire him. Then he'd sneak back in with another band and before long they would get rid of him for the same reason. He had this drum case with all the names of the bands he'd been with on it, and they were all crossed out. And the names would get smaller and smaller so that he could get them all on. All this was before bands had PA systems and drums were amplified. He just played them acoustically. But he hit those skins so hard, blimey, it was incredible. He was just so bloody loud!

The Rockin' Chevrolets had long since broken up, but I was still with Alan Meredith's sister, Margareth.

I was very jealous back then and I was very protective of Margareth. One night I was on stage playing away with The Rest when I saw somebody bothering her. I put my guitar down, jumped off stage, went around, punched this bloke out, got back on stage and carried on playing.

The stuff you do . . .

One time we were walking around Aston. I went to the loo and she waited outside for me. When I came out there was a gang of guys hassling her. I saw red. I went straight to the guy closest to her, grabbed him, and bang! Luckily, the others backed off. I used to do that a lot in those days. Always in a fight somewhere. But I've calmed down now. At last.

My relationship with Margareth even outlasted The Rest. They fizzled out because the bass player got married and decided to quit. The Rest was just a little band that had done all right for a while playing pubs. Little did we know it was the stuff Mythology was made of . . .

Later on in early Sabbath days I went out with Margareth's younger sister, Linda. It was very strange going around to the same house, but then to pick somebody else up. There'd be me, sitting outside in my car waiting for Linda, and another guy would pull up in his car to pick up Margareth.

Linda and I broke up when I went off to tour Europe for the first time. I came back and told her that I wanted to end it, because for me Europe had opened my eyes to a different life altogether, something I had never seen before, living in Birmingham.

9

Job-hopping into nowhere

After leaving school I was expected to join the workforce. The first job I got was through a friend of Dad's who owned a plumbing company. It was on a building site and I lasted no time at all. I couldn't handle it because I don't like heights.

My next big career move was getting a job treadmilling, which was making those rings that have a screw on them and if you put them around a rubber pipe and you tighten them, they close up on it. It was piecework, so you got so much for however many you did, but you cut your hands to pieces doing it. I thought, I have to play with these! So I got out of there in a hurry as well.

I then got a job at this big music shop called Yardley's in the centre of town. All the musicians met each other there, and the people who served them were playing away to show them how everything worked. I thought that's what I'd be doing: 'This is how this guitar works, this is the sound it's got.'

But instead they had me getting all of the stuff out of the windows, cleaning all the drum kits, putting them back, cleaning the guitars, putting them back, and I thought, hang on, when can I sit and play? Then they had a burglary and they thought I was involved, because I was the new one there. They interrogated me and remained suspicious until they finally found who actually did it. I didn't like what they had me doing, because all I did was menial tasks, and I didn't like what had happened. So again I went and got another job.

Me quitting all these jobs didn't go down at all well with my parents. They would both have a go at me: 'When are you going to get a proper job instead of this playing the guitar thing!?'

After working at Yardley's I got the welding job that cost me my fingers. And after my hand healed I got a job at B&D Typewriters. They taught me to drive and they gave me a van. I had to wear a suit and go to offices and service the typewriters on the spot. When I repaired stuff there'd be screws everywhere: where's the screw for this and where's that bit, oh no, little screws from here and there, oh my God!

But I really liked it, because I met a lot of girls that way. As long as I was repairing their typewriters they couldn't work and they'd be chatting away, so I had no option but to chat them up. That actually backfired on me, because girls were phoning our office saying their typewriter had broken again. So the gov'nor would say: 'You were only there a couple of days ago, I thought you repaired it!'

'I did!'

'Well, they want you back because there's something not working on it, so get over there.'

I'd find out there was nothing wrong with the typewriters, but because I had been chatting them up these girls thought I was going to ask them out. It was fun. It ended because I was getting too many gigs with The Rest and came in late too often, so it was not working out any more.

And after that I never had another job.

10

How three angels saved
heavy metal

After I passed my driving test I bought an MGB sports car. I was eighteen or nineteen, I was working and I paid so much towards it every week. My mother never wanted me to have it, because I was a bit frantic in that thing. And I actually had a serious accident in it.

Driving along a dual carriageway I overtook this other car. I looked over and it was a girl driving. And suddenly ... bang! I'd driven over something and two tyres went and it pulled me straight off the road. I went flying over into some trees and saw the wings coming off the car as I was sitting there. As I remember it, it all happened in slow motion. It sounds mad, but I saw three figures come down, one to the left and two to the right, like angels. And I thought, this is it.

I hit a tree, the car flipped over and I was knocked out. When I came to, I smelled petrol and I thought, fuck, I hope it doesn't blow up. It was a convertible and it had no roll bars. It was upside down, but I managed to get out because I had landed in soft earth. It was a big drop and I scrambled up to the road. I had concussion and I didn't know what was going on. Some guy picked me up and apparently I was ranting to him: 'Don't tell my parents, don't tell them!'

The next thing I knew my mum was screaming at me in my hospital bed: 'You barmy bastard, fancy doing that. You should have never bought that car!'

Bloody hell.

Everybody who saw the car said: 'You should have been killed.' They brought the wreck to my house, on a trailer. Mum saw it and just burst out crying. Even the people who towed it said: 'How the hell did you get out?'

I said: 'I don't know.'

I should have been killed, but all I had was concussion. I was bruised a bit, but nothing very serious.

Seeing those three figures, it was so vivid. It made me think, Christ, I've been saved here. And saved for a purpose: to do something. Someone once suggested it was to invent heavy metal. What a great purpose. The angels must have said to each other: 'Oops, that went wrong!'

It took me a while to get back into a car after that. But I had to drive the band's transit van, so I didn't have all that much time to get over it. And I did have sports cars again later.

But I don't look at women now when I overtake them.

11

Things go horribly
south up north

After The Rest fell apart I got this offer to join a band called
Mythology. They were from Carlisle, then a town of maybe
70,000 people on the border with Scotland, about a three-hour
drive from Birmingham. I went up there and Chris Smith came as
well, as Mythology also needed a singer. The band had been
reduced to Neil Marshall, the bass player and band leader, and a
drummer who soon left, so I thought, well, I know a drummer!
Enter Bill Ward. Then most of The Rest moved to Carlisle and
became Mythology. It was a logical step for us. In Birmingham
there was a limit to what we could do, but Mythology was the
biggest band up there, so there were gigs to be played.

I'd never been out of bloody Birmingham before, where I was
still living with my parents. To move out and live up in Carlisle
with the rest of the band was a big step. I didn't know anybody, so
having Chris there, and Bill a little later on, was great. We lived in
Compton House, a big place that was divided up into flats. We
had a lounge and a little kitchen on the top floor, and a bedroom
underneath that we all shared.

The landlady and her daughter also lived in the house, but they weren't the only ones there. One day we were about to order fish and chips and we counted out how many portions we'd need: 'You want chips, you want chips, you want chips . . .'

We counted one more than we actually needed, because there was a young boy there who we took into account. I said to Bill: 'Hang on, did you see that?'

'Yeah, a boy.'

Blimey, that was weird. It was really puzzling who this lad was. I said to our landlady: 'It sounds mad, but we think we saw a young boy upstairs.'

She said: 'Did he look about seven or eight years old?'

'Yeah.'

'Oh, he died in the house many years ago.'

She was completely aware of it. He'd had a bad death right there. But he wasn't the only one. We saw this young girl there as well. Apparently she had drowned in the bath . . .

It didn't frighten us. If it had been ghosts jumping at us, screaming, we'd have probably shat ourselves, but they were just young kids.

We were fairly careful with what we did there, with the noise and stuff. We got drunk on cheap wine a few times, for which we duly got told off, and we weren't allowed to bring girls in. No way: women in there? You couldn't do that! I was twenty years old, and Neil was about twenty-four at the time. His claim to fame was that he used to play with Peter & Gordon. Neil was leading a much more grown up band than The Rest had been. Mythology had its own style. We played more guitar stuff than I was used to, blues with lots of solos. It gave me the opportunity to really start playing, to actually learn to play solos. And as we gained more popularity, I gained more popularity; people liked what I played.

Mythology had a great agent, Monica Lynton, who used to get us quite a bit of work. Of course she would always go: 'You could play a bit more popular stuff, you know.'

We rehearsed in the lounge, just quietly, to put a song together. But most things we played were covers. We extended them or changed them around a bit, so that we could put a solo in. We'd try it out in the house and then do it during the gig the next night.

We had some blues and rock albums. One record we played a lot was The Moody Blues' *Days of Future Passed*, even though we didn't play any of the songs ourselves. And we had *Supernatural Fairy Tales*, an album by a band called Art. Their singer, Mike Harrison, later became famous with Spooky Tooth. We certainly played a couple of tracks off that in our set, because they were big up there, so people wanted to hear that.

We played places like the Town Hall in Carlisle, one of those horrible sounding buildings; the Cosmo, the biggest club there, like a big ballroom; and the Globe Hotel on Main Street, a place we later played with Sabbath as well. We did about two or three gigs a week, not just in Carlisle but travelling to Glasgow, Edinburgh, Newcastle and all the little pockets and places in between. We had tough audiences up there. They could drink like Scotsmen and shout like them as well: 'You know any Rolling Stones? Play some Rolling Stones!'

They fought all the time; that was their night out. Bottles came flying in, but if you stopped playing that would be it: they'd smash your stuff up. So you had to play on, no matter what. It was just like that movie *The Blues Brothers*: you'd dodge bottles galore. All the audience were fighting and it'd be really ridiculous. Then the next week they'd all be back and everything would be right as rain and they'd be talking and then it would all start over again. It's weird to see everybody fighting and the girls screaming and *girls* fighting!

Living away from home, we were free to do and look as we pleased. I started to grow my hair and it just went mad. People would actually be frightened of us, because nobody had long hair like that. Also I had this buckskin jacket that I *lived* in. I was proud of it and wore it everywhere. Bill Ward took that one step further: he'd wear a T-shirt for I don't know how many days *and* go to bed in it. He was a dirty bugger, and he hasn't changed much since. We actually called him Smelly for many years. We even bought gas masks and wore them when he was there. And Bill went: 'Hang on a bit!'

The joke backfired on us when we got stopped by the police in Hartlepool. They spotted these gas masks in the back of our van and thought we were going to do a robbery. We got arrested and were hauled off to the police station. Imagine that happening in Park Lane: they would have talked about it for ages.

Up in Carlisle I smoked my first hashish. It made me go weird, almost paranoid. I thought, oh God, I don't know if I like that. And I sure didn't like what it would lead to in the end. This dealer came around to the house maybe three times, because Neil would buy a little bit of hash off him. One day this guy, who was from out of town, turned up with these suitcases. He said: 'Can I leave these here, because I've got to do a bit of running around.'

We said yes and never saw him again.

The next morning, around seven o'clock, bang! The police busted the door down and came into our room. They found these suitcases, full of dope.

We were shocked: 'It's not ours!'

They locked us up and there was all hell to pay. I was petrified. Oh no, what are Mum and Dad going to think now!

It was actually the first time I had some of my own and it was maybe the third time I had ever smoked it. We tried to explain that the suitcases weren't ours. They knew that, because they'd been following this guy. That's what led them to our house. They arrested him but they were still trying to charge us with it, saying: 'If you don't tell us what's going on . . . all this was in your possession, you know!'

They really laid it on and frightened us to death. They separated us and asked us all questions. Of course we were thinking, I wonder what the others have said? Very awkward.

It was splashed all over the newspapers, because it was a big thing then: 'Band caught with drugs'. It made the national news and also reached Birmingham, so my parents found out. Imagine the neighbours: 'That Iommi boy is a drug addict!'

I called my mother and she went absolutely potty at me, crying and screaming and shouting: 'You brought disgrace to this house!'

Sergeant Carlton was the one who busted us. He found out soon enough we weren't the hardened criminals they were looking for. He helped us sort it out.

The drug fiasco was the main reason Mythology broke up. Getting gigs became difficult, so me and Bill just came back to Birmingham. I had to live at home again. It was embarrassing, but I had nowhere else to go.

Bill and I stuck together. We wanted to start another band, so we looked around for singers. We went into a music shop and we saw this advert saying: 'Ozzy Zig requires gig, owns his own PA'.

I said to Bill: 'I know an Ozzy, but it can't be him.'

We drove around to this address, knocked on the door, his mother answered and we said: 'Is Ozzy in?'

She said: 'Yes. Just a minute.'

She turned around and shouted: 'John, it's for you.'

And when he came to the door I said to Bill: 'Oh no, forget it. I know this guy.'

12

Down to Earth

'What do you mean?' Bill said.

I said: 'I know him from school. And as far as I know he isn't a singer.'

I suppose Ozzy was shocked as well. I hadn't seen him since school, so the only thing he remembered about me was me going around beating people up. Ozzy is a year younger than me, so he was in a class one year below mine. He always hung around with his friend Jimmy Phillips. Albert and me never associated with them at school.

Me and Bill talked to Ozzy for a bit and then we said: 'Okay then.'

And off we went and basically forgot about it. A few days later Bill came over to our house and Mum made him a sandwich. Suddenly Ozzy and Geezer turned up, looking for a drummer. I said: 'Bill is a drummer, but we're going to stick together. But if Bill wants to do it, fine.'

But Bill said: 'No, no, I want to stick with Tony.'

I said: 'Why don't we all have a go? Get a band and see how it goes.'

We got together for a first rehearsal. Ozzy's friend Jimmy

Phillips was there as well, playing the slide guitar, and some guy was honking away on a saxophone. Geezer was a guitar player but he decided to switch to the bass. Trouble was, he didn't have a bass and neither did he have the money to buy one. He tuned down his Fender Telecaster, trying to play the bass parts that way for that one rehearsal. I thought, oh blimey! To my relief he then went and borrowed a Hofner bass off his old band later. He only had three strings on that, but he only played one string then anyway.

We rehearsed some blues stuff, did a few songs and called ourselves The Polka Tulk Blues Band. Jimmy Phillips and me were going to try and get some gigs. We were in our lounge with the phone on the boxes and I said: 'Well, Jimmy, you phone this one, this Spotlight Entertainment sounds interesting.'

He phoned up and he went: 'Can I speak to Mr Spotlight please?'

We started laughing and that was the end of that. Just disastrous. I then called Mythology's agent Monica Lynton up in Carlisle, saying: 'We've got this band, give us a try.'

She said: 'Okay, but you've got to play some Top 20 stuff, in order to get away with playing some blues.'

'Okay, okay.'

Off we went to Carlisle. Near there, in a place called Egremont, we played at the Toe Bar. This big Scottish bloke came up to me and said: 'Yer singer is crap!'

'Ah, right. Thanks.'

We must have looked a right bloody bunch: me in my buckskin jacket, Bill in his smelly gear and then there was Ozzy who had shaved his head bald. Geezer wore a long Indian hippie dress. Peace, man, and all that stuff. I thought, that's weird, a bloke in a dress. What have I let myself in for?

Geezer dated this girl who lived down the road from our shop, so I saw him walking past a lot. I saw him more often when I was in a band that played at this nightclub and Geezer's band, Rare Breed, played there as well. You'd see him crawling up walls, because he did acid in those days. I thought he was a loon. When we played the Globe Hotel in Carlisle, some idiot came in who had already knocked a couple of policemen out and killed one of their dogs. We were getting the equipment out, Geezer was coming down the stairs in his hippy clothes carrying a couple of guitars and this guy came after him: 'You-ou-ou-aargh!!'

Geezer went: 'Huh!'

He let go of the guitars and shouted: 'Don't hit me, man, I'm peaceful!!'

And then he ran. It was unbelievable, this completely frantic big bloke running after Geezer and Geezer in his kaftan trying desperately to get away from him. It took a whole gang of policemen to get the bloke down and to jail. Bloody hell: what a great way to start off with a new band!

It didn't last that long with Jimmy Phillips and this saxophone player. There would be a solo and everybody would be playing it at the same time. It was a right row. These two guys just seemed to do this for a bit of a laugh, and that upset me. I had a little meeting with Bill, Geezer and Ozzy and said: 'The sax player doesn't really work and neither does Jimmy Phillips.'

They said: 'What do you want to do?'

We didn't want to hurt anybody's feelings by firing them, so we told them we were breaking up. After that we didn't see each other for a couple of days and then we got back together with just the four of us.

Those first gigs were crap. This band was not nearly as good as Mythology, but I said: 'Give it time, it will be all right.'

I could see there was some potential. It was an odd combination: somebody I knew from school who I didn't get along with back then; Geezer, who was from another planet; and me and Bill, who were probably from another planet as well. But it all seemed to jell. We rehearsed and rehearsed and did a few gigs and things started working for us.

We dropped the name The Polka Tulk Blues Band and changed it to Earth Blues Band, which quickly turned into Earth. We were doing twelve-bar blues, Ten Years After-type stuff. I just liked anything with guitar. We had blues albums by artists I'd never heard of, but there would be a guitar solo on one of them and we'd go: 'Ah, we'll do this track, it's good, another twelve-bar!'

The guitar work became more jazzy and Bill really liked big band music, so we also went into more jazzy stuff. Ozzy was doing that fine. I used to be on at him a lot, because at first he didn't know what to do. I was always saying: 'Go on, talk to the audience, say this, say that.'

And Geezer learned to play the bass very quickly: before you knew it he was playing away. But because we played the blues, we didn't work a lot. In Birmingham soul was big then, so there were only a couple of places where we could play. For us, Mothers club was probably the best venue in Birmingham. We played it, but I also saw Chicken Shack, Jon Hiseman's Colosseum and Free there. The Town Hall had a funny sound, but we played that a few times as well. In fact the *Volume 4* album's inside cover has a picture of us performing there. A lot of places we played at were in pubs, where they'd have this big room that they didn't use, and so they'd rent it out to somebody who'd organise a gig in there. Like Jim Simpson, who rented a room over a pub in the centre of Birmingham and called it Henry's Blues House. He had it maybe a couple of nights a week, but it became very popular.

Because the stages were so small, we all kind of grouped together. Ozzy hovered in front of me somewhere, but later, when we got to the bigger stages, he stood to the left in front of my stack and I moved to the middle of the stage. Don't ask me why, I never knew. It seemed weird, but I liked it: centre stage was the best spot to hear how everything sounded. It stayed that way until we broke up. Ozzy only went to the middle when we got back together many years later, in the nineties.

The first thing the band bought was a huge Commer van with blacked-out windows. It was a wreck, an ex-police van that had a great big hole in the floor on the passenger side. I once used the van to pick up this girl. We had put a carpet over the hole, trying to do it up a bit. She came out all dolled up, stockings on, climbed in the van, and went straight through the floor. The metal ripped her stockings and cut her leg. So that was the end of that romance.

Mum helped us get the deposit for it. We decked it out and put a couch in the back. We'd drive up to Carlisle in this thing, which was unbelievable. The van broke down constantly. It was shit but the roads were shit as well back then. To go to Carlisle or London seemed like never-ending journeys.

As I was the only one who had a licence and we couldn't afford a chauffeur, I was the one driving it. I'd pick everybody up to get to rehearsals and gigs, but because it was all down to me I'd get absolutely shattered, so we're all lucky to have survived that, really. They'd all be asleep in the back and I'd be slapping my face trying to stay conscious. The worst thing was, when I opened the window to keep awake, they'd go: 'Oy, it's cold in the back!'

Driving home one night when everybody was asleep, I found this road that was identical to the one Ozzy lived in. I thought it would be great fun to drop him off there! It was four or five o'clock in the morning, Ozzy was asleep and I said: 'All right, Oz, you're home!'

'Weuhh . . .'

He got out of the van and I shouted: 'See you tomorrow, ta ra!'

I pulled away, looked in my rear-view mirror and saw Ozzy trying to get into the wrong house. By the time he realised it wasn't his, we were gone. And he had to walk a mile or so to get to his own house. The next night I picked him up again and he went: 'You dropped me off at the wrong road yesterday!'

I said: 'Oh, did I? Oh my God, I thought that was your road!'

'No, no, it was the wrong road.'

Later that night, on our way home, he fell asleep again in the back and I stopped at the same wrong street.

'All right, Oz, you're home!'

'Weuhh . . .'

He got out, we drove off, same again. He fell for that umpteen times.

Mum helping out buying the van was one side of the coin; the other side was her moaning: 'A bloody nuisance you are. You ought to get a bloody proper job!'

But she did a lot for us and she looked after everybody. She'd always offer sandwiches or something else to eat, so the band loved her. And both Dad and Mum liked all the guys in the band. They took a particular shine to Ozzy. Dad thought he was funny, and he was right: Ozzy was a very funny guy.

Ozzy's dad also helped out. Ozzy did have his own PA, but we needed a bigger one, so his dad signed a thing called a pay bond. This meant he guaranteed payment and Ozzy could borrow the money to buy it. He bought a Triumph amp and two cabinets. And we had a Vox PA. In those days you didn't have a sound man twiddling the knobs in the middle of the hall; all the sound came from your own gear on stage so you'd start and you'd turn the volume up and then everybody would start screaming: 'Turn it down!'

We'd get complaints because we were always too loud. Always. If you were standing in front of your own cabinet you couldn't hear anybody else any more, so you'd move over to hear what else was going on. You could never really hear the vocals, even though Ozzy turned up his amp so loud it would start whistling.

We played at Henry's Blues House a lot, where we quickly developed a draw. Jim Simpson, the guy who ran that place, took an interest in us. He was a jazz guy, a trumpet player, and we played jazzy blues. He liked that, so he approached us for management. We didn't have anybody else, he had his Blues House where we could play, so we thought, if we don't sign with him we won't have the gig.

Jim Simpson started managing us around the end of 1968, beginning of '69. So here we were, in possession of PAs, a huge wreck of a Commer van, a set list filled with jazzy twelve-bar blues and a manager. All dressed down and no particular place to go but up.

The first thing Jim Simpson did was put us on the Big Bear Folly, a UK tour with four bands playing, and the night always ended in a jam with everybody back on stage. In January 1969 we played the Marquee club, but we didn't go down very well with John Gee, the manager of the place. The guy was into big bands and, when Bill claimed he was also into jazz, John Gee played him some of that music and said: 'Who's this then, who is this?'

Bill gave him a totally wrong name and John Gee really got the hump.

Ozzy had a pyjama top on and a tap around his neck. John didn't like that either. He probably thought we were really scruffy. Well, we were. We didn't have the money to look good. Ozzy actually used to walk around in bare feet. Geezer was the fashion guru who'd get the latest trend. He had these lime-green trousers. They were his only pair and he washed them all the time and wore them over and over again. One day he dried them by the heater and one of the legs caught fire. Because he loved this pair of trousers so much, his mum sewed another leg on and from then on he walked around with one green leg and one black leg. Mad!

Bill actually won an award for the worst dressed rock star once, 'The Scruffiest Rock Star Out There' or something like that. He was really proud of it as well. And there was me in my buckskin jacket. What with the clothes and lots of hair, we certainly looked heavy. We all grew handlebar moustaches and Bill grew a beard as well. There was no conscious thought behind that. If you're in a band you develop a similar look.

'Oh, your hair has got a little longer, looks good, leave it like that.'

The downside of it was that we didn't have any women coming to the gigs. Scruffy long hair, only blokes sitting there . . .

Come to think of it, you did see some. But they looked like blokes!

13

A flirt with Tull in a
Rock 'n' Roll Circus

Earth had gigged for just a couple of weeks when we opened for Jethro Tull, who were already getting very popular. I thought they were really good, but obviously there was something going on, because during that gig their guitar player, Mick Abrahams, passed this note to Ian Anderson. It said something like: 'I'm leaving', or: 'This is my last night'. After the gig they asked me if I'd be interested in joining.

I went: 'Oh, bloody hell. I don't know.'

And I didn't. I was shocked by it all.

On the way home in the van I said to the others: 'I've got to tell you something. I've been asked to join Jethro Tull. And I don't know what to say.'

They were really supportive and said: 'You should go for it.'

Tull got in touch and I said: 'Well, yeah, I'll give it a go.'

But it wasn't as simple as that. They said: 'You've got to come for an audition.'

I protested, but they said: 'Come down to London. You'll be all right.'

I went down there and I walked into this room and there were so many guitar players from known bands there that I panicked . . . and walked out again. I knew John, one of their crew, from his time with Ten Years After. He rushed after me and said: 'Look here, don't worry, just go and sit in the caf across the road and I'll come and fetch you when it's your turn.'

'Well, I don't feel comfortable with this.'

But he insisted: 'You've got to have a go; they really want you to play.'

So he came and fetched me from the caf. Everybody was gone by the time it was my turn. We did a twelve-bar blues and I got to solo. We did another two or three jams and then they said: 'You've got the job.'

Before I knew it I was in rehearsals with Jethro Tull for the recording of their *Stand Up* album. The song 'Living In The Past' from that album would go to No. 1 in the British charts. I came up with a couple of the riffs for 'Nothing Is Easy'.

Because I felt so out of place in London and I really felt bad about leaving Earth, I took Geezer down with me for moral support. He would sit at the back of the room, and they were fine with that. John put us up in his flat and took us to the rehearsals. They started at nine o'clock in the morning sharp. I had never heard of nine o'clock in the morning with our band, none of us had. With Earth we would just straggle in whenever we felt like it. But with Tull it was: 'Gotta be there, on time!'

The first day we got there maybe ten minutes late and I could hear Ian Anderson screaming at John: 'Nine o'clock, I said!'

I thought, bloody hell, this is a bit serious. I hadn't even plugged in and already the tension was palpable. At twelve o'clock sharp it was: lunch. I just sat down with Ian at a table. The others were at another table whispering to me: 'No!'

I thought, what's the matter with them?

They went: 'You don't sit with Ian. You sit with us.'

'What do you mean?'

'He likes to sit by himself. And we sit together.'

I thought, bloody hell, that's a weird set-up. This is supposed to be a band!

That night Ian Anderson took me to see Free play at the Marquee. He introduced me to everybody as his new guitar player, so I thought, this is wonderful. I felt like a pop star. From being a nobody from Birmingham to people at the Marquee taking an interest – it seemed great. We watched Free for a bit and left early. Rehearsal again the next morning, nine o'clock. And don't be late!

But it just didn't feel good. The thing that put the nail in the coffin for me was a meeting with the band's manager. He said: 'You'll get £25 a week and you are really lucky to have this position.'

That pissed me off. I said: 'What do you mean I'm really lucky? They want me because they like what I play, not because of luck!'

After that I thought: I want to be a part of a band that's going to make it all together, not be put in a band where they've already made it and I'm 'lucky to be in there'. I went back to the rehearsal room and said to Ian: 'Can I have a word with you?'

We went outside and I said: 'I don't feel comfortable about this whole thing.'

He said: 'What's wrong?'

'I'm not happy with the situation. And I don't feel right about being "lucky" to be in a band and all this sort of stuff.'

Ian was great, I can't fault him at all; he was very nice about the whole thing. He said: 'Look, if you are definitely sure you want to leave . . .'

'Well, I am.'

'We're in trouble now, because we're doing this film, *The Rolling Stones Rock and Roll Circus*, and we don't have a guitar player. Would you do that at least?'

I felt bad walking out on them, so I said: 'Yes, I'll do that.'

And that was it. As soon as I came out of that last rehearsal I said to Geezer: 'Let's get the band back together.'

He said: 'Are you sure about leaving Tull? You ought to give it time.' He was pushing me, but then he said: 'I'm glad you're not doing it.'

I said: 'Let's make a proper go of it. Do what they're doing: rehearse in the morning, really get down to it.'

He agreed. So we phoned the others from London and made a plan to get back together.

I still had to do this *Rolling Stones Rock and Roll Circus*. The opening of the whole thing was in the Dorchester Hotel. There was me with the same buckskin jacket again. I wore it for the film as well. The Stones had all their gear set up on the floor of a ball-room. The Who were there and Taj Mahal and all the people who were in the movie, but I didn't know a soul and felt like a spare dinner. Marianne Faithfull must have sensed that; she came over and went: 'You'll be all right, I'll talk to you.'

And so she did, she was great.

The Stones started playing but within a minute or so they stopped. They started arguing and had the biggest row. The whole room went quiet. Brian Jones and Keith Richards were screaming at each other: 'You are fucking out of tune, you fucking . . .'

Because he was with Marianne Faithfull, Mick Jagger came over to us, saying: 'They can't even fucking tune their fucking guitars.'

It was a sure sign of troubles to come.

The next day we filmed in a big warehouse somewhere. They had a stage set up and something that looked like a circus ring. They wanted people to dress up in silly hats and circus stuff, which seemed ridiculous to me. Even Eric Clapton said: 'I feel fucking silly wearing this stupid thing.'

They gave me this bloody clarinet and we all had to come out pretending to play as we were going around the ring. Clapton, The Who and John Lennon – everybody had to go around this thing. After we all did that I don't know how many times to get it right, people started chatting and it got a bit more comfortable.

We were all eagerly awaiting the much anticipated jam with Clapton, Lennon, Mitch Mitchell, and Keith Richards playing bass. I said to Ian Anderson: 'I'm really looking forward to seeing Clapton play.'

They started jamming on this instrumental thing, bloody Yoko sitting at John's feet, and they weren't good at all. So Ian said: 'What do you think of your hero now then!?'

We shared a dressing room with The Who, so that was my first time meeting them. They were nice enough and when they started to play they were really good. I was completely surprised when I heard Pete Townshend playing lead, because you never normally heard him do that very much and he played great.

Not everybody played for real; we did 'Song For Jeffrey'. Ian Anderson got this hat and he said: 'Try that on.'

I said: 'It looks all right', but I felt pretty embarrassed and kept my head down while I was playing so people couldn't see me.

It was ages before that ever came out. I bumped into Bill Wyman two or three times and he said: 'Oh yeah, I'll get you a copy of that for you.'

He never did, so I never saw it until years later and it was horrible. It's so out of date. But it's a classic now; half the people who were in that show are dead. There's John Lennon, Keith Moon, Brian Jones and Mitch Mitchell . . . it's a Rock 'n' Roll Circus, all right.

14

The early birds catch
the first songs

After I came back from London I said to the rest of the band: 'If we're going to do this, we're going to do it seriously and really work at it, starting with rehearsals at nine o'clock in the morning. Sharp!'

We booked a place in the Newtown Community Centre in Aston, across the road from a cinema, and started a whole new regime. I'd pick everybody up to make sure that we got there on time. Geezer didn't live that far away, so he'd walk down. Occasionally he'd be a little bit late, but on average we were there at a sensible hour to start work. And that's when we began writing our own songs. 'Wicked World' and 'Black Sabbath' were the first two that were written during those rehearsals. We knew we had something; you could feel it, the hairs stood up on your arms, it just felt so different. We didn't know what it was, but we liked it. I just came up with this riff for 'Black Sabbath'. I played 'dom-dom-dommm'. And it was like: that's it! We built the song from there. As soon as I played that first riff we went: 'Oh God, that's really great. But what is it? I don't know!'

Just a simple thing but it had a mood. Only later did I learn that I had used what they call the Devil's interval, a chord progression that was so dark that in the Middle Ages playing it was forbidden by the Church. I had no idea; it was just something that I had felt inside. It was almost like it had been forced out of me, these things were coming up just like that. Then everybody started putting bits to it and afterwards we thought it was amazing. Really strange, but good. We were all shocked, but we knew that we had something there.

Geezer was going to be an accountant. That's why he had the job of sorting all the money out every time we had a gig. He was the clever one, so it was him that came up with the lyrics as well. I certainly wouldn't be able to sit down and write stuff and Bill would be on it for twenty years to write one line. Ozzy would come up with the vocal melody line. He'd just sing what came into his head and so it might very well have been that he sang: 'What is this that stands before me' at the time. Geezer would then use that and put the rest of the lyrics in. So both of them really would come up with stuff.

Back then we did a lot of dope. One night we were at this club, in the middle of nowhere. Ozzy and Geezer saw somebody leaping around outside, being silly. To them it was like an elf or something. I fear it must have been the drugs, but that's where I think 'The Wizard' came from, another one of those early songs. They simply put what they saw into lyrics. Those first songs are often described as scary. I liked horror films and so did Geezer. We used to go to the cinema across the street from our rehearsal place to see them, so maybe it was something that subconsciously directed us to that sort of thing. I know there is a Boris Karloff movie called *Black Sabbath*, but we never saw it at that time. Geezer came up with the name Black Sabbath and it just sounded like a good one to use.

We always thought there was something there that led us into this music that we were playing. I played that 'Black Sabbath' riff straight off, dang-dáng-dang, and that was it. It just came up, as a lot of my riffs have. It was like somebody was there, saying: 'Play that!'

Something or somebody was providing ideas and guidance from some other dimension, like an invisible fifth band member . . .

15

Earth to Black Sabbath

When we played near Carlisle at the Toe Bar, they always put us up in a caravan. In winter it was so cold we burned the furniture to keep warm. One day we turned up at this gig in Manchester and there was a guy on the door wearing a suit and a bow tie. We thought, this is weird for a blues club. He said: 'Oh, you're Earth, come in.'

In we went and he said: 'I really like your new single.'

'Oh, thanks!'

We didn't have a single out at the time, but we took no notice, got all the gear in and set up. Then we saw all these people coming in in bow ties, suits and ballroom dresses and we realised they had booked the wrong band. We soon found out that there was another Earth, and that was a pop band. The manager caught on to us but said: 'You might as well go on and play.'

We played one song and everybody out there, all expecting to dance, was going: 'What is this crap!'

They pulled us off. Then the manager wouldn't pay us, so we nicked the tea urn, we took the rug out of the back of the dressing room, we took knives and forks, we took whatever we could. And we said to each other: 'That's it, we're never going through this again. We need to come up with a name that nobody else has.'

Jim Simpson came up with Fred Carno's Army. Fucking hell, it was getting worse! Fred Carno was some old-time music hall impresario who had worked with Charlie Chaplin and Stan Laurel. Ozzy's idea was Jimmy Underpass and the Six Way Combo. So much for that. Geezer came up with Black Sabbath and it just sounded like a good name to use.

Jim Simpson got us our first gigs in Europe. The very first trip over there, we picked up Ozzy and he showed up with just a shirt on a hanger. We said to him: 'We're going away, you know.'

'I know.'

'We're going to be away for a few weeks.'

'I know.'

He only had one shirt and one pair of jeans, and that was it.

On our way over there we decided to change our name. Or maybe it was in one of the first clubs we played, the famous Star Club in Hamburg. It held 400 or 500 people. Because they had us back a few times we were able to build a following and we ended up holding the attendance record there, after The Beatles.

It was after the Jethro Tull thing and inspired by Ian Anderson that I had bought a flute and tried to play it on stage. We were smoking dope there a lot and I was pretty pie-eyed. I held the flute way too low so I was just blowing air into the microphone. Ozzy went backstage and grabbed this great big mirror, brought it out to the stage and put it in front of me. He tapped me on the shoulder and I went: 'Ooohh!!'

Another high point came when Ozzy found this tin of purple paint and he painted his face with it. There was a big ladder behind the stage and he climbed to the top of it until his head was over the curtains and all you could see was this purple head popping up over the backdrop. Crazy stuff like that helped us maintain whatever sanity we had.

We did a couple of European tours in those early days. The first one took us to Hamburg, Denmark and Sweden, and following tours also saw us travel to Switzerland, where we played in St Gallen for six weeks. We played there for maybe three people, four or five spots a day. All we'd get would be a glass of milk and a sausage. No money: we were poverty-stricken. Geezer was a vegetarian, but he had to eat the sausages because we didn't have any money to buy him any other food. We all stayed in this one room above this cafe across the road from where we played. If you weren't in on time they'd lock you out. One night me and Ozzy went off with these two girls and stayed with them. Geezer came back from somewhere and couldn't get in, so Bill tied sheets together, trying to pull Geezer up. As they were doing this the police came by. It took quite some explaining in two different languages to sort that one out.

We then moved on to Zurich. When we arrived there the place was packed. This band was up there playing away, looking happy and they even had champagne. We thought, this is marvellous, we'll have some! Little did we know they had been there for six weeks and it was their last night. All these people were there seeing them off, so it was a big party night. As soon as we started the place was dead. We went, wait a minute, what happened? Where's all the people? They had this one nutter coming in every day. He'd stand on his head, all his money would fall out of his pocket, he'd pick it up again and leave. And there was this old hooker sitting at the corner by the bar and that was it.

Because it was deserted anyway, we started making stuff up. And we thought, hang on, if Bill does a drum solo for one set and I do a guitar solo for the next set, the other guys can have a rest. That was great for a couple of days but of course they caught on. During Bill's solo the owner's daughter came up and said: 'Shut that noise! We're paying for you to play, not all this!'

It was a really grim place. We all slept in one room, together

with a bunch of rats. The owner of the club had taken our pass-
ports, so we couldn't get out. It was like slavery, with us playing
five forty-five-minute spots and seven on the weekends with
hardly any pay. But we did have a lot of laughs, also because we
had the occasional joint. And Bill smoked banana skins. He used
to eat the banana, scrape all the residue off the skin, put it on to a
piece of tin foil, put that in the oven, cook it and then smoke it.
He claimed it got him high, thought it was great and was really
proud of it.

'What's Bill doing?'

'Oh, he's cooking his banana skin.'

16

Black Sabbath records
Black Sabbath

When we played at Henry's Blues House we had music business people coming to see us. We went to London to play at the Speakeasy once for that reason as well; Chrysalis came down to check us out, but the place was empty and the gig was dismal. It was all to try and get a deal. We got turned down, but that wasn't the end of the world. You've got to stick to what you believe in, just carry on and don't change because you think that's what people want. That's how something new comes up. Doing what everybody else is doing is the easy way out; you've got to do your own thing.

Tony Hall came to Henry's Blues House, liked what we were doing and wanted to sign us. He had been quite a well-known DJ originally and he now ran Tony Hall Enterprises, whatever that meant. We signed with that company, which in turn signed us to the Fontana label. I'm sure they did very well out of that deal. We only saw him on a few occasions afterwards. He turned up once at *Top of the Pops*, but I haven't seen him since. Another figure from those early days was David Platz, who signed us to Essex Music. It was a crap deal but I've been told they all were back then. Anyway, he certainly made a few bob off us. On very rare occasions, we'd go and see him. Strange, he had a button that he'd push that opened a door to a secret room behind his desk. He managed to survive a long time. Probably thanks to that room. After getting a proper record company, it was time to record our first album. We received £100 each for our efforts, which to us was a lot of money, but of course we would gladly have done it for free. Having an album out there would mean that people could hear us. We recorded a couple of demos in the autumn of 1969, 'The Rebel' and 'Song For Jim'. 'The Rebel' was a song that Norman Haines from Jim Simpson's band had written, and Jim wanted us to do it. And I can't even remember how 'Song For Jim' goes, but we named it after him as a bit of a joke. We first auditioned for Gus Dudgeon, already a well-known producer at the time, at the Trident Studios in London. We didn't see eye to eye with him at all and he turned us down.

A couple of days later we had a gig in Workington and that's where Ozzy announced our name change to the audience. It wasn't a big deal, we didn't have a celebration or anything; we just changed the name to Black Sabbath. And our first Black Sabbath gig was on 30 August 1969, but as far as I'm concerned the band has been together since 1968. I always forget about the fact that we were first called Earth; to me the four of us getting together is the only thing of importance.

By that time we already played 'The Wizard', 'Black Sabbath', 'N.I.B.' and 'Warning', basically the songs of what would become our first album. We didn't want to play other people's stuff any more. A twelve-bar blues in the middle of all our new songs just didn't sound right any more anyway, because our own stuff was so different. Nevertheless, we did record 'Evil Woman', a cover of an American hit by The Crows. Jim Simpson wanted us to do that because he said: 'We need something commercial.'

We reluctantly agreed to it, but things were changing our way already, because during that same session we also recorded our own song 'The Wizard'. Simpson used these demos to get disc jockey John Peel interested in us. In November we played his show *Top Gear*, performing 'Black Sabbath', 'N.I.B.', 'Behind The Wall Of Sleep' and 'Sleeping Village'. We were on national radio. Things started to move, things were happening!

We didn't choose to record with producer Rodger Bain, he was chosen for us. We met up with him beforehand and we liked him; he seemed like a nice enough guy. He was as green as we were, and he hadn't done much before. He was in his early twenties, just like us, maybe a bit older. Being the producer, Rodger was overseeing the whole thing. He was good to have around, but we didn't really get a lot of advice from him. He maybe suggested a couple of things, but the songs were already fairly structured and sorted.

Our roadie, Luke, drove our gear to the Regent Sound studio off Tottenham Court Road in London on 16 October 1969, and put up the amps. The studio wasn't much bigger than a small living room and we're all in there playing away, with partitions between us and Bill. Ozzy was singing in a little booth at the same time as the band played. Everything was performed just like a live band. It was the most important thing we had ever done, so we were all pretty well on the case.

I had never been in a studio before and didn't know anything about recording and where to put microphones or anything. By the same token, I think it must have been hard for Rodger Bain and engineer Tom Allom to come in and work with us just like that. Two guys who had never travelled with us, did not know what we were like, did not know what we sounded like, but came in and suddenly were adding their thing to it. The biggest problem we've always had is explaining to the people who recorded us how we have our sound set up. My guitar and Geezer's bass have to very much agree with each other, to make the wall of sound. All of them just see a bass as a bass, dumm-dum-dumm, clean and neat. But Geezer's sound is more crunchy, more raw, and he sustains stuff and he bends notes the same as the guitar, to make it fatter. Some of them would try to get him to take the distortion away, and it would be like tum-tum-tum.

'Fucking leave it! It's a part of our sound!'

It took a lot of convincing for people to understand that. They'd always separate the sounds as well. They'd hear the guitar on its own and go: 'Oh, it's so distorted!'

'I know! But play it all together as a band and see what it sounds like!'

People couldn't grasp that we were a band that sounded good together, no matter how an individual player sounded. Rodger Bain understood it to a point, which is why those early albums we did with him have a very plugged-in sound. It was basically a case of what you see is what you get: we just walked in, plugged in and played; thank you and good night. And that was it, there wasn't much fiddling around with the sounds we had. The drums as well, they were just mic'd up and off we went, giving it that real, honest sound. And that was the sound that took off.

Everything was done very quickly. We thought, bloody hell, we've got a whole day to record these tracks, great, that's fucking brilliant! Later I heard Led Zeppelin spent a week recording their first album, but they were more experienced than us. They had Jimmy Page who had recorded with The Yardbirds and God knows who else before that. He had been in and out of studios, but we certainly hadn't, so we didn't have a clue.

We did a track called 'Warning', with a long guitar solo. Because it was such a long song you had to capture it in one take, or else we'd run out of time. After the first one, Rodger said: 'Okay, that's it.'

'Well, I wanted to try something else . . .'

'That's it!'

'Can we do it just once more? I think I can get it better.'

Eventually Rodger said: 'Okay, we'll do another one.'

So we had another crack at it and that was it: take it or leave it.

That whole album was done exactly like that: play like you play at a gig. You play it once, you don't have ten goes at it. As we played it in the studio then, 'Warning' was fifteen minutes or something ridiculous. Rodger and the engineer edited it down to about ten minutes. They cut a big section and plucked out a couple of smaller pieces in places I wouldn't have edited. I was upset because I felt it originally had a more natural flow, but you have to have a certain length for a vinyl album and maybe a fifteen-minute piece was too much.

The funny thing is, after we put a song like that down on record it became the version we would play from then onwards. It gets accepted like that. So forty years later we're still reproducing on stage what we happened to do in the studio on that particular day. When we recorded 'Electric Funeral', for instance, Bill would play it differently every bloody time. He didn't know how many times to come in, and in certain parts he plays three instead of four and we kept the three. And to this day we still play it that way.

A lot of people think 'N.I.B.' stands for Nativity In Black, whatever that means. It's a typically American thing; they always have to go: 'Oh, it's gotta be something satanic!'

We called Bill 'Smelly' and we also called him 'Nib', because with his beard his face looked like a pen nib. It just sounded humorous to us and when it came to the title of the track we said: 'What shall we call it?'

'Uh ... Nib?'

It was just a joke.

I loved my white Fender Stratocaster, because I'd worked on it so much. I had it in bits and put it all back together again, I potted the pickups, filed the frets down on it and basically did everything to try and make it easier for me to play on. One fateful day I bought a Gibson SG as a backup guitar. Two guitars: it was getting a bit flash, really! In the studio, right after recording the first track of the day, 'Wicked World', the bloody pickup went on the Fender. I thought, oh God, I'm going to have to use the SG, which I never really played! I recorded the album with it and that was it, I just stuck to it. I actually swapped the Strat for a saxophone. I can't believe I did that now. That was a classic guitar and it really had a different sound from the regular Strats because of all the work I did to it. Years later, Geezer saw it in the window of a second-hand shop and went back to buy it for me. But it had been sold and I've never seen it again.

It was a right-handed Gibson SG that I played upside down. Then I met this guy who said: 'I've got a friend who is right-handed, and he plays a left-handed guitar upside down.'

I said: 'You're kidding!'

I met this guy, we swapped guitars and we were both happy. The Gibson SG had single-coil pickups which, because I used a treble booster, caused a horrendous racket: 'Shghghghghghghghggg!!!'

I then potted and encased the pickups and later on I put in different ones altogether. I was fiddling about with the guitar again, doing the stuff I had done to the Strat. That SG was very dear to me, but I don't have it any more. It's been put out to pasture at the Hard Rock Café. But the deal is, if I ever want it back, I can get it back.

We didn't have the time to get involved with the final mix of the album, because we were off to tour Europe. There really wasn't a lot to mix anyway; it was recorded on just four tracks, it didn't have hundreds of drums on it or overdubs, so it was really very basic. Rodger Bain and Tom Allom did add the bells and the thunder and lightning at the beginning of *Black Sabbath*. One of them got some sound-effect tapes and said: 'What about putting these on it?'

We went: 'Oh yeah, that's great!'

Because it is, it really sets the mood for that track.

We didn't have anything to do with the cover art. The photo was taken at the Mapledurham Watermill. We weren't there when it was taken, but we did meet the girl featured in the picture. She came to a gig once and introduced herself. I thought it was a good cover, really different. But inside the gatefold sleeve you have the inverted cross, which opened all sorts of cans of worms for us. We were suddenly satanic then.

But most of the excitement we felt at the time had nothing to do with that. We were just happy to have an album.

17

Now under new management

The record company switched us from Fontana to one of their other labels, Vertigo Records. They pushed it more because it was a new label with more progressive acts. But we didn't have a lot of contact with them; they only wanted to talk to the manager. At least, that's what we were told. Sometimes you'd see people from the label turn up, but you wouldn't know who they were.

The marketing people made sure the album came out on Friday the 13th, February 1970. We did interviews around the release, but that ended after Patrick Meehan took over management from Jim Simpson. He stopped us doing press, because us being unavailable for interviews made it more of a special thing. We hardly had any radio play because the only one who played us was John Peel. Even so the album sold 5,000 copies in the first week after release thanks to underground word of mouth, especially in the places in which we had built up a following by playing live.

The press hated us, and we got slagged left, right and centre. You obviously get concerned, but it's not like we thought, oh, we're going to change the music then. The album was selling, so obviously we'd done something right. We believed in what we did and we loved it, so there was nothing else we could do apart from carry on with what we were doing.

Only when grunge became popular, and all those musicians said that Black Sabbath was a great influence, did we become the flavour of the month, or flavour of the time. So here we were, reading good things about ourselves, going: 'Hang on, what happened? They can't write good things!' Because we always said: 'As soon as they start writing good things about us, we better give up.'

The single 'Evil Woman' didn't do much, but the album went to No. 8. Jim Simpson had booked us a lot of gigs before it came out and we were still honouring them for something like £20, next to nothing. We said to him: 'Hang on, how many more of these gigs are we going to be doing?'

'Oh, we've got months of these to go.'

It was getting silly. Even the people who ran the clubs we played at were going: 'You should be getting more than this! What are you doing playing here?'

We thought, well, fuck this, we've done enough! So when heavyweight manager Don Arden called, telling us he was interested in working with us, we went up to London to see him. Wilf Pine picked us up in a Rolls-Royce. Wilf was a nice bloke when you knew him, but, on the other hand, he was quite vicious. Fucking hell, I've heard tasty stories about what he did for Don Arden. Everything looked really heavy around Don. You saw lots of gangster-like characters floating about. We got to his office and it was a bit overpowering, with Don going: 'You're going to be great. You're going to have billboards up everywhere. I'm going to get you to the top!'

And so on. He went: 'Sign here!'

We just couldn't do that. It was all too bombarding. So we came away, thinking, oh God, what are we going to do now? He'll probably have us killed! He kept getting in touch with us, arranging to take us out to dinner and all that sort of business. He never let go. Then one day, Wilf got in touch. He said: 'I've got another guy that wants to meet you. I'm going to bring him up to Birmingham.'

It was Patrick Meehan. He seemed a lot calmer than Arden and said the things we wanted to hear: 'You've got an album out, nobody is pushing the record. You should get better gigs . . .'

All that stuff sounded good to our ears. Instead of being up on billboards, we just wanted to be out playing. He just had the right way about it at the time, so we ended up signing with Patrick Meehan.

Looking back at it now it was quite strange that Wilf, who worked for Arden, would suggest Meehan to us. Wilf probably thought, oh well, they don't want Don but maybe they're interested in Patrick. Which we were. But we didn't know how close the relationship between Arden and Meehan really was. In the past Patrick Meehan's dad had worked for Don Arden, so there certainly was a connection.

Wilf wrote a book a few years ago. There's a picture of me and him in it, and then on the other side of the page there's one of Wilf and John Gotti, then the head of the New York Mafia. I thought, fucking hell, how did I get mixed up in this?

Patrick Meehan had learned the ropes from his dad, who also had a management company. It was all very much roses at first. Meehan talked a good talk and in the early days he really got things going. He was the one who got us to America. The whole thing changed for us. We were travelling in private jets everywhere. Any time we wanted anything, we'd just phone him up: 'I want to buy a new car.'

He'd go: 'Oh, okay, what car?'

In my case a Lamborghini or a Rolls-Royce, or whatever.

'Where is it?'

I'd tell him where it was.

'How much is it?'

I'd tell him how much it was.

'I'll send them a cheque and I'll arrange to get the car over.'

And that was it. If I wanted to buy a house: 'Where is the house? How much is it?'

And I got the house. That's how we lived. But we never saw any significant amounts of physical cash, even though there was a lot of it about. We got some money put into the bank, but not a lot. But for us, coming from what we came from, a few hundred quid in the bank was brilliant. I believe that we never really knew how much money we actually made. We had accountants involved with us, but we never really questioned what their role was or who they were taking instructions from.

'Oh, it's a big accountancy firm, it must be all right!'

We knew nothing at all about the business side of things. When we went down to the office it was always come in all's great: 'By the way, sign these papers. It's basically so-and-so, I'll tell you about it, all from the accountant.'

And you'd think it was all above board.

But I liked Meehan. We all liked him at first and we believed in him.

18

Getting Paranoid

After recording *Black Sabbath* we immediately started writing songs for our second album. Some of them were written when we were on the road in Europe, like 'War Pigs'. When we played that grim place in Zurich, we jammed a lot and that's where the initial idea came from. Later, during rehearsal, we turned it into a song. We had writing sessions in whatever rehearsal place we used at the time, putting tracks together. We also did some work for *Paranoid* in Monmouth, in Wales, because we wanted to go somewhere where we could lock ourselves away. We were one of the first bands there, after Dave Edmunds. At the other places we'd have to go in and then go home, but here we could all be together and around each other all the time.

The recording of the *Paranoid* album went pretty quick. We went back to Regent Sound, working with Rodger Bain again. It didn't take much more than three or four days, just a bit longer than the first one. Because we were in a fight a couple of nights before that, I recorded that album with a great big black eye. It was the days of Mods and Rockers and we were playing at this seaside resort. We had finished and Geezer went out to make a phone call. He soon came rushing back in, going: 'Fucking hell, loads of skinheads trying to get me, they're all waiting for us to come out!'

We went out to see what was happening and it was serious stuff. Ozzy grabbed a hammer and I said: 'Who is the one that got you then, Geezer?'

He pointed at some guy and said: 'It was him!'

I went down and, bang!, I hit this bloke and then they all came from nowhere. Fucking horrible, but you're in the midst of it then, fighting. Some bloke got me around the neck and I shouted: 'Ozzy, hit him with the hammer!'

Ozzy hit him and at the same time he got jumped from behind and he slammed the bloody hammer backwards over his shoulder in that bloke's face. It was brutal. They were wearing these big metal-tipped boots and we were getting kicked in the face with them. We managed to get away, but we were a bloody mess.

Ron Woodward, my old bass-playing neighbour, had driven us to the gig because he had just bought this new car. We jumped in screaming: 'Quick, drive, fucking get away!!'

But he took off like a slug on Valium, with us screaming our heads off, big black eyes, blood everywhere: 'Put your foot down, drive, drive!!!'

All these skinheads were rushing down the hill, catching up with us, bats in hand, and Ron was making a getaway in slow motion. It turned out he was afraid to speed because you're not supposed to do that with a brand new car. We got away, but it took us ages to get home because he drove so slowly. I finally walked in the house and Mum was in the bedroom.

'How did the show go?'

I opened the door.

'Oh, great!'

Lyrically, the album *Paranoid* was political, or certainly 'War Pigs' was. That wasn't because of any negative reactions to the supposed 'occult' first album, because we never ever regretted what we've done. It just happened that way. But not all of *Black Sabbath* was, for lack of a better word, occult, and not all of *Paranoid* was political. 'War Pigs' actually started off as a song called 'Walpurgis', which suggests it might have been a supernatural song. This is not necessarily the case. Maybe it was just a working title, with no lyrics written for it whatsoever. I don't know why Geezer changed it from 'Walpurgis' to 'War Pigs'. The lyrics were definitely his department. I always liked what he did, so I never questioned him.

Rodger Bain and Tom Allom speeded up the ending of 'War Pigs'. When we first heard that, we thought, that's strange, why would they do that? But we had no say in it in those days.

We smoked a lot of dope, so that might be why some of the lyrics are a bit unusual. Like 'Iron Man', which came from a comic about a robot which became alive. I suppose there was a serious thought behind that, really, that somebody living couldn't get out of that body, couldn't get out of this thing. And look at 'Fairies Wear Boots'. What a lyric! But nobody questioned it, people accepted it.

After we recorded all the tracks, Rodger said: 'We don't have enough. Can you come up with another song? Just a short track?'

'Oh? Yeah, I suppose.'

The others popped out for lunch, and I started playing DadaDadaDadaDada DadaDadaDadaDadada, dudududududu-dudu, Dada da: Paranoid. When the others came back I played it to them and they liked it. Geezer came up with the lyrics, I can't remember if Ozzy had any input in that one. When we'd start playing a new song, Ozzy would improvise and just sing anything, 'Flying out the window' or whatever, and probably wouldn't even know what he was singing. And then Geezer would go: 'Oh yeah, I can use that!'

Geezer would do the lyrics before we started recording or, in some cases, even in the studio. And then it would be up to Ozzy to get it right. He would come up with the melody, and he'd follow the riff in a lot of cases. I don't know how Geezer came up with the idea for the 'Paranoid' lyrics, but he had quite a wide imagination. He would sit and listen to the music for a bit, and sometimes he'd want it to be quiet. He'd write a few things down, cross some out and write something else. And then he'd give it to Ozzy, and of course Ozzy would go: 'What the fuck does this mean, Geez!'

Paranoid: I doubt we even knew what the word meant at the time. Ozzy and me went to the same lousy school, where we certainly wouldn't be around words like that. We knew what 'fuck' meant, and 'piss off', but 'paranoid'? That's why we left it to Geezer, because we considered him to be the intelligent one.

All our tracks were five minutes-plus. We had never done a three-minute track, so 'Paranoid' was like a throwaway: 'This will fill the gap.'

We never thought that it was going to be the hit. Out of all our stuff, that's always the one that people put on compilations, use in TV themes and in films. And it took probably four minutes to write. It's that basic, simple thing, that catchy theme, that seems to appeal to people. 'Paranoid' even brought us to *Top of the Pops*. We were very nervous doing that, because it was such a prestigious thing in Britain to be on that show. We were probably the loudest band they'd ever had on. I didn't like the atmosphere there at all, with the BBC people telling you what to do and all this rubbish. Things came to a head when I said: 'Get that light off of me, it's driving me mad.'

'We can't turn that off.'

I was like: 'Well, get it off!'

Of course I played in the dark then. We never did it again after that. We weren't really a *Top of the Pops* band anyway.

If the *Black Sabbath* album with the inverted cross on its sleeve caused some controversy, *Paranoid* did its best to top that. At first we were going to call the album *War Pigs* and they'd done the

album cover up with a guy with a shield and a sword: the 'war pig'.
But then they wouldn't accept that title and changed it to
Paranoid. We asked: 'What's that got to do with that cover?!'

But it was too late to change it, because they needed a title
quick.

'No, we can't use *War Pigs.* What are we going to call it?'

'It's got to be *Paranoid*!'

And that was it.

19

Sabbath, Zeppelin and Purple

John Bonham and Robert Plant were both from Birmingham. Me and Bill, when we were in The Rest, played gigs together with Bonham a lot. He'd be in one band and we'd be in another and we'd play the same clubs. And Geezer knew Robert Plant more than I did in those days. Geezer and myself were out shopping one day and we bumped into John and Robert. They said: 'We got a new band, we're getting together with Jimmy Page.'

'Oh, great!'

We didn't know Jimmy personally, but we knew him from The Yardbirds, so we were happy for them.

The first time I heard Led Zeppelin's first album I thought it was really good. Their heaviness was in Bonham powering the drums. Jimmy Page played great riffs, but he didn't have the heavy sound; his was a different sound. But it was a great combination. However, our direction was the other way round; it was the riff, the heavier sound of the guitar. Where Zeppelin relied on thundering drums, we had our massive guitar and bass wall of sound.

Bill Ward has said that at the time we decided to out-heavy Led Zeppelin. I don't remember that, but we may well have. As you did in those days. But in reality there's never been much rivalry between Sabbath and Zeppelin. We were both from Birmingham, we were all from the same gang if you like, so we always wished them well, as I'm sure they did us.

Nowadays everybody communicates with everybody else in other bands, but you never did that much then. We talked to the guys in Led Zeppelin because Bonham and Plant were mates. There was always this thing between bands from London and from Birmingham, from the Midlands. London musicians always thought that their bands were better than your bands. They looked down on people from the Midlands, and we in turn looked at Londoners as being snobby. There was a lot of competition because of that, with bands trying to outdo each other. It was always Zeppelin and Sabbath and Purple, but the rivalry was with Deep Purple, certainly later on, when we had *Paranoid* in the charts and they had 'Black Night' out. It was then, when we were both climbing the charts, that we felt real rivalry.

We were such good mates with Led Zeppelin that they even wanted us on their Swansong label. I don't know why that didn't happen. Maybe we couldn't get out of the deals with Warner and Phonogram, because we did sign ourselves to them forever. We would have loved to have had Peter Grant as our manager as well, but it wasn't to be. I think he only managed Zeppelin and of course later on Bad Company, who were signed to Swansong. In the early days there weren't that many managers who managed a lot of bands. There was just one manager for one band. We had Patrick Meehan and he didn't manage anybody else, at least not in the beginning.

When the guys from Zeppelin visited us while we were recording *Sabbath Bloody Sabbath*, we had a jam together. Bonham wanted to play one of our songs, I think it was 'Sabbra Cadabra', but we said: 'No, we're playing our songs already. Let's just jam and play something else.'

I don't know if any tapes exist of that. That would've been a different one: Black Zeppelin. It's the only time the two bands played together. John did get up and jam with us in the early days, but Bill never liked him playing his kit. It was his pride and joy and Bonham always broke something.

'Oh, Bill, let me play them . . .'

'No, you're going to break something.'

'Let me have a go, Bill.'

'No!'

They were mad, really.

We're still mates with Zeppelin, even though Bonham really upset Ronnie when they came to see our show at the Hammersmith Odeon back in May 1980. John was on the side of the stage having a good time and drinking Guinness, getting more and more sloshed as the show went on. We came off stage and he said: 'That guy's got a great voice for a fucking midget!'

Of course Ronnie heard him. Bonham meant it as a compliment really, but it didn't come out as one. Ronnie turned to John and said: 'You fucking cunt!'

It nearly came to blows. That would have been a lopsided fight because John was a bit of a hooligan. So I said to him: 'Look, please don't.'

He said: 'What's the matter with him!'

'Well, he didn't much like that. Just go back to the hotel and I'll see you later. It's not a good time right now.'

He went away then, but blimey, it could have been quite nasty.

Pagey is a mate. A couple of years back he wanted to see our gig at Fields of Rock in Holland and he flew out with us. We hung out, he saw the gig, we watched Rammstein together and we flew back. I've seen him many times at various functions since.

20

This is America?

Our first album was in the charts for quite a while in America, even though we had never been there. After we recorded *Paranoid*, we finally went. One of the stupidest things we ever did was take over our own PA. We took a Laney PA, Laney columns, and we had no flight cases or anything for them, so all the amps and cabinets suffered greatly from being thrown in and out of the plane's cargo hold. We got to New York and our expectations were sky-high: 'This is the real thing, ah, great, I can't believe it!'

But our first gig was in a poxy little club called Ungano's on West 70th Street in Manhattan. It was supposed to be *the* place to play, like when you're in London you do the Marquee, but we didn't think that when we saw what a shithole it was. I guess they booked us in there because agents and record company people were supposed to show up.

Our roadie, Luke, didn't realise it was a different mains in America, so when he plugged the equipment in, it blew up.

'Oh bloody hell, what are we going to do now?'

It was chaos, but they soon managed to get the fuses going again. We had two nights at this club and I thought, well, this is it? This is America? It was such a disappointment. But on the third

night over there, we played the Fillmore East, which was fantastic.
Bloody hell, monitors . . . what a difference! It was the first time we
heard each other properly on stage, the first time I could actually
hear Ozzy sing. It was brilliant and after that we never looked
back.

We played the Fillmore with Rod Stewart and The Faces. We
really went down well and Rod Stewart came on and he was practically booed off stage. We did two gigs with him and the same
happened the second night. He was not a happy chap. But that's
when we realised we were grabbing them . . .

The Americans, they really liked us!

Us being not very well known yet, some people thought that
Black Sabbath was a black band. That didn't last very long, as they
soon found out we weren't much of a soul group. As the tour progressed, we used to hang around and see other bands, like the
James Gang. We did the Fillmore West in San Francisco with
them and Joe Walsh was smoking this bloody angel dust. Right
before the gig Geezer said: 'I'll just have a puff of that.'

Ozzy joined him. They thought they were just smoking a joint.
Geezer said he was hallucinating on stage. It frightened him to
death. Most of us were pretty out of it half the bloody time. I
didn't partake as much. I was certainly no saint, but I thought it
wise to try to maintain a clear head. Up to a certain point.

21

Happy birthday witches to you

There were people in whatever country out there who wouldn't even understand our lyrics at that time, because they couldn't speak English. But it was because of the vibe of the music that they felt it was satanic. We were actually invited to join satanic sects. Alex Sanders, the head witch of England, 'the King of the Witches', came to the shows trying to get us into his thing. And the first time we played San Francisco, Anton LaVey, founder of the Church of Satan, held a parade for us there. I still have a picture of that. LaVey with a Rolls-Royce and a big banner that read: 'Welcome Black Sabbath'. I thought, what's all this? That's nice of them to do that!

When we turned down an invitation to play Walpurgis at Stonehenge, this sect put a curse on us. We took that very seriously. That's when we started wearing our crosses. First Ozzy wore this kitchen sink tap around his neck. Soon it would develop into a real cross. At the time we often talked about our dreams and many times it turned out we dreamed about the same situations, which was really weird. Maybe it was the Walpurgis thing, but one night we all had this dream about wearing crosses to protect us from evil. And so we did.

Ozzy's dad gave us these aluminium crosses that looked like they were made of silver. After the first four he made, he started mass production because we started selling them at gigs to make some money. Later Patrick Meehan gave us the gold crosses. He saw us with these aluminium things on bits of string, so I suppose he thought, I've got to get them something a bit better looking than that.

I never go on stage without wearing my cross. When I go on tour I always have two things that I really look after: the cross and my thimbles. The cross is big, in fact I've hit myself in the face with it a few times. You bend down to get into the car and, bang! That really hurts. Geezer lost his gold one at an Aston Villa football match. Bill still has his tucked away somewhere, but he actually still wears his original aluminium one. I lost my original one. I probably did what I usually do: put it away somewhere and forgot where. I can just see some new owner of one of my old houses suddenly discovering it: what's this cross . . . and this gram of coke?

Of course, neither us nor our music was satanic. Geezer and his family were very religious, Irish Catholic – he still is – but at the same time he was interested in occultism. He read a lot of books by the English occultist, mystic and author Aleister Crowley. We both had an interest in what happened beyond and got involved in it quite a lot. So he'd get his ideas from that. This certainly played a major part in that first album. I think Geezer felt that the music was portraying such a heavy thing, that the lyrical content had to be about something that went with the music. Everywhere else, it was all flower power and everything nice and happy and people weren't writing about real life: wars and famine and all the other things nobody wants to face. So we saw that and thought we should be doing it. But being accused of having made an occult or, worse yet, a satanic album, was simply ridiculous.

Still, we got a lot of flack. Certainly in America, because there the Church is such a big deal. We'd get to the gig and there'd be ministers and their congregations holding up banners: 'Don't come and see this band. They are satanists.'

Then there was a case there of a nurse who killed herself in her apartment, and what did they find? *Paranoid* on the turntable! So it was our fault. There was an inquest. *Paranoid* was mentioned and they found it wasn't to blame. But it was a shock to hear about this case, because it wasn't what we were about. We weren't trying to kill people! Besides, if people are depressed and put an album on, they're certainly not going to kill themselves because of the music.

Then there were the people from the dark side. One night, three witches came to the gig. Well, supposed witches. They saw we had proper crosses on and they cleared off. A bit later, back at the hotel one night, we went up to our floor and there was a whole crowd of people with black cloaks on and candles, sitting in the hallway outside our rooms. We thought, what's going on here? They really take you too seriously. Bloody hell! We climbed over them and got into our rooms as they held on to their candles, murmuring. We phoned each other up and said: 'What are we going to do? Let's give it half a minute and we'll all go outside.'

So we did. We all went into the hallway, blew out the candles and sang 'Happy Birthday' to them. They were disgusted, got up and left. But it could have gone the other way. They could have stabbed us!

Later on, around *Volume 4*, we were playing at the Hollywood Bowl. After the sound check we got back to the dressing room. It was locked up and there was a big red cross on the door.

'Fucking hell!'

We finally did get the door open and we never thought any more of it. We got on stage and after a while my amp started crackling. It was one of those days. I got really pissed off, turned around and I booted my stack. Luke the roadie was behind it and

I pushed it and tried to kick the thing over and then I just walked off. I was like that in those days, I had no patience. As I stormed off, I didn't even notice there was a guy on the side of the stage with a dagger. He was about to stab me. They eventually wrestled him to the floor and took him away. It turned out he had cut his hand and put that cross on the dressing-room door in blood. He was one of these religious freaks, really out there. They showed the dagger to me and I couldn't believe it: it was huge. Those were the sort of people you had to deal with a lot, but this one was a bit extreme.

Also in America the head of the Hell's Angels came to give us his blessing. He said: 'You get any problem at all, with anything, call me and I'll get it sorted out, whatever it is.'

What can you say to a man like that making an offer like that? 'Fuck off!?' Blam! So we just went: 'Great! Thanks!'

Maybe we should have taken him up on his offer with the guy with the bloody dagger . . .

22

Ozzy's shockers

Ozzy just had a weak bladder. One night we went to a club and we had a skinful of booze. Ozzy fell asleep on a couch and as they were closing the doorman said: 'You'd better get him.'

I said: 'I ain't getting him. If you want him out, you'd better move him.'

He said: 'I'll fucking move him.'

He picked him up, put him over his shoulder and Ozzy pissed himself, all down this guy's suit.

Eventually we could afford two to a room. Geezer and Bill shared one room and me and Ozzy shared another. That was better, but I'd be in bed, sound asleep, and Ozzy would wake up at all sorts of funny hours. He'd put the TV on full blast and then take a shower. I'd jump up wondering what the hell was happening, turn the TV off and get back into bed. He'd get out of the shower and turn it back on full blast again. I'd hear him bumping and banging and fiddling around and I'd think, I might as well get up myself now.

When we did get our very own rooms, I thought, this is great! But nothing changed: I'd be in bed at God knows what time, and there'd be a bang on the door. I'd answer it and it would be Ozzy, going: 'You haven't got a light, have you?'

'Do you know what time it is? And you bloody woke me up for a light!'

Ozzy and hotels . . . We were on tour, travelling for hours and hours through a lot of desert land. We came to this shop in the middle of nowhere, so we all piled out of the bus to have a look. There was a big sign saying: 'Fireworks'. Ozzy went in and bought all the fireworks they had. I said: 'What are you going to do with them?'

'Oh, I'm probably going to let them off later.'

When he said 'later' I didn't know he meant as late as he did, and I didn't know where. It turned out to be in the hotel at four o'clock in the morning. We were in our rooms and I heard these whizzing sounds of rockets flying past. I looked through the peep-hole of my door and I saw that the hallway was full of smoke. Then it started coming under my door, so I went out. By this time the bloody sprinklers had come on in the hallway and all the rooms. The guests came out in their pyjamas, screaming, not knowing what the hell was going on. It was such a mess.

Meanwhile, Ozzy, absolutely out of his skull, was still in the hallway letting his fireworks off. Of course the police came and took him away. They said to us: 'You better come down and bail him out!'

We said: 'You keep him tonight. We'll bail him out tomorrow. We've got to get some bloody rest!'

It was a newly refurbished hotel, but Ozzy's fireworks had burned the carpets and damaged the walls. They made him pay for it big time, so he learned his lesson there.

Or maybe he didn't.

And he's still the same now, always mooning everybody. Even when we were inducted into the UK Music Hall of Fame and we played 'Paranoid', Ozzy mooned the crowd. Well, the crowd – there weren't that many people there, but he didn't think they were enthusiastic enough so he decided to pull his pants down again.

You're playing to people in your business, so what do you expect? They're not going to jump up and shout and scream; they just sit there politely. And The Kinks were in the front. You don't expect them to leap up!

It didn't piss me off, though, it didn't bother us. We're used to seeing that.

I've seen Ozzy's arse more times than I've seen my own!

23

An Antipodean
murder mystery

In January 1971 we flew to Adelaide to headline the Myponga
Open Air Festival. We were lured into doing this by the promoter,
who said: 'Why don't you come and stay for a week's holiday? All
expenses paid!'

Really great for us. We got there and he turned out to be a very
generous host. He said to us: 'While you're here: whatever you
want.'

We wanted! Caviar and champagne, it was over the top.
There were four limousines at our disposal and on top of that
he gave each of us a brand new car. He said: 'For you to use in
case you want to drive anywhere yourselves and have a look
around.'

The wrong thing to do. We decided to go down to the beach to
have a race along the water's edge. One of the cars got stuck. I
tried to tow it out and I got stuck.

'Ah, fuck!'

Then the tide came in. As the water got closer, we started to panic. We got these oars off this bloke's boat and we were trying to get them under the wheels. 'Kchch!' Broke both his oars. No matter what we did, the cars couldn't be moved. We watched help-lessly as, finally, the water covered both cars. I phoned the promoter up and told him what had happened. He took it in his stride and sent a truck to tow them out. Of course the cars were completely knackered.

In the run-up to the festival I did some radio interviews and at one of them I said: 'Oh, we're very lonely, we could do with some women here.'

Live, on air. And what happened? Loads of girls turned up at the hotel. Me and Patrick Meehan ended up with this one girl in our room and then . . . she passed out.

Meehan went: 'She's dead!'

Oh, fucking hell! I thought, Christ, she's dead. She's *dead*!

I could see the headlines: 'Girl found dead in hotel room with two guys'. I just thought, they'll think it's us!

Meehan went: 'We got to get rid of her! We got to get rid of her!'

His idea was to throw her off the balcony and say that she had fallen off it. We were really high up. The thought of it now is absolutely frightening, but in my panic I went along with it. We got her to the balcony, we were trying to pick her up and then . . . she came round.

'Bloody hell, she's alive!'

She was probably high on drugs, but, we could quite easily have just tossed her off of there and I would have become a twenty-two-year-old murderer.

'But your honour, she was dead already!'

I bet that girl doesn't even know what happened. I'll probably be arrested now. She will read this book and come out of the woodwork: 'Yes, there he is!'

'It was Meehan! It was Meehan!'

Such a shame, really. It was a big festival, everything there went great and the promoter looked after us like you wouldn't believe. We later heard he went bust.

I wonder why . . .

24

Flying fish

In February 1971 we started our second tour of America. It was great, also thanks to our friends from Mountain. They were a good band, they treated us well and they had plenty of drugs. I really liked their guitar player, Leslie West. Still do. I once said to him: 'I really like the sound you're getting, I love the guitar.'

He looked and found me a Gibson that was the same as his. He came over to England and gave it to me. But it was stolen. You have a break for a while and your guitars go into storage somewhere. I had about four guitars go from storage once, and that was one of them. Leslie's guitar going: that broke my heart.

It was on this tour that we first stayed at the Los Angeles Hyatt, better known as the 'Riot', where we met our first groupies. We didn't really know about that. In Europe the women weren't as forward as in America. As soon as we walked into reception at the Hyatt these girls came up to us, saying: 'How are you? Are you from England?'

Before we knew it, everybody had a girl. We couldn't believe it. 'Blimey! Is this what America is like?'

And then, later, you'd see them again, with somebody else. We were like: 'So, that's what they call a groupie!'

In Seattle we stayed at the infamous Edgewater hotel, where you could fish out of the window. The hotel was built on stilts and leaned over the water. You could get a fishing line at reception, so that you could fish out of the window. And that's what we used to do. I don't know why really. Ozzy was fishing out of the window once and caught a shark, which he put in the bath while we did the gig. Of course it died, because the thing was as long as the bath and sharks have to move to breathe. Ozzy then proceeded to cut it up. Blood and shit were everywhere. He tried to . . . I don't know what he was doing.

Bill was below my room and he had his window open. I caught this shark, it dangled on my line and I swung it into Bill's room. He was very surprised. Not pleasantly, but very surprised! To have a bloody shark come flying through your window: 'Ahhhh!'

He threw it out of the window back into the sea, but the room smelled of fish from then on. Actually, all the rooms smelled of fish. You couldn't wash the floor down or anything, it was all carpeted. I don't know what they expected their guests to do with the fish they caught.

Another time we tied the line to one of the standard lamps there. We left, came back later and the standard lamp was gone. Gone out the window! So we picked up the bill for that one.

During the last tour we did with Sabbath, when we were in Seattle me and Bill went down to the Edgewater again, just for old time's sake. They showed us around: there was a Zeppelin room and they were doing a Sabbath room as well.

In the early days there were only certain hotels that allowed bands in, because of the reputation that everybody had. But now we stay all the time at the Ritz-Carltons and Four Seasons, the top hotels. And at sixty-plus years old we don't throw televisions out of windows any more.

Can't pick 'em up now.

25

Number 3, Master of Reality

Paranoid went to No. 1 in the UK album charts and, although it hadn't even been released in America yet, we did feel pressure when we had to come up with our next album, *Master of Reality*. Because once you've had a No. 1 album, where do you go? If you don't go to No. 1 again, you're not doing as good, so you've got to come up with songs that are going to make the next album at least equally as popular.

Management had us out on the road all the time, with weird schedules. Sometimes we did two shows a day, in different cities. We hardly had any breaks at all. Because of this, and because we didn't have any songs lying around from previous studio sessions, we went into a rehearsal room and started writing them. I'd come up with riffs and once we got started we came up with songs quite easily. Sometimes it was a bit of a struggle to get enough for an album, because you needed some time to think about them and live with them. And we didn't have that time. Especially after *Paranoid*. If we didn't have enough songs for an album, we'd have to write an extra song in the studio. We'd add little guitar bits to songs as well, to extend them a bit. I also liked to come up with some instrumental guitar tracks, like 'Embryo', which serves as an intro to 'Children Of The Grave' on the *Master of Reality* album. It's a little classical thing to give it all a little space and create some light and shade. If you listen to an album or even a song from start to finish and it's all pounding away, you don't notice the heaviness of it because there is no light in between it. And that's why, sometimes in the middle of songs as well, I put a light part in, to make the riff sound heavy when it comes back in. 'Orchid' served a similar purpose, leading into 'Lord Of This World'. It was just me on acoustic guitar, a nice little bit of calm before the storm to make the dynamics pop out. At first everybody thought, hmm, that's a bit odd. But we liked doing stuff outside the box. We wouldn't think, you can't do that, you can't do acoustic stuff, you can't use orchestras, so we did much more than heavy stuff.

When we recorded *Master of Reality* in February and March 1971, I got quite involved in it and really started coming up with ideas. We did some stuff that we had never done before. On 'Children Of The Grave', 'Lord Of This World' and 'Into The Void' we tuned down three semitones. It was part of an experiment: tuning down together for a bigger, heavier sound. Back then all the other bands had rhythm guitarists or keyboards, but we made do with guitar, bass guitar and drums, so we tried to make them sound as fat as possible. Tuning down just seemed to give more depth to it. I think I was the first one to do that.

We just weren't afraid to do something unexpected. Like 'Solitude', maybe the first love song we ever recorded. Ozzy had a delay on his voice, and he sang that quite nice. He has a really good voice for ballads. I'm playing the flute on that song as well. I tried all sorts of things in the course of doing albums, even though I couldn't play them, and after being with Jethro Tull for that short stint, I thought I might try the flute. I did it only to a very amateurish extent, I must admit. But I've still got that flute.

We all played 'Sweet Leaf' while stoned, as at that time we were doing a lot of dope. While I was recording an acoustic guitar bit for one of the other songs, Ozzy brought me a bloody big joint. He said: 'Just have a toke on this one.'

I went: 'No, no.'

But I did, and it bloody choked me. I coughed my head off, they taped that and we used it on the beginning of 'Sweet Leaf'. How appropriate: coughing your way into a song about marijuana . . . and the finest vocal performance of my entire career!

'Into The Void' is one of my favourite songs from that line-up; 'Sabbath Bloody Sabbath' is my other one. The structure of those songs is really good, because they have lots of different colours, there's lots of different stuff happening in them. 'Into The Void' has this initial riff that changes tempos in the song. I like that. I like something with interesting parts in it.

For Ozzy getting Geezer's lyrics right wouldn't always be easy. He certainly struggled on 'Into The Void'. It has this slow bit, but then the riff where Ozzy comes in is very fast. Ozzy had to sing really rapidly: 'Rocket engines burning fuel so fast, up into the night sky they blast', quick words like that. Geezer had written all the words out for him.

'Rocket wuhtuputtipuh, what the fuck, I can't sing this!'

Seeing him try, it was hilarious.

Just like our previous albums *Master of Reality* had some controversial moments. 'Sweet Leaf' upset some people because of the reference to drugs, and so did 'After Forever', thanks to Geezer's tongue-in-cheek line 'would you like to see the Pope on the end of a rope'. The cover was unusual again as well: this time it just had words in purple and black on a black background. Slightly Spinal Tap-ish, only well before Spinal Tap. Although this time we were allowed two weeks to record the album, what with Rodger Bain producing and Tom Allom engineering again, musically *Master of Reality* was a continuation of *Paranoid*. At the time I thought the sound could've been a bit better. That's the thing when you're a musician: you like things to be a certain way, to sound a certain way, and therefore it's difficult to leave it up to other people. When it goes into somebody else's hands you've got no control over it, and when you hear it it's not like you expected it to be. That's why I got involved more and more after those first albums.

26

No, really, it's too much . . .

When we recorded *Paranoid* I still lived at home. My parents had bought another place in Kingstanding, near Birmingham. They planned to move there as soon as they got rid of the shop. Mum wanted to get out of it. It was just a burden. You'd wake up in the morning and the shop opened and after you closed you'd go to bed. They could never go away. We never went on a holiday as a family, they had never been abroad.

I was proud of that new place. Before they moved in I had a key and if I had met a girl I'd take her up there: 'This is our new house!'

After all, I couldn't take anybody back to the old house: 'Here, come and sit on this box of beans, and I'll get you a nice drink.'

Wouldn't think of it.

But it was time for me to find my own place. At first I didn't have the money to do that, and when the money came in I was out on tour all the time. The first big cheques went towards a flash car anyway. No sooner did I get my hands on some serious cash than I bought myself a Lamborghini. So here was this Lamborghini outside the house in Endhill Road, Kingstanding. The house cost £5,000 when they bought it; this thing was like five times more than that. That car outside, we were mad in those days.

We were all car crazy. Geezer always said: 'When I pass my test, I'm going to buy a Rolls-Royce.'

One day I came home, and there was this Rolls parked outside our house on Endhill Road. I thought, oh hell, he's done it! Geezer's passed his driving test! Bill also bought a Rolls-Royce. In the ownership book there was Frank Mitchell, the famous Mad Axeman, who killed a lot of people, Sir Ralph Richardson, the well-known actor, and then Bill Ward! He'd have crates of cider in the back of it, like a travelling bar. Ozzy didn't have a driving licence, but he still bought my Rolls off me. His wife drove him and he came over to my house with all his dogs on the back seat. It was an immaculate car when I sold it to him, and the state of it when he came over! Dogs shitting in there and everything.

Geezer didn't manage to keep his car in mint condition either. It was the days of platform shoes, and Geezer's were very, very big. How on earth he drove that car with them I just don't know. He was driving around Devon, where the hills are quite steep, and he stopped off at a shop that was on top of one of these hills. He parked the car, went in on his platform shoes, and somebody in the shop suddenly said: 'Look! There's a car rolling down the hill. And it's a Rolls-Royce!'

Geezer went: 'Oh my God!'

He ran out, hobbling along on his platform shoes as fast as he could, trying to get next to his car so that he could open the door and stop it. Of course Geezer couldn't keep up with it and the car went flying down the hill and crashed through a fence, straight into a tree. On his way home he drove past my house, and I heard his car go 'kchh, kchh, kchh', this scraping sound of the fan hitting the radiator. The front was completely smashed up, and Geezer said to me: 'Now I see why they call it a Rolls . . .'

I bought my first house in 1972 in Stafford, north of

Birmingham. It was a three-acre property with a swimming pool. I soon noticed that they were building this modern house right behind it and I thought, fuck, it's right behind my swimming pool! Instead of allowing it to bother me, I bought it for my parents. They moved in there from their house in Kingstanding. It was a lovely place, brand new, all carpeted, modern bathrooms, the whole lot. I let Dad use some of the land where he could have his chickens, so he quite liked it there. But Mum felt like she was stuck in the middle of nowhere, too far away from the city. It was brilliant giving them that first house, but they didn't like it, so that was a huge disappointment to me. I said: 'Okay, you find your-selves a house you do like and I don't want anything to do with it. You tell me about it and I'll get it.'

So they did. They found this house that they liked at an auc-tion. I was in America at the time, so I sent this guy along to bid for this place. And who was he bidding against? My aunt, who was trying to get it as well! I didn't find out till afterwards. It was just the two of them bidding. I couldn't believe it! But we got it in the end and they were absolutely thrilled to live there. Dad had horses and chickens there, so he was in his element. It was almost too late for him, because he was starting to get too ill to enjoy it, but he did have a few good years there.

I tried to look after them, but that wasn't easy. Earlier, when we lived in Kingstanding, I saw my father outside with this old handle trying to crank-start his car and I thought, oh God, every morn-ing he's out there doing it, cigarette in his mouth, really horrible, we can't have this. So I bought him a Roll-Royce. Mum said: 'He's not going to like that!'

'Of course he will!'

I went to this dealership and bought him a Rolls-Royce for his birthday. They delivered it to the house with a crate of champagne in the back. Dad just went: 'What's that? I don't want that! Can you imagine me going to work in that? What would all the people say, and the neighbours, what are they going to think? Me with a Roll-Royce!'

Bloody hell. I had to phone the Rolls-Royce people up and say: 'He doesn't want it.'

'What do you mean he doesn't want it? It's a Rolls-Royce!'

'Yes, but he won't even get in it.'

So they came and picked it up. I said to Dad: 'What do you want then?'

'I don't want anything.'

'Wouldn't you be better off with another car? What about a Jaguar?'

'Well, it's better than that thing.'

So I bought him this Jaguar 3.4, the classic one with all the nice wood and switches and stuff. He still didn't want it, but I said: 'Dad, you got to have it. I can't get my money back now. I bought this car; they won't just forget about it, I have to buy something off them.'

He used that for a while, but it was a struggle. I thought, blimey, I try and help him out and he says: 'I don't want that bloody thing.'

My father died in 1982, he was only about sixty-five years old. Mum survived him by nearly fifteen years. He was a stubborn man, very proud, and he never complained. He'd just plod on. He had worked hard all his life. That's what he believed in, work and nothing but work. And he would never stop smoking. He smoked himself to death. He died of a collapsed lung and of emphysema.

One day I noticed he was looking ill. Because Sabbath had done some charity work for the hospital in Birmingham I had met these specialists. I told them about Dad and they said: 'Well, get him to come in.'

Dad hated doctors, so I said: 'There's no way he's coming to hospital. Would you come out and see him?'

They did and he went absolutely mad. He hit the roof, going: 'Don't you ever bring them around here again!'

They checked him over anyway and said: 'Well, he's in a bad way.'

But there was nothing you could do for him, he just wouldn't have it.

Couldn't buy him a house, couldn't buy him a car ... couldn't buy him his health.

27

White lines and
white suits

In England it was all hash and dope and pills, but when we head-lined the Los Angeles Forum in the autumn of 1971 I was introduced to cocaine. I said to one of our roadies: 'I feel really tired.'

He said: 'Why don't you have a little line of coke?'

'No, I don't want to do any of that.'

He was American, so he was familiar with it. He said: 'You'll be fine. Just have a little toot before you go on.'

I had a toot and I thought, ah, this is wonderful! Let's get on stage and play! And that was it. Bloody hell! I felt great on stage and of course the next time I had a little bit of that stuff before going on again. And then I started doing it more and more. As you do.

To do something special around that gig we also performed at the Whisky a Go Go on Sunset Strip. Patrick Meehan said: 'Why don't we wear something different? White suits and top hats and canes!'

We hired all these white suits and they were absolutely covered in dirt after no time at all. Most people take these things back all nice on hangers, but the people at the rental place must have thought, who's had these?

The Beach Boys came to see us that night and I didn't know what they looked like. I was coming out of the dressing room and somebody walked up to me and said: 'Can I come in and see the rest of the guys?'

'No, no, there's nobody allowed in the dressing room.'

It was a little bit embarrassing afterwards, when I found out he was a Beach Boy.

LA and movie stars and sunshine – it made quite an impression on us. We ended up at these well-to-do parties where we saw lots of movie stars, like Tony Curtis and Olivia Newton-John. We'd be coked out anyway, as a lot of them were as well. Floating around there . . .

I think it was at the end of that third tour of America that we played the Hollywood Bowl for the first time. My memory is not crystal-clear about that show, because I collapsed at the end of it. I passed out because of exhaustion. I just remember going to the last song and then urrrggh, boing, and gone. The doctor who examined me said: 'You've got to go on the next plane back to England, go straight home and just take it easy.'

I was about to have a nervous breakdown, so they prescribed Valium in high doses. I was a fucking zombie all day. I really had to just rest. It had been too much with the lifestyle we were living, all the touring and not getting a lot of sleep. And the drugs, I suppose. Bill was diagnosed with hepatitis and ended up in hospital. He carried this rusty knife with him all the time and he opened some clams with it and cut his hand. He claims he got it either from his knife or from a shell. Being a vegan, Geezer couldn't get half the food he wanted, so a combination of that and drugs made him awfully thin. He got these kidney stones and ended up in hospital as well. We were all falling to bits. Ozzy probably had the most unhealthy lifestyle of all of us, but he was the only one still standing.

We were all out for the count, but Ozzy? He was right as rain.

28

Air Elvis

We started off 1972 with a nineteen-day UK tour with Glenn Cornick's band Wild Turkey. We had them supporting us, because Patrick Meehan had teamed up with Brian Lane and they managed the band. Lane was the manager of Yes, which was why we had them on the next tour with us: thirty-two shows throughout the States and Canada, starting in March, the Iron Man tour. Us and Yes: it was an extremely unlikely combination. They hated us, because I'm sure in their minds they were the clever players and we were the working class. Sometimes they talked and other times they would walk straight past you. Very strange. Years later we all got along fine, but it took a long time. And they were funny on stage. If anyone made a mistake, the daggers would be out. We thought, what's all that about? Music, somebody's made a mistake, so what? It's a good thing they weren't in our band. We would make mistakes every two minutes. Here we were, with them as supporting act with all their clever stuff coming out, and we're going 'boing', 'clunk', 'zzzzz'. They must have gone: 'What the fuck? What are we doing here?'

Their keyboard player, Rick Wakeman, didn't get on with them, so he travelled with us as much as he could. We liked Rick. I think he was interested in playing with us, but he would have been too good, too much for what we wanted. We only wanted something very basic, that just went 'duh-duuh-duh'. It wasn't like Yes music.

On our previous tour one night, Elvis was staying at the same hotel we were at. We would see him come in with all this security and go to the top floor. We were invited to go and see Elvis perform. I had a bird that night, so I said: 'I'm not going.'

I regretted that afterwards, because I didn't see his show then and I never would.

On this tour we flew from LA to Vegas and back in a plane that belonged to Elvis. Really strange: all leopard-skin seats in there, very flash. The stewardess on the plane came out with a plate of all different coloured sandwiches. I went: 'Blimey. What's this then?'

'Well, it's coloured bread.'

'Ah!'

It must have been something that Elvis liked. But it was a nice plane. We used it, behaved ourselves, left it in one piece as, of course, we were very respectful. I mean, it *was* Elvis!

29

Going Snowblind

We took quite a long time to write and rehearse for the *Volume 4* album. It's not like it was becoming harder to come up with stuff, but the pub was only a mile away, so we'd start to come up with ideas, and it was: 'Ah, oh . . .'

And they'd all go down to the pub for 'a' drink.

I'd think: I'm not going to go; I'll just sit here and try to come up with something. I'd play for a bit, an hour, two hours, three hours, and they'd all come back plastered: 'You got anything?'

Oh, great! I felt really pressured.

When it was suggested we go to the States to record, we were all very much in favour of the idea. It was a way to avoid the English taxman and the studio rates were better, cheaper, out there as well. More important than that, we thought it would be nice to really go somewhere else to try and get a different vibe. We went to Los Angeles in May 1972. Patrick Meehan knew John Dupont, from the Dupont company, lighters and paints and all that. A big – *huge* – company. We rented his house in Bel Air. It was a great place with a big ballroom-type room overlooking the pool. It had a magnificent view of LA, the works. We all lived together there, the band, Meehan and these two French au pair girls who came with the house.

The vibe in America was great. The Record Plant, where we recorded, was a state-of-the-art studio and far better than what we were used to. We decided to produce *Volume 4* ourselves. It's not like we were fed up with Rodger Bain or anything, I thought he was all right. But we had done so much studio work by then, that we felt we knew how to do it ourselves. I've heard Rodger has since disappeared and won't talk to anybody any more. I don't get that. I wonder why that would be.

Patrick Meehan put himself down as producer as well. I don't know why he did that either. But he was there, he was in the control room and I suppose he thought, oh I'll just add my name to it. Once or twice he may have said: 'What if we try . . .?' and that was it, his part in the production.

Producing it ourselves was everybody going: 'I want my bass up', or 'I want this' and 'I want that', but it worked out okay. It was only later, from *Sabbath Bloody Sabbath* and onwards, that I started really poking my nose in more.

Recording took six weeks, maybe even two months. During that time we also set some gear up at the house in Bel Air, where we wrote the last of the songs. It was a different environment, everybody had a brighter attitude and there was a schedule: 'We have got to get it done.'

We were still fucking about and doing stupid jokes, but ideas and the songs were coming out quickly. Perhaps having loads of cocaine helped speed things up as well. And we had a lot of it. It came in a sealed box the size of a speaker, filled with files all covered in wax. You'd peel the wax off and it was pure, fantastic stuff and loads of it. It was like Tony Montana in the movie *Scarface*: we'd put a big pile on the table, carve it all up and then we'd all have a bit, well, quite a lot. Word got around, and soon other musicians, lots of women and new 'friends' came to the house and everybody was diving in.

One sunny day we were sitting in the TV room around a table

with cocaine tipped out on it and grass as well. This house had all these buttons around all the rooms. Bill thought it was the maid's button and pressed it, but it was an alarm button for the fucking Bel Air police. Only a few minutes after that I stood up, looked out of the window and there were about six or eight police cars in our drive. I shouted: 'Quick, the police!'

Everybody went: 'Hahaha!'

'I'm serious, it's the police!'

Again: 'Hahaha!'

I had literally to get one of them and go: 'Look!'

And then: 'Oooh, it's the police!'

We quickly scraped all this coke and dope off the table. We had our own little stashes in our rooms as well, so we all rushed up there, trying to snort as much as we could before flushing the rest down the toilet. Then we said to one of the au pairs: 'Quick, answer the door!'

She did and, of course, the police came in. We were sitting in the ballroom, all quiet-like, eyes wide open. They said: 'What's going on in there?'

'Mmmm, nothing . . . Why?'

You could obviously tell we were out of it. They wanted to know what we were doing there, and we told them we'd rented the house and so on and so on. It was hell on earth. If they'd have searched us, we would have gone down very badly. But they left after we explained about Bill's button mistake.

We flushed a lot. Afterwards, of course, it was: 'Oh fuck! It's all gone, man! Quick, phone the bloke up again. Get him over!'

In the Record Plant, though, we were a bit more serious. Being in control in the studio we were free to experiment a bit more. The first three albums could've all been from the same batch really, but *Volume 4* was when we started introducing different things. I'd found a piano in the ballroom up at the house and I used to play that thing when I'd had a million lines of coke. I'd never played the piano before and I started learning it right there and then, within a couple of weeks. Mind you, I was up all bloody night every night with a line of coke, play for a bit, another line of coke, play, so I was probably up for the equivalent of six weeks. And while doing that I came up with 'Changes'. Ozzy came in and said: 'Oh I like that', and started singing to it. We got the Mellotron in and Geezer started playing that, like an accompaniment, an orchestral thing. And that was it, we decided to record it. It sounded really weird; I couldn't believe it was us. I actually felt pretty embarrassed, because when we recorded it at the Record Plant, Rick Wakeman came in and he said: 'Who was that playing the piano?'

I thought, oh no, he's going to say: 'That's crap, that is.'

But he liked it.

I suppose we could have asked somebody like him to play these keyboards, but Geezer and me wanted to do it ourselves. Both of us were learning, it was a challenge.

If 'Changes' was unusual, 'FX' certainly was way out there. We were mostly naked at the time when we recorded it. When you're in the studio for hours on end smoking dope, you go a bit mad. We started playing and were dancing around half naked, just being stupid. I hit my guitar with my cross, it went 'boing!' and we went: 'Ooh!'

'Boing!'

'Aah!'

Everybody then danced past the guitar, hitting it. We were just playing about. We didn't think of using this as a track, but they recorded it with a delay and we thought, oh, yeah, hmmm, and we put it on the record. I always put so much work in every song, putting all the different changes in and everything, and here we had a track that came about accidentally because a couple of stoned people were hitting my guitar, and it ended up on the album. A total joke! If only we'd had videos of it, it would have been amazing.

Or not.

'Laguna Sunrise' was actually inspired by a sunrise at Laguna Beach. I was there with Spock, one of the guys of our crew who was a good guitar player as well. We were up all bloody night and I just started playing this acoustic guitar and came up with this idea. We also tried to work out the orchestra bit for it. I had never done that before, as we had never used orchestras up until then. I don't know how to write music out, but Spock did, so we tried to work out the notes for the orchestra to play: 'What's that dot there? Okay, put that down.'

We went into the studio and, of course, the orchestra wouldn't accept it. They wanted all their parts written out properly and once we got somebody in to do that, they were great. On the end of 'Snowblind' we also used orchestras, and again later on 'Spiral Architect' off the *Sabbath Bloody Sabbath* album. And 'Supertzar', off *Sabotage*, is me playing heavy guitar with a choir and a harp player. I did things like that to get a different sound into our music.

Bill nearly didn't make it to the end of the recording process. We were rummaging around the house one night and in the garage we found all this Dupont paint. We grabbed these spray tins of gold paint and this clear lacquer. We got back into the house and there was Bill, pissed as a parrot and on the floor. We said: 'Can we spray you?'

Of course he said: 'Yes.'

We took all his clothes off, sprayed him, and he had everything gold. We then got this clear lacquer and sprayed him with that as well. It was bloody funny. Bill was lying there, all shiny, then he started making these weird little noises. Then he started throwing up and he went into this violent seizure.

Oh, fucking hell.

We phoned for an ambulance and we thought, how the hell are we going to explain this?

'What's wrong with the chap?'

'Well . . . he's sort of lying there and he's . . . gold.'

And then trying to make it sound serious: 'And he's being really sick.'

'Excuse me, what exactly is wrong with him?'

'Erm . . . he's sprayed gold and he's on the floor, naked.'

They came out and gave us a right bollocking: 'You idiots. Don't you realise you could have killed the man!'

Everything was gold, his arse, his beard, the whole lot. Apparently it blocks all the pores up and you can die from it. They made us show them the tins of paint that we sprayed him with, and this lacquer as well. They read the tins, all seriously worried, and then they injected him with something. Meanwhile, we were standing there like naughty boys, going: 'Is he going to be all right?'

We dashed back to the garage again, found some thinners and used that to get the gold off him as quickly as possible. It was quite a job cleaning him up. It was a fun idea, but it really backfired.

Recording *Volume 4* was great. We had the Dupont house, the sun was shining, there was the swimming pool, women, everything. And coke, lots of coke. We had such a good time that we didn't want it to end.

Towards the end of our stay one day we partied a little too hard. We were at the house and started messing around. First we threw a few things and in the end we got the hosepipe in, squirting it at each other. Ozzy painted himself in all these different colours, which caused such a mess. And then the doorbell rang. It was the owner of the house, John Dupont. Ozzy answered the door, soaked and with all this paint on his face. Dupont went: 'What the hell is going on in here?'

He came in and it was a total mess. I was standing there with the hose, going: 'Ah. How are you? Nice meeting you.'

He had a go at Patrick Meehan and we had to pay him. The

situation was solved by money. As if he didn't have enough, this John Dupont.

But crazy stuff like that happened because we were happy there. We rehearsed and came up with ideas and wrote stuff during the day and at night we went to the Rainbow Bar or whatever and partied.

That whole period was one of the most enjoyable times ever, and a song like 'Snowblind' makes it clear that it was also because of a certain drug. That's why we wrote on the album sleeve 'We wish to thank the great COKE-Cola Company'.

Just a little thank-you nod to our suppliers. I rented a house in Bel Air again a couple of years ago, when we were working on songs for the *Heaven and Hell* album, 'The Devil You Know'. The Dupont house was on Stradella Road and, because I went out for walks a lot, I passed it every morning. Apparently it's now owned by former Charlie's Angel Jaclyn Smith, so I used to look in, trying to catch a glimpse.

But I never did.

30

This is your captain freaking . . .

When we toured America in the summer of 1972, we travelled around in a private plane. We'd fly somewhere, stay there for a few days to do the gigs in the area, and then we'd fly off to somewhere else to do the same thing. If at all possible we'd stay in Florida so we could be on the beach during the day. Flying private planes was a Meehan thing. We had already used them back in 1971 on the *Paranoid* tour. In March of that year we toured the States with Fleetwood Mac, and they hopped on a flight with us. Ozzy sat in the front and we were all chatting away in the back. Suddenly the plane dived and went: 'Vroooom!'

Ozzy had taken the controls. I don't know why on earth the pilot let him do it! I shat myself. Bloody hell! But of course Ozzy thought it was hilarious. Everybody was screaming and shouting so he did again: 'Woo-hoo!'

It didn't do much for Bill's fear of flying. He used to get terrified and needed to take Valium to get on a flight. He soon started driving instead of flying. He had a GMC mobile home and his brother, Jim, drove him from one gig to the next. Occasionally they'd have to stop at one of those places where you have to dump all the contents from the toilet. One day Jim was pushing the button that was supposed to release all the shit and nothing was happening, so Bill decided to get underneath to see what was wrong. He had got into CB Radio, like the truckers, and he was going through a stage of talking like that, with all this 'breaker 1-9, come in Bulldog, 10-4' stuff. So Bill was under the bus, going: 'There's a negative on the shit, Jim, a negative on the shit. Nothing's happening, negative.'

He was banging away at stuff, then his brother pulled a lever again and all this shit and blue sewage stuff just went all over him.

Blwerkk!

Bill just went: 'I've got a positive on the shit, Jim, positive on the shit.'

Jim pulled the bus forward and there was the outline of Bill on the ground with this pile of shit around it. His face was covered in it and he looked like the Creature from the Black Lagoon. It was one of those classic moments.

Typical Bill.

31

A rather white wedding

My first wife was Susan Snowdon. I met her through Patrick Meehan in his office in London. Meehan was from a very well-to-do family himself. He mixed with high-society people, had the suit and the Rolls and went to all the in places. I presume that's how he met Susan. She wanted to do some singing, so I said: 'I'll write you a song.'

Of course I never did. She came up to my house one day and it was a bit awkward: I found out she couldn't sing at all and she found out I hadn't written a song for her. But we did go out to dinner, and that's how it all started.

We were totally opposite people. Susan's parents and her family were all right, but some of her friends, bloody hell: 'Oh, what do you do then, you play the, ah, what is it, a plink a plonk, ah, you do this?'

Very condescending. I really did not want to go near these people. Susan reacted to my friends in much the same way as I reacted to hers, so she'd go and see her friends and I'd go and see mine. That might not sound like a very solid basis for a relationship, but we lasted for eight years, a fairly long time. Of course I was on tour most of that time. We had a very peculiar relationship. She was always too posh for me, really.

We planned to get married on 3 November 1973. Before I could marry Susan, I had to meet her parents at their enormous mansion and ask her father for his daughter's hand. I was really nervous when I got there. They brought the cakes out and the tea and teapots and little cups and I thought, God, I hope I don't knock something over. But her father and mother were very down-to-earth, honourable people. I got on really well with them. Of course, when we got married, we were going to have the reception at their house. I was thinking, oh bloody hell, what's going to happen when they see my friends?

But first I needed to survive my stag night. It was only John Bonham, me and a driver. We went to clubs around Birmingham, and the last one we hit just before closing time was Sloopy's on Corporation Street. John said: 'Let's go and have one last drink.'

Right, one last drink ... he had the bloody bar lined up with twelve bottles of champagne and twelve glasses, and he said to the bartender: 'Pour them out!'

I thought he was going to treat everybody in the club, but, no, he said: 'This is for you.'

'Fuck off, John, I'm getting married in the morning. If I drink that, you're never going to see me there!'

'Well, I'll drink them then.'

Which he duly did. Of course, within half an hour he was absolutely paralytic, and he was going: 'Whuehheu ...'

To make matters worse, the club was closing and we had to get out. Sloopy's was upstairs and the stairs to the exit were steep. On our way out John grabbed the owner of the club around the neck and of course the bloke fell down the stairs. He hurt himself so he wasn't very happy. Our driver and me finally managed to get Bonham out of the club and into the car, and we took him home first. When we got to John's house he didn't have his keys on him. It was four o'clock in the morning. I pressed the doorbell: nothing.

Again: nothing. Then the lights went on upstairs. His wife, Pat, opened a window and shouted: 'He's not coming in!'

I said: 'Pat, please, let him in. I'm getting married in the morning and he's got to be there.'

'He's not coming in!'

'Please!'

Finally Pat said: 'All right, but he's not coming upstairs then! If he's coming in, he can sleep downstairs.'

'Okay.'

She came down, opened the door and ran straight back upstairs. We carried John in, put him in the hallway, sat him against a radiator and I said to him: 'You're not going to make it tomorrow, are you?'

He put his thumb up and slurred: 'Yeah, I'll be there.'

The driver took me home and I thought, bloody hell, John's never going to turn up and I'll be without a best man.

I had to be there at some silly hour and I couldn't believe it: eight o'clock sharp I saw Bonham coming up the drive, with his top hat and tails on, all dressed up. He lived a good thirty-five minutes from my house and I hadn't even had a shave or anything yet. I opened the door and he was all chipper and energetic, going: 'I'm ready. Are you?'

I actually felt worse than him. We got in the car and of course we immediately did a quick couple of toots. I thought, oh dear, so this is how the day is going to be. We got to the bloody church and, before we went in, all our lot kept disappearing behind the building, one after the other, having a line. Come back, snort and go: 'Right!'

And then somebody else would go: 'I'll be back in a minute.'

On my wife's side they were wondering where they kept going off to and I was thinking, Christ, I can't do this! Once inside, my friends were all sniffing and snorting, all those sounds going on in the church, it was terrible. And then you had her side, all immaculate and straight.

I had written this instrumental thing called 'Fluff'. They played the tape when Susan walked down the isle and it started going wrong. First it came on and then it went off and it came on again and everybody started giggling. A total disaster.

When the guy said: 'Is there anybody here who's got anything to say about why these two should not be joined in matrimony?' I was convinced somebody was going to shout out. But they didn't. They were just sneering. I was bloody glad to get out of that church.

When we got back to the house for the reception, they were all disappearing again. More lines. My mother-in-law said: 'It's funny, none of your friends are eating.'

Of course I said: 'Oh really? I wonder why.'

John Bonham and Ozzy and a few others were notorious drinkers who'd play up once they'd had a few. That's why we thought it best just to have a toast in champagne and after that not to have any more alcohol. It really didn't go down very well. We had the champagne toast and then a top-up with apple juice and Bonham spat it out and went: 'Fucking apple juice!'

Susan's side never swore, so I thought, oh no, this will upset the cart. My mother saved the day. She said to Bonham: 'Don't worry, John. We'll go back to my house. I've got plenty of booze there.'

They all sneaked off to Mum's house and carried on drinking there. If it weren't for her there would have probably been antiques going through the walls, on account of all that apple juice.

32

Going to the big house

Susan didn't want to live in my house in Stafford, so we decided to move to a place between London and Birmingham. We were looking at houses to buy, but couldn't find anything we liked. One day her dad said: 'Why don't you come and live here? This house is far too big for us.'

Sue went: 'That's an idea.'

And so we did. We had a major part of this massive, 200-room house. My father-in-law built a partition between their living quarters and ours and we lived there for quite a few years.

Just like in Carlisle, we weren't the only ones there. I saw an apparition going up the stairs one night. It wasn't like a three-dimensional person, it was more like a figure. And I had more weird things happening there. We had these big, old-fashioned keys in the doors to all the bedrooms. I was in the lounge one night and I had my briefcase open. I closed it and I went upstairs to bed. I heard this big bang and ran downstairs again. One of the big paintings had fallen off the wall. I walked into the lounge and my briefcase was open. And I went to open the door and the keys had gone. All of them. Never found them again. I talked about this to my in-laws and they said: 'Yeah, there is a ghost here. But he's a friendly ghost.'

Things like that make you really think. A poltergeist, for a start, can be horrible, but . . . they can move an object! I've always been able to see things that most other people can't. It's hard to talk about it, because people think, right, he's had too many drugs. But I actually did see things, like the Carlisle ghost. Saw him as clear as day.

I always wondered about what happens when you die, when you're beyond this world, and tried to find information about that in books. While living at the big house, I read a lot of books by Lobsang Rampa. He was a writer who claimed to have been a Tibetan monk before spending his later years in the body of an Englishman, or so he wrote. I started getting into all this leaving the body stuff, astral travelling. I really believed in it and that made me want to do it. I planned it and thought about it and I tried it a few times, but nothing happened. When I finally managed to do it for the first time, I came out of my body and, with a jolt, suddenly jumped back in. You feel it pulling you back as your astral is leaving your body; you feel this pull up your spine. I must have got frightened and I came straight back in.

Once I had done that I was determined to make it work properly. I kept practising. You've got to be by yourself in a room and you have to really, really relax, but not to the point of falling asleep, because you have to stay conscious. And then you will yourself to leave. At first it's funny, because you feel like you're falling. Most people have had that feeling when in bed. You go, oohh: you experience a jolt. That's when your astral comes back in your body when you dream. You're asleep and you're just about to leave your body, and if you move, whoof, it comes straight back in and you get that jolt.

After a while it worked. I came out my body. It was weird. I floated around the room and looked down on myself from the ceiling. And I could leave the room, go through walls and go off to the roof. It sounds mad, but once I even went along the beach.

You come back. You're attached by a silver cord that pulls you back. If that's ever severed, you don't, so it can be risky. When you dream and your astral leaves your body, and an entity is in the lower-class astral, and it pulls on your silver cord and annoys you, you get these horrible dreams. It could be caused by drugs or drink, just anything. I know it sounds odd, but I have experienced all that and it opened another world to me.

I don't know why I don't do it any more. I didn't follow it through. I have actually tried it a couple of times and: nothing. I can't leave my body any more. But in those days I could do it quite easily. I got to a point where I could do it without falling asleep.

I still believe you can go to a non-physical plane of existence. When you die you can go there, and you can look back on your life in a thing called the akashic records. I really think that's what happens: you can go and see whether you've achieved what you wanted to achieve, and if not you can be born into another body and try again . . .

Back to the reality of living in that huge house, I tried to rebuild and redecorate it. I phoned up this one company and I saw this painter and decorator's van come up the long drive. He came to the house, looked at it, turned around and drove straight off. I just couldn't find the people who could take on a place that size, so I had to get contractors in who normally did schools. You wouldn't be able to buy huge properties like that any more, but in those days they were still quite affordable. And now it's a wonderful hotel, Kilworth House. The old snooker room is now the dining room, and the conservatory is still intact as there were only three of those in the country and there is a preservation order on it. All I did with it at the time was grow tomatoes in it, and some exotic plants. But probably the most exotic thing in that place at the time was a long-haired guy from Aston, who only a few years earlier had shared his tiny bedroom with a lodger who came from nowhere, a million boxes of peas and a phone that kept disappearing.

33

One against nature

On 2 January 1973, we flew off to New Zealand for the Great Ngaruawahia Music Festival of Peace near Hamilton City, followed by a few shows in Australia. On our way there the plane stopped in New Delhi and bloody Singapore and everywhere in between and beyond, and we'd have to get off the plane, wait an hour, get on again. It took forever. We got pissed, sober, pissed, sober . . .

At this Ngaruawahia Festival somebody erected a huge cross on a hill and set it on fire. I don't know why he did this, but it looked really good. I can't remember much else about that. The trip to it is still etched on my mind, but the memory of the gig itself must have gone up in flames together with that cross.

After New Zealand we had a gap before the next shows in Australia. Patrick Meehan said: 'Let's take a break and go to Fiji!'

So off we went. Again, it was a real pig to get there and after we landed the drive along a dirt track to the hotel in the middle of nowhere was diabolical. It was a lovely place, close to an equally lovely beach, but at night it took on another life.

This hotel had an outside bar. There were no drugs at all in Fiji, but there was plenty of drinking going on. In the middle of the night I went back to my room and there were so many bugs and cockroaches scurrying across the footpath that walking along all you'd be hearing was 'crunch, crunch'. I went into my room and I got into bed. I put the light out to go to sleep and I felt something on my chest. I put my hand there and it was a cockroach about three inches long. I shot up, put the light on and I could hear 'krrch, krrch' – all of them running across the stone floor to go down this drain in the room. It was absolutely awful. In a panic I phoned the reception, screaming: 'Get over here!'

This guy wandered in, all casual, with a tin of spray. He gave me the tin and off he went, just like, well, what's he moaning about?

I said: 'Is that it?'

You couldn't kill them either. It's like they were made of stone. I was hitting them with my shoe, and it was just like ... nothing. Still going 'krrrrch!' A bloody army of them.

Horrible!

In Fiji it was also the first and the last time we all played golf. We were merrily shanking our way to the first green when I saw this toad hopping around and I picked it up. This bloke came running towards me, screaming: 'No, no, no!'

Apparently this was a deadly poisonous toad. It had all this stuff coming out on to my hand. I shot back to the hotel in a panic, to wash it off in a hurry.

Meanwhile, Bill stepped into an anthill and suddenly all these ants were marching up his leg. They bit him so he was dancing all over the place, going: 'Aah, uh, oh, oohh!'

A leisurely game of golf and I nearly got poisoned to death and so did Bill. We packed up after that. I don't think we even made it past the second hole.

Apart from all that, it was lovely in Fiji. We went out on a boat, sat on the beach and then to this bar at night, just doing the things you do while on a holiday.

But I never got a proper night's sleep there.

34

The well runs dry

We'd had such a great time doing *Volume 4* in Los Angeles, and we wanted to recreate the experience for what was to become our next album, *Sabbath Bloody Sabbath*. We all went back to LA and rented the same house. After us ruining the place the first time, John Dupont must have got a wad of money to allow us back. We also returned to the Record Plant, but the room was different.

'What's happened? It's really small now!'

'Oh, we built this Moog in here for Stevie Wonder.'

'Oh, no!'

Back at the house I tried to come up with ideas, but I couldn't think of anything. I don't know what it was. I just couldn't get it. Then I started panicking: 'Oh, no, what am I going to do!'

Up until that time, when we went somewhere to write and rehearse, I felt that most of the time everybody was dying to go down the pub instead of working at the songs. But you need to get stuff done. It's quite easy to sit around, telling jokes and boozing, but the money is going out of the window like this, sitting in some studio for bloody two grand a day or whatever it was. So I was really aware of that.

It was already getting harder around the time we were working there on *Volume 4*, because we were established by then. In the past I'd say: 'Come on, we've really got to work on this!'

The guys would listen to me, because I had always been looked on as the leader of the band. But at best I was a very reluctant leader. It was a role that eventually got to me, because if something went wrong I had to be the pillar everybody leaned on and to say: 'Everything's fine, it's going to be all right.'

If I had broken down, I think everybody would just have fallen to pieces. Me believing in what we did and not letting things get to us, I think the other guys looked at it as a strength thing. Maybe me being physically the strongest also had something to do with it. If we had a fight it would always be me they'd call for. It happened quite a few times. I came back to the hotel one night and Bill came running towards me, shouting: 'Oh Christ, you're back! Ozzy and Geezer are fighting upstairs, you've got to come up quick!'

'Oh, fuck!'

I shot up there and they were drunk and really going at it. Ozzy was on top of Geezer and he was wearing this long mink coat. I grabbed Ozzy by the collar to pull him off. The next thing I knew I was standing with the collar held high, while Ozzy was still down there pounding on Geezer – I'd torn the thing clear off. I picked Ozzy up and he took a swing at me, so I landed one on his jaw and he went down. I felt bad, because I didn't want to do that. But I was put in that position; somebody had to be in control because otherwise it would go all over the place.

Ozzy has said in the past that he felt that I always had a barrier around me. That's probably because I tried not to get involved with the partying so much. We used to stay in these poxy hotels where you could hear everything through the walls. I often heard people screaming and smoking dope and having a good time, but I felt that if I went and joined them we'd all be in the same boat, so I didn't. Somebody had to be in control if something went wrong. If I'd become the same, nobody would have listened to me any more. I think you have to maintain some sort of separation. It's a bit like being the office manager: when people have a problem they go to his office. With Black Sabbath it was a bit the same, really. I didn't want that, but that's the way it was. I can't say I was responsible all the time because I've certainly done my share of stupid things and in my own little world I was as bad as Ozzy, but I couldn't let the whole thing get too close.

I think for many years Ozzy was frightened of me and if I said: 'We need to this and we've got to do that', he would listen. I became the bully again, which I didn't want to be. But somebody had to do it. The whole purpose of it was to function, get the band on the road and work, with as little aggravation as possible. If somebody went: 'I'm not playing tonight, I'm tired', someone had to say: 'Fuck it, you've got to play!'

Being in a band isn't all fun, it's bloody hard. I think you've got to deal with everything life has in store for you, no matter how bad that might be. I tend to fight through a lot of stuff, so it's hard for me to understand other people not doing the same. I wouldn't expect something to solve my problems, going: 'I'll take one of these pills and everything will be all right.'

It's like these rehabs: I would never go to one. I just think it's a cop out, going into rehab and walking out and saying: 'Ah, I've been to rehab.'

Ozzy went into the Betty Ford Clinic and they had him scrubbing the floors. How was that going to rehab him? You could do that at home! I just think a lot of it is brought on by yourself; you can control it to a point. Like with me, at some point I was taking loads of coke. I could have said: 'I'm going to go into rehab' but I didn't. I stopped on my own.

It does take a lot of determination and that's something I really do have. That comes from the way I was brought up. I was always being told by Mum and Dad: 'Oh, you're never going to do any good.'

My other relatives chimed in as well: 'Why don't you get a proper job like your cousin!'

Because of that I became very determined to achieve something, no matter what got in my way, if only to prove to them that I could. It gave me the determination to fight on. It's like when I cut the ends of my fingers off and they told me I could never play again. I wouldn't accept that.

I'm sure it has actually helped Black Sabbath. I was the driving force in the band, I made them rehearse and got them off their arses to do everything needed to achieve what they wanted to achieve. I saw that it needed some control. You can't just all go off willy-nilly and expect everything to happen just like that.

But as we got more popular, I was less and less in a position to firmly take the reins any more. And with nobody there to control it, it just got out of hand. If we were working in the studio but they decided to go down the pub, they'd go down the pub. If there was a particular part where I was trying to think of something for maybe fifteen minutes, they'd get impatient and say to each other: 'Oh . . . shall we go and have a drink?'

The rest of the day would be shot, and then the next day it'd be the same, until I came up with stuff to work on. That became harder and harder. If you have no one to bounce ideas off, it becomes almost impossible, and I didn't have that any more. In the early days, when we jammed I'd come up with riffs and then everybody would be enthusiastic, putting stuff in. We had now reached a point where it was like: 'Oh, we got to do another album', and nobody was motivated enough to really do it.

My role was to come up with the music, with the riffs. That probably stopped the others from writing music. If I didn't come up with anything, we wouldn't do anything. I felt the pressure of that, but I had always been able to cope with it. However, it got to me when we needed to do *Sabbath Bloody Sabbath*. We were all back again in Bel Air, sitting in the ballroom of John Dupont's house. Everybody was looking at me and I couldn't get into the vibe at all. It was totally different. I just couldn't function. I got writer's block and I couldn't think.

So we knocked it on the head and moved everything out. We got back home to England all depressed. The other three thought, that's the end of that now. I remember Geezer and Ozzy talking like it was all over. I panicked. I thought, blimey, it's never going to happen again. My God, I've lost it all!

After a couple of weeks or so we rented Clearwell Castle in Gloucestershire to see if we could get the vibe back and write again. We were just looking for something different. Everything in this place was dismal, especially its dungeons. It was really creepy down there. It was a big space with an armoury, another room with something else in it and a lounge. We set our gear up there and tried to get a vibe. We certainly got one: I walked down this long corridor with Geezer and we saw somebody coming towards us.

'Who's that?'

'Don't know.'

We had no idea who it could be, because we had rented the whole castle. We saw this bloke coming up, just this black figure, and he went into the armoury. We looked at each other, followed him into the armoury and ... nothing! It was just a bare room with a big table with weapons on it and swords and shields all over the walls. And that was it. No other doors out. It baffled us: 'What happened to him? Where's he gone? Bloody hell, this is really weird!'

We looked everywhere but there was ho trapdoor or anything in there. He couldn't hide under the table either, because you could see under that. We got in touch with the woman who owned the castle and she said: 'Oh, was it a guy with a hat on?'

I said: 'Well, we just saw this figure coming up.'

'Oh, that's so-and-so, the castle ghost. You may occasionally see this person.'

As if it was the most normal thing in the world. Bloody hell. But we didn't see him again.

About the same time we saw our ghost, Ozzy fell asleep in the lounge, which had a big fireplace. He had stoked the coal fire up really high and one of the pieces of coal fell out on to the rug and set it on fire. We came in and he was spark out on the couch and about to burn to death. It's a habit of his, building the fire up too high. It happened in his own house. He set the chimney on fire and they had to get the Fire Brigade out because the house started burning down. And this time, if we'd come in a little later, Ozzy would've become a ghost himself.

After telling the others about the ghost, we started frightening each other. Our roadie, Luke, stayed in one of the rooms. It had this big bed and nice curtains, and there was this model of a big ship above the fireplace. I got some fishing line, put it under the carpets and fixed lines to the curtains and the ship. Then I labelled them all outside the door and put the carpet over the line. I waited until Luke went to bed and started with the ship, pulling that a bit. Then the curtain. And I heard him going: 'What! Who's there! Who is that?'

He was absolutely petrified and came flying out of the room. And there I was, holding the line.

'Oh!'

The woman who owned the castle had said to Bill: 'You might feel something strange sometimes, because there is a bit of a funny feeling in that room.'

Bill went: 'Ah, oh, why?'

She said: 'Well, many years ago . . .'

And she told him a story about this maid who used to live there and had a baby by the owner. She got the baby and jumped out of the window and killed herself. It happened in Bill's room and apparently sometimes you could see this woman run through the room and jump. Bill got so scared he had this big dagger stuck in the side by his bed.

I said: 'What are you going to do with that thing?'

'If that ghost . . .'

'Bill, it's a ghost. How are you going to stab a ghost, for Christ's sake!'

Geezer actually liked it at first. He stayed in this room that was supposed to be haunted and was trying to see if he could get a vibe. But at the end of the day nobody knew if it was something in there or if it was somebody playing a joke and none of us dared stay there any more. I thought, fucking hell: we got this place in the middle of nowhere so we could go and start writing, and everybody has terrified themselves that much that they're driving home at night!

But the vibe there did lift my writer's block. As soon as we started working the first song I came up was 'Sabbath Bloody Sabbath'. First day we were there, bang! I went: 'Bloody hell!'

35

Sabbath Bloody Sabbath

We recorded *Sabbath Bloody Sabbath* in Willesden, north London, and produced it ourselves. The 'direction Patrick Meehan' credit was on the album sleeve again. We felt there was less 'directing' than ever, as Meehan was expanding his business more and more and we were probably not getting the attention we should have had. That began gradually and the first cracks in our relationship started to show. I really worked hard on that album. I tried a lot of different stuff. It was a matter of constantly being in the studio creating sounds. Back then you had to make them yourselves and it took a while. Now, with the computer, it's bang, okay, next.

The riff of 'Sabbath Bloody Sabbath' was the benchmark for that album. It was a heavy riff, then the song went into a light bit in the middle, and then back to the riff again: the light and shade I'm always looking for. Ozzy sang very well on it, actually on all of the songs on the album. Very high!

Geezer wrote lyrics for the song with lines like 'the race is run, the book is read, the end begins to show, Sabbath Bloody Sabbath, nothing more to do'. I don't know what inspired him to write that, but it could be about him thinking it was all over when we got writer's block. But after that song the rest followed without any great problems. The other guys came up with ideas as well. Ozzy had bought this Moog synthesiser. It was like the top of the range, but he didn't really know how to work it. I don't know who could understand it either, it seemed really complicated to me. But he got this one sound out of it and he came up with 'Who Are You?'. It worked really well. I just put a piano bit in the middle of that one. And the initial riff for 'A National Acrobat' was written by Geezer, and then I added bits to it. Geezer can write some great stuff. It's just getting it out of him. This was probably the first one he did that got on to an album.

Rick Wakeman played on 'Sabbra Cadabra'. He wouldn't accept any money for that, so we paid him in beer. We'd always have a bit of a laugh with him. On the end of that song Ozzy's saying stuff like 'stick it up her arse' and all that, just as a joke. It was never meant to be on the album as this track was supposed to finish well before Ozzy started ranting and raving, but, because Rick was playing on it, we just kept it going. Then we thought, we'll be crucified doing an album with all that on it, so we put phasing over it so you can't tell what he's saying. But all that foul language is on there, just jumbled up a bit.

Apart from the single 'Paranoid', we couldn't gain any radio airplay. One of the few who gave us a chance was Alan Freeman, the BBC DJ whose nickname was 'Fluff'. He liked us and played 'Laguna Sunrise' as the theme tune for his programme, *The Saturday Rock Show*. So when I came up with another quiet instrumental I thought, well, I'll call this song 'Fluff', after him.

On 'Spiral Architect' we used strings again, arranged by Will Malone. Will has a nice, weird way of thinking. It was again a bunch of serious people coming in and playing those strings. I didn't play bagpipes on this song, although I tried. I just thought for a minute I could play them, so I sent one of the crew out to buy me some bagpipes at this Scottish shop. I started blowing, without any result. This went on and on; it was a real waste of studio time. I went: 'Take them back to the shop, tell them they're not bloody working!'

He took them back, the bloke at the shop played them and said: 'Nothing wrong with these.'

I thought, oh no. I then attached them to a vacuum cleaner, to see if we could blow the bag up so I could just play it. But of course the only noise you got was 'Wuuuuuhhh', from the vacuum cleaner. I tried for ages, but all I could get was something that sounded like a dying cat: 'Wiiiihhuhhwiiiuh.' So in the end I gave up on that. Of course we could have got a Scotsman to do it, but we always tried things like these ourselves. The first time me and Geezer wanted strings, we thought we could play them ourselves, multi-track the instruments and make this into an orchestra. We got a violin and a cello and it sounded awful: 'Wooohhooo, yieieiehieieieieh.' I could hear what I wanted in my head but it wasn't coming out in our hands. We tried until we said: 'Oh fuck it, we've got to get an orchestra in!'

It was the same with the sitar. I couldn't play that either. I had all these great ideas, but they never materialised. I've still got that sitar somewhere. Got rid of the bagpipes, though.

The album ended with a little bit of applause. Our engineer put that on and we thought, oh, that's funny, and it ended up on there. Sometimes these little things did, and sometimes they didn't. Actually, on one of the earlier albums, when we were working with engineer Tom Allom, we spent an hour and a half marching up and down these stairs, singing: 'Hi ho, hi ho, it's off to work we go.' We were coming all the way down these three flights of stairs and there was a microphone at the bottom, so the sound we made was getting louder and louder. And Tom kept going: 'No, no, go back, do it again.'

We were dead at the end, but we kept doing it: 'Hi ho, hi ho.'

The idea was to walk down and eventually slam the door and

'duh-duh-duh-duh' come into a track. It looked like a good idea until we tried it and it sounded awful. So we scrapped it.

The album cover had great paintings by Drew Struzan, with the good on one side and the evil on the other. On the inside it had a picture of the band in what should have looked like an ancient room, except there was a three-point power plug down there on the wall. That sort of blew it a bit, really.

Even today, I find that the music, compared to the previous records, has more class about it, more arrangements, more shine if you like, and it's more adventurous. It was a leap forward. We used strings and God knows what else; we really expanded. That's why, for me, *Sabbath Bloody Sabbath* was the pinnacle. And then the next one would be *Heaven and Hell*, which created that same vibe for me again.

36

The California Jam

We rounded off 1973 with a couple of UK dates in December. After the Christmas break we did a few European gigs before flying to America for a lot of shows in February. We often got stuck with the same bands when we went to the States. We always seemed to have Edgar Winter, Johnny Winter, Brownsville Station or Black Oak Arkansas opening for us. It was like: 'What, Black Oak Arkansas? Oh dear, not again!'

After America we went home to take some time off. Next up was the California Jam on 6 April 1974 at the Ontario Motor Speedway in Ontario, near Los Angeles. We were going to be rehearsing out there prior to the gig and we sent Spock and the rest of the crew over there first. But then this almighty row broke out between Deep Purple and ELP about who was going to close the show. They were trying to involve us in it as well. We thought, we better hang on, this whole thing is blowing up. Purple wanted to close it, and then ELP as well, so Patrick Meehan at some point said: 'We're not going out, it's off.'

We agreed: 'We don't want to get involved in it, we'll pull out.'

Then Spock phoned me at something like four in the morning:

'You've got to come! Everybody wants to see you! It's going to be an almighty ruckus if you don't show!'

I phoned the other guys, going: 'We got to get out there, get on a flight!'

They thought I was joking: 'Oh, hahaha!'

'Seriously. We've got to get out there. I've heard from Spock . . .'

We got on a flight at the last minute. We got out there and we just said: 'Look, we don't care. We'll just go on, whenever.'

And that's what we did. We went on and ELP closed the show. It was strange: one moment you're home in bed and the next you're flying to a gig. We hadn't played for five or six weeks, we didn't rehearse; it was a one-off, so it was a bit hairy.

We all get stage fright on certain occasions. It depends. The first gig of a tour usually makes you go: 'Ooooh!' The second gig is much more relaxed. And that's the one where everything goes wrong. You also have the gigs where everybody you know comes to see you, like the Hammersmith Odeon in London, the Forum in Los Angeles and Madison Square Garden in New York. All your friends and the press are there and you get worried: 'Oh fuck, everybody's coming down tonight. If anything goes wrong . . . I'll be glad when this one's over!'

It's like when you're recording a show. Nine times out of ten when you think about being recorded you make a mistake. It's that edgy feeling you have. At regular shows you don't care, you just get on and do it, and it becomes second nature. But the California Jam, what with the weird lead up to it and hundreds of thousands of people there, was nerve-wracking. And it was televised, which made it even more terrifying. But stagefright never lasts. We got on stage, played, and it was okay.

But the gig was good. It was just the shock of it all. But I think it worked.

After the California Jam we toured the UK in May and June, taking a break from the road until November, when we rounded off our Sabbath Bloody Sabbath tour with about eight shows in Australia. AC/DC were supporting us. I didn't really meet them then, but we certainly got acquainted a couple of years later when they opened for us during our European tour in the spring of 1977. We got on all right with Bon Scott, but there just seemed to be a little bit of friction between the two bands as that tour went on. There was something going down quite heavy between Geezer and Malcolm Young. They were in the bar, got paralytic, got into an argument and somebody pulled a knife. I think it was Malcolm who drew that knife. I don't think it was Geezer, but it could have been.

We were in Sydney to start the tour and the promoter took us to this really flash restaurant. They closed it especially for us, so we were the only ones there. We were eating this exquisite food using all this nice silverware and everything, and then somebody flicked a pea at somebody else.

He then flicked one back.

Then it was something else, a potato ...

At the end it was just ridiculous. The dinner was flying everywhere. Everybody was ordering: 'Can I have another salad, please, with loads of oil and vinegar?'

Kggg, on somebody's head.

Bill, of course, him being the one who always gets it, was absolutely covered: cake, olive oil, sauce and chocolate all over his face and all down his clothes. He was an absolute mess. We all looked pretty bad. Ozzy had yellow trousers on, we got hold of them and, *kggg*, ripped the legs all the way up past the hip. The owner of the restaurant was absolutely in bits. One of our guys went over to him and said: 'They're going to take care of it.'

He gave him a bundle of money. The owner was suddenly all right then, going: 'Ah, carry on, carry on!'

We then got the waiters involved even more: 'Go on, give me a big cream cake under the table!'

And then: 'Whoa!' *Kggg!*

We walked back to the hotel afterwards. We looked awful. Such a picture. With all the drink and everything as well, I actually thought they wouldn't let us back into the hotel. We walked into reception and the doors opened and there was a ball going on. We walked in on a whole crowd of people in suits and bow ties and ballroom dresses and their mouths dropped. Of course security came rushing in and we were going: 'It's all right, we're guests!'

I bet that promoter hasn't invited many people out since. He certainly didn't invite us again.

37

Where did all the money go?

We said to each other: 'Does anybody know what's going on? Has anybody seen any accounts?'

None of us knew how much money we had, because it was always a case of anything you wanted, you got. We'd phone Meehan up and any money we wanted: 'I'll arrange it.'

Sometimes Meehan sent a cheque and the bloke at the bank would go: 'It's bounced.'

'Aye?'

And I'd phone him up.

'Oh, I'll put it in again. Go and put it in again now, it's all right.'

He was very careful. He always had a wad of cash in his pocket, never used a credit card, I think because that way he wouldn't have any kind of record of what was being spent. That's the way he worked. We thought, why can't we just have a lump sum put into our bank so we know how much we have and work with that? We met these people in the office one day and Meehan said: 'These are your accountants. They are going to look after all your stuff. You talk to them. Don't talk to me, talk to them.'

And then all our money went to the accountants. We never had it coming to us direct. We'd have these meetings with them and they'd say: 'You can't just get everything you make and put it in the bank. We want to take some of your money and put it in a Jersey account, because of the tax.'

We just said: 'Oh, well . . .' We didn't know anything about that side of it and it all seemed above board. When somebody from a big accountancy firm tells you what they're going to do with your money, you go along with it. We found out later that they also worked for Meehan.

And then, when we found out that our management contracts with Meehan weren't signed by him, they were only signed by us, that was even worse. He really caught us with that one, a trick from the early days.

We were so gullible about everything. All we wanted was to play and tour everywhere and go to America and all that. That's why in the beginning we never questioned Meehan's way of doing things. And, of course, most of the time we were on tour, so we didn't require much. It's only when we came out for another break that we went: 'I want to buy a new house' or whatever it might be. Or he'd go: 'I'll send another ten grand down' and everything would be roses.

We started seeing things change a lot at the office. When we got involved with Patrick Meehan at first, it was just him. Then he got more money and bought companies like NEMS, the old Beatles thing, Brian Epstein's label. He also got on board with David Hemmings, the actor famous for the movie *Blow-Up*, with a company called Hemdale. So then Meehan was also making movies. One day he said to me: 'I'm auditioning today. I've got all these women coming around.'

I came downstairs and saw this whole queue of gorgeous women outside the office.

And he got into a building company, housing and all that stuff. Of course, when we bought houses, we bought them through this company. Meehan was involved with so much stuff I could never tell what it all was. He even bought a racehorse called Black Sabbath and a racing car as well. We were seeing him flying around in private jets and he'd always have the latest Rolls-Royce. And so would we if we wanted them, so we didn't argue.

We were told that 'All the money was put in the London & County Bank', which went bust at the end of the day.

And apparently our money disappeared with it.

We really started to think when we saw what we thought was a bunch of pretty unsavoury characters getting involved with Meehan at NEMS. These people were nice enough with us, but it made us very nervous. I think David Frost, the very well-known TV personality, was a client and Dave Hemmings also.

Eventually, when we went on tour in Europe, one of them came with us. Willy his name was. Maybe he was there to make sure nothing happened to us, or maybe he was seeing what we were up to, spying for the mob or whoever they were. It was a bit frightening, certainly when one fan tried to approach us and Willy pulled his gun out. It was really heavy.

We hadn't a clue about what was going on.

The fact that Meehan was gambling like there was no tomorrow didn't help either. When we had Yes with us on our American tour, we played Las Vegas. It was a very involved situation. We thought, fucking hell, what's going to happen? How are we going to fight this one?

We were unhappy with the situation, so we had to do something about it. We finally decided to leave Meehan. Somewhat surprisingly, he seemed all right about it at first. I think he'd got what he could out of us and was happy to let us go. So many things went on that we were just not aware of and I think that's why we felt we were screwed over. We sued Meehan but when it came to it, for whatever reason which I never really understood, we didn't have a leg to sue on. He sued us in turn and he won. It seems to me that from the moment we became successful we've been in court. Jim Simpson sued us after we left him and that case dragged on for ever. The Simpson case only got settled around the time we split up with Meehan and Simpson was awarded something like £35,000 that we had to pay him. He also sued Meehan, who had to give him a similar amount.

So much for the old management, but what about a new one? It was hard to trust anybody. We did have managements approaching us, but how do you know they are straight? In those days there were no music lawyers you could turn to for advice, people who knew about the business and who could look at the contracts. A lot of the things that were signed back then had loopholes galore. We decided that the only way to do it was to run it ourselves and have Mark Forster, who already worked for us, do the day-to-day stuff. We just got another accountant and all that rubbish and started again. We had band meetings, but it soon got to be too much for us. We said to each other: 'Look, we're not business people, how are we going to do this? We don't know how this all runs and works. We're musicians and what are we trying to do?'

We met with lawyers and accountants. That got boring because we weren't into that stuff at all. Within five minutes Ozzy would be asleep or he'd stand up and walk around and then go out and come back in and go: 'We're going to get something to eat or what?'

'Well, we'll end this meeting then?'

'Oh, uh . . .'

'Sit down.'

'All right.'

He'd sit down for a bit and you'd see him fidgeting and then he'd ask a few questions: 'Is that it then? We're finished?'

Mr Impatient. It was very hard. But we had no option. It was the only thing we could do.

38

Everything's being Sabotaged!

At the beginning of 1975 we got together to write and rehearse for what was to become *Sabotage*. The making of that album took a long time because we were in the studio one day and in court or meeting with lawyers the next. A writ is a summons to appear in court and we were being handed writs even while we were working in the studio. It was so distracting. It felt like we were being sabotaged all the way along the line and getting punched from all sides. We were constantly in some problem or another with management or somebody. It made the band into a tighter unit, because it was us against them. We were trying to do music and it was hard to create it in that situation, unless we wrote a song about it, which sort of relieved that situation. That's why one track is called 'The Writ' and the album is called *Sabotage*.

Apart from legal harassment, we were also having technical problems in the studio. We had a hard time recording 'Thrill Of It All' and eventually we got it down after no end of takes. Soon after we went to a bar across the road to play darts and Dave Harris, the tape guy, came over and said: 'We've got a problem.'

I said: 'What?'

He said: 'One of the technicians has aligned the tapes up on the master tape.'

'You're kidding!'

'I'm not, honestly!'

Their job was to put this series of reference tones, basically a bunch of beeps going from higher to lower pitch, on to a master tape so it's all aligned and ready for you to use. You had to in those days: align the heads and everything, make sure it was all right. He would set it all up on the tape machine and go: 'That's fine, you can use it.'

But he had mistakenly put the tones on to the master tape of 'Thrill Of It All'. We listened to the recording of the song and suddenly it was: 'Doo-doo-doo-doo.'

He'd wiped enough off so we had to record the whole thing again. It was such an ordeal. We didn't kill Dave but did actually give him a nod for his screw-up on the album sleeve: 'Tape operator and saboteur – David Harris'.

We produced *Sabotage* ourselves. The band disappeared most of the time so it was sort of left to me and the engineer. I got more and more involved with the production side of things, but it wasn't like I would sit there and tell the other guys what to do, because they knew what to play, they put their parts to it. I just spent a lot more time in the studio because, when it came to doing the guitar bits or mixing, it would take longer and I'd be more into it than they were. I didn't mind so much. I'd be there to the death.

Sabotage has a couple of unusual tracks, like 'Symptom Of The Universe'. That has been described as the first progressive metal song and I won't disagree with that. It starts with an acoustic bit, then it goes into the up-tempo stuff to give it that dynamic, and it does have a lot of changes to it, including the jam at the end. That last bit was made up in the studio. We did the track and after that finished we just started jamming. I started playing this riff, the others joined in, we kept it going and we ended up keeping it.

Then I overdubbed it with acoustic guitar. A few things we've recorded came from jams like that. We'd just keep going on the thing and so the end of the song sometimes became longer than the song itself. A lot of our songs tended to be long anyway. Like 'Megalomania': we carried on and on with that until we just faded it out. Some of those tracks were probably twice as long as you hear on the album, but we had to fade them out.

I wrote 'Supertzar' at home with a Mellotron, to create choir sounds. I put heavy guitar to that and it really blended well. I thought, I'd love to try this in the studio, it would be great if we could use a real choir. So I booked the London Philharmonic Choir. They came down and were all set to go at like nine o'clock in the morning. Ozzy didn't know anything about this. He walked in, saw all these people and he walked out again.

'Fucking hell, it's the wrong studio!'

He came back and went: 'What's going on, who are all these people in here?'

'We're just trying this song.'

'Uh ... Oh.'

This woman came along with a harp, because I had a harp at home and I could only play 'ding, dong'. She said: 'What do you want to hear?'

'Well, sort of like "ding, dong". That's what I am playing.'

She said: 'Ah, something like this ...'

And her fingers flew over the strings.

'Yeah! That's it!'

I felt like such an idiot. What was I doing, asking her to play 'ding dong'? But to my knowledge it had never been done before: a heavy guitar riff with a choir and this harp. It was a challenge. I thought, there's a fifty-piece choir here and this harp player, this better work out. But we did it and it sounded really different and really great.

The *Sabotage* sleeve is probably our most embarrassing one. It had us posing in front of a mirror that reflected the wrong way round. We turned up at this photo session for it and Bill said: 'I don't know what to wear.'

He turned to his wife: 'Can I borrow those tights?'

He put her tights on, but he had this checked underwear underneath that was shining through. Typical Bill. Ozzy didn't do much better, dressing up in some sort of Japanese mourning gown. I've even heard it being described as 'the homo in the kimono'. Such a naff thing; we're all so different there. Fucking hell, we've had trouble living that down over the years!

On *Sabotage* the sound was a bit harder than *Sabbath Bloody Sabbath*, and my guitar sound was harder as well. That was brought on by all the aggravation we felt over all the business with managements, lawyers and writs. *Sabotage* did all right, but it didn't sell as well as the previous albums. It's the way it goes with everybody: you can't go up and up and up, things go up and down. Other people come in and other music takes over. The taste of people moves, it changes. And yet we still plod on, doing what we're doing. Even so, we've been pretty lucky with our fans because they've been very loyal. We did go through a period, certainly in the *Paranoid* days, of attracting a lot of screaming teenagers, which wasn't our sort of audience at all. But they go for anything in the Top 10. We didn't want to be involved in that because it wasn't us. We weren't about the pretty boy image; it was purely the music for us. That's one of the reasons all our albums keep selling really well after all these years. I can't believe the way it goes, it's just phenomenal. It must be that new kids are coming around to buying it.

39

Bruiser in a boozer

My old friend Albert Chapman was the manager, doorman and
whatnot of a club in Birmingham. I said: 'Do you fancy coming
and doing a bit of work with us in Australia?'

He went: 'Oh, I'd love that!'

This was in November 1974. After travelling with us to the
other side of the world he stayed on, doing the 1975 Sabotage
tour, which took us to America for the summer. On a couple of
dates we had Kiss supporting us. Their show was really interesting
to watch. I couldn't believe what was going on, all these costumes,
the make-up, fire breathing, fireworks shooting out of the end of
guitars and God knows what else. I had never seen anything like
it.

At first we didn't get on with Kiss. We even changed the first
letter in the sign with their logo from a K to a P. We didn't even
know who the guys in Kiss were then, because we'd never seen
them without their make-up. They'd be at the airport the same
time as us, waiting for a flight, a group of guys, long hair, spots all
over them probably because of all the make-up, and we'd go:
'Yeah, I bet that's them!'

As time went on, we came to know them and got on with them

quite well. Years ago I did an American TV show called *Rock School* with Gene Simmons. They recorded it over here in England and the idea of it was to teach kids how to play. Gene's done a series of them. He's all right. Every time I see him now I just take him with a pinch of salt. He's telling me how much money he's earned and how to earn this and how to do that. But that's the way he is. It's just him.

After this very extensive American tour we did ten dates throughout the UK, some of them with Bandy Legs from Birmingham opening for us. I had met their guitar player, Geoff Nicholls, through Albert Chapman, who managed them. They later changed their name to Quartz. Albert signed them to Don Arden's label, Jet Records, and he asked me if I would be interested in producing them. I liked some of their songs and I ended up doing it. When you're involved in your own stuff, you have a routine with what you're doing. When it comes to somebody else, you've got to put a different hat on. All in all it was a good experience for me.

Geoff Nicholls was their main songwriter. He reminded me of myself, how he liked to get things done and work hard at it. He was creative, he loved playing guitar and keyboards and he sang as well. After Quartz fell apart, Geoff would work with Black Sabbath for quite a long time, playing keyboards and so on.

As a matter of fact, the Sabotage tour was the first time we took a keyboard player with us. We had always been a four-piece and the other guys wanted to keep it that way, which was understandable. Ozzy simply said: 'We don't need keyboards.'

I just thought that having somebody there to back up the solos would bring more flavour to the songs. Also we were using more and more keyboards and orchestras on our records, and with a keyboard player we could reproduce some of it on stage. So we hired Gerald 'Jezz' Woodroffe. He was from Birmingham, where his family owned a well-known shop called Woodroffe's Music

Shop. And, God, did he get some stick! Our crew played him up something terrible. You never knew where he was going to end up; sometimes he was on the side of the stage, sometimes he disappeared from view completely. He had a big nose so he sort of looked like a parrot. We had all these smoke machines and the crew put one of the tubes of a smoke machine facing him. They covered it up so he couldn't see it and then, when we were playing, we saw this toy parrot flying across on a wire, with its wings flapping. It stopped right in front of Gerald, still flapping. We were in stitches. Then we got to 'Black Sabbath', 'da-daa-da', and all this smoke blew in his face. The poor bugger took it on the chin, but he wasn't happy about it. He's a great musician, but he kept getting all these wind-ups. Funnily enough, to this day it's happened with every bloody keyboard player we've had.

After the UK it was off to Europe. We hit Düsseldorf on 2 November, Albert's birthday and my wedding anniversary, so we decided to celebrate. We went down to the Why Not Club. Geezer and Ozzy joined us and so did Dave Tangye and Luke from our crew. Roger Chapman, who used to sing with Family and supported us with his band, Chapman Whitney Streetwalkers, and Nicko McBrain, now of Iron Maiden fame, who was his drummer at the time, were in a different part of the club.

Our lot were sitting there drinking, having a good time and minding our own business. Then some bouncers from the club started circling our table.

'Funny, isn't it?'

'Wonder what's going on . . .'

It turned out they'd come to watch what we were doing, because there was some trouble caused by some of the Streetwalkers and their lot, and to them we probably all looked the same: 'Oh, they're all in that group.'

Ozzy went to the toilet and Dave Tangye went with him. Somebody said something, or grabbed him, and Tangye dived in to stop it and it turned into an almighty fight. Me and Albert rushed out to see what was going on. We ran downstairs and the bloke at the bottom of the stairs shot Albert in the mouth. The guy put a gun by his face and bang! Albert had a lot of teeth missing from boxing anyway, so there wasn't too much damage to be done. He was all right. The bullet had gone clean through his cheek. I'll never forget the bloke who did that. He was wearing a suit and black gloves. Albert then hit him so hard, the guy got covered in blood. It was a bad fight.

I ended up hitting this one bloke and between punches I noticed he was the chef from the restaurant. I don't know how he got involved but it was a free-for-all. Like in one of those old westerns, someone would turn around and bang! There were fucking people going over the banisters and falling off the balcony, it was unbelievable. It just went from nothing to this.

The fight moved outside, into the street. We called this one bloke that Albert was fighting Bumble, because he had a striped shirt on. He was one of the security people over there. He just wouldn't go down. He'd go down and then get up again, down, up again, down, up, and Albert beat the shit out of him. Then this other bloke stepped in and Albert beat the shit out of him as well. Just horrendous it was.

Meanwhile, this bloke who had shot Albert went to hit Ozzy on the head with a metal bar. I put my hand in the way and it hit my fingers.

'Aargh!'

Fucking hell, that hurt. And then I started hitting him. It was mad. I thought, we've got to get out of this. These cars pulled up and I screamed: 'Quick get in the car!'

I grabbed Albert, jumped in the back and shouted: 'Hilton hotel!'

The two guys in front turned around and I was looking down the barrel of a gun. It was the police.

Ah, fucking hell.

They put me and Albert in jail. We got out in time for the gig the next night and the audience must have wondered about the state of us. Black eyes and everything. It was a terrible fight, and we got the blame!

So that was my wedding anniversary and Albert's birthday.

We had a fantastic time!

After Europe, Ozzy hurt himself in a motorcycle accident, so we had to postpone a couple of UK gigs. When he healed we went back to America. We started off in Madison Square Garden, with Aerosmith supporting us. All sorts of strange stuff happened that night. The worst of it was somebody jumping off a balcony. We were told about it after the show. Apparently the guy broke his neck.

Over the years many things like that happened. We've had people climbing up the side of the sound system and falling off, hurting themselves. In America, in the very early days, we had gigs where people got squashed against the railings in front; they'd go underneath and get trampled on. You'd see them being pulled on stage and then carried off over the stage, dead. We heard of kids driving home from the gig and getting killed. And then they had all this Black Sabbath stuff with them . . .

It's horrible, but it has happened a few times.

That same Madison Square Garden show, I got hit on the head by a full can of beer and all this blood poured down my face. I still kept playing away, we finished the song, I went off stage and somebody said: 'Look, the guy who works for Muhammad Ali is here, who does all the repairs.'

Being a huge boxing fan, I thought, what's good enough for Muhammad Ali is good enough for me: 'Yeah, I'll have that!'

He stitched it and put all this sealer stuff on it and he did it in no time at all. I came back on stage and carried on. But I had a hell of a headache.

Some people go a bit mad; they throw all sorts of stuff. They don't think about hurting you, they just get a bit stupid. After it happened Ozzy shouted: 'Fucking idiots!' but he was allowed to. It was his birthday that day. A cake was wheeled on to the stage to celebrate this, and a girl jumped out of it.

As Madison Square Garden shows go, this one certainly took the cake.

40

Me on Ecstasy

When we wrote the songs for what was to become *Technical Ecstasy*, Gerald Woodroffe was a great help to me because I now had somebody I could try out ideas with. The band didn't get up until something like 2 p.m., so I often went into our rehearsal room earlier to run over some ideas with Gerald. It was good to have somebody along who could play the chords as I was playing the solos.

Again a pub was not far away, so quite often everybody would go down there, including me. We still managed to write *Technical Ecstasy* in six weeks and get it all rehearsed and ready to go. Off we went to the Criteria Studios in Miami. We'd heard that The Bee Gees, Fleetwood Mac and The Eagles used it. In fact, The Eagles were recording *Hotel California* while we were there. They sometimes had to stop because of us, because we were too loud and it was leaking through into their studio: 'Wrrooaarr!'

But it was a great place. Again, I was in the studio full time, being very much involved in the production. I was in there night and day, to the point that Ozzy even said: 'It's a Tony album.'

We stayed in West Palm Beach and everybody else was always on the beach. I know it sounds like I'm blowing my own trumpet, but that's what happened. They wanted to leave it to me, they trusted me to do it and so I was left to do it.

We also had some bloody laughs there, especially when we played jokes on Bill. He would never allow the maids in to clean his room. One day we got a big load of this really horrible, smelly Gorgonzola cheese, and while somebody kept him talking I sneaked into his room and piled it up under his bed. Many days later I came in again and the smell was atrocious. I went: 'Phew, Bill, what's that smell?'

'I don't know what it is, it must be my clothes.'

Bill is a dirty bugger; he'd pile his filthy clothes up in a corner.

'When are you going to clean them?'

'I will, yeah.'

He never sussed out the cheese under the bed. It smelled absolutely vile. He actually started smelling like cheese himself. When the maids eventually went into his room, they must have died.

One night in the studio, we dressed Bill up as Hitler. He'd had a few drinks, so it was easy. We got some gaffer tape, really strong tape that sticks to most things, and we put it on his head, making his hairstyle like Hitler's. We made him a skinny moustache as well. We gave him this uniform and whatnot, and he was enjoying it all until we tried to take this stuff off him. We couldn't get it off his head, because pulling the tape off would mean ripping his hair out. So we basically cut all his hair off. By this time he was well sloshed and he didn't even realise what we'd done until the next day. He wasn't very pleased. He looked even scruffier than he usually did.

Andy Gibb was recording in the studio next to us. He had a doll out at the time, all immaculate with the blond hair and the nice clothes. We decided to buy one of them and transform it into a Bill Ward doll. One of the guys who worked for us was a real artist, and he messed up the hair, put a beard on it and ruined the clothes. It really looked like Bill. We set it up on the recording desk. One day Andy Gibb came in to have a listen to what we'd been doing. He saw this doll and went: 'Who's that?'

We said: 'It's Bill Ward.'

Andy was all taken aback, going: 'Bill's got a doll out as well?'

One time we all came out of a club in Birmingham at some ridiculous hour. We'd had a few drinks and we went down to a nearby lake. Bill was completely rat-arsed and we put him on this boat and shoved him out on this lake.

And left him.

Another time we carried a very drunk Bill into a park, put him on a bench and covered him with newspapers so that he looked like an old tramp.

And abandoned him again.

Once when he got sloshed we put him to bed and tried to take his trousers off. As we pulled at them, one of the trouser legs just ripped off. The next day he came down still wearing the same trousers, one leg on and one leg gone. He just didn't care.

One time at the Sunset Marquis hotel in Los Angeles we made a big banner saying: 'I am gay, come and visit me.' We climbed up on his balcony on the third floor and hung this banner from it. One of those stupid things you do. The manager of the hotel saw it and wanted him to take it down, but Bill didn't know anything about it and didn't know what he was going on about. The manager said: 'There's this big banner I want you to take down.'

And Bill went: 'Banner? What banner!'

Of course he went out on the balcony and saw it.

'Aargh!'

He used to put his shoes out to air on the balcony. He would get up so late, I'd have been up for hours already, so I'd climb over to his balcony, fill his shoes up with soil and put plants in them. And he'd fall for it every time.

It's a wonder we didn't drive him loony. It was always Bill who got it. And if you didn't do anything to him for a while, he'd actually say: 'Is something wrong?'

'No, why?'

'Well, you haven't done anything to me today.'

He's different now. The last tours at least he was actually up for breakfast. He's changed his lifestyle and he's a lot more healthy now. Since his heart attack he had to stop smoking and, well, he had to stop everything.

'It's Alright' was Bill Ward's song. Although he used to be the singer with The Rest all those years ago, this was the first song Bill ever sang on a Sabbath album. We encouraged him to put it on because we thought it was a good song and Ozzy liked it as well.

'Dirty Woman' was a song about prostitutes, because we were in Florida and Geezer had seen all these hookers around there so he wrote about that. It's not like we were into prostitutes. Well, we did have one or two in the early days. One night back then we were in the Amsterdam red-light district and I went into one of these places. I was sloshed and I fell asleep. Soundly snoring away, I went into extra time and the next thing I knew this guy was screaming at me: 'Where's the money!'

And then he threw me out. I hadn't done anything, except pass out in there.

There were keyboards on all of the tracks, which was a bit different for us. I liked it, but *Technical Ecstasy* didn't sell as many as the previous albums. *Sabotage* hadn't broken any sales records either, but with this one the decline really started. It was especially disappointing for me, because I was really involved with the album from start to finish. But it was just one of those things. It was 1976, it was the time of punk, and there was a whole new generation of kids.

41

Ecstasy on tour

For the Technical Ecstasy tour we didn't have a very big production; just musical equipment, a snow machine and dry ice. Nothing fancy, no coming in through the stage or flying in from the rafters. But Bill had this brilliant brainwave of having a big sea shell built behind his drums. It was made out of fibreglass and it was loud, as it projected the sound. And every night he had tons of fresh flowers around his kit as well. He started getting more loony, but the shell was better than his original idea, where he wanted all these tubes around his kit with water going through it, changing colour. He had all these fancy ideas. They were great until you tried to get them to work: impossible.

We started touring America in October. We had acts like Boston, Ted Nugent, Bob Seeger and the Silver Bullet Band supporting us. The shows were all sold out. At the Halloween gig in Denver, Heart opened for us. When we were playing two girls stood on the side of the stage to watch us and Albert threw them off because he thought they were groupies. He said: 'I fucked them two off. They were on the side of the stage, dancing around.'

I said: 'That was the other band!'

'What band?'

'Heart!'

'Oh no!'

Linda Blair from the movie *The Exorcist* came to our gig in New Haven, Connecticut. Ozzy was a bit infatuated with her, probably because he'd seen the movie. Or maybe he identified with her, because in the movie she also peed all over the place.

As a matter of fact, we all were very impressed by Linda once. We went to see *The Exorcist* at a cinema in Philadelphia a couple of years before and it scared the shit out of us. Back at the hotel we went into the bar to have a drink to calm ourselves down. The television there showed a programme with this priest talking about exorcism. That made it even worse. We got so scared that none of us could sleep, so we spent the night in the same room. Just pathetic.

The bar of our hotel in New Haven had a glass wall behind it, so you could see into the swimming pool. Albert Chapman and me had a few drinks and we got this great idea: 'Why don't we go out there and jump in with no clothes on!'

And so we did. It was one of those stick your arse against the window deals. I don't know what they must've thought in the bar. Absolute madness.

When we got out we needed a quick getaway, so we nicked a golf cart that was parked there. Two grown-up naked men in a golf cart driving around the hotel grounds! We made it back to the room, dried off, got dressed and went back into the bar like nothing had happened. Most of the people didn't even know it was us, because all they'd seen was two arses up against the window.

A pretty picture.

We had met Frank Zappa at a party in New York a couple of years before. He took us all out to a restaurant, telling us how much he liked 'Snowblind'. It was very kind of him and we became friends. On 6 December we played Madison Square Garden, with Frank introducing the band. He wanted to play as well. We'd put his stuff on stage but we had a really bad night. Frank was waiting to walk on and I thought, he can't, it's disastrous, everything is going wrong, my guitar is going out of tune, there's noise and crackles and God knows what. So I said to him: 'It would be best if you don't play, really.'

We got on well with him. In fact later on with Ronnie James Dio I phoned Frank, because Geezer had left. I said: 'You don't know any bass players, do you?'

He went: 'Yeah, you can use mine.'

'No, we want a bass player that might be with us for a long time.'

Me and Ronnie went over to his house. Frank opened the door with a parrot on his shoulder. He said: 'Do you want a drink? A soda, ice tea?'

We were thinking more along the lines of a beer.

'No beer.'

All he had were the more hippie sort of drinks. We went down to his studio and he said: 'Can I play you my new album?'

'Yes, please do.'

I like some of his stuff, like *Hot Rats*, but when he played me this new album it wasn't my cup of tea at all. There was so much going on and it was such off-the-wall stuff that I couldn't absorb it. I thought, well, I don't want to be rude, what am I going to say to him when it stops? Because he's going to go: 'What do you think?'

And he did: 'What do you think?'

'Erm . . . what was that . . . on the third track . . . that eh . . .'

'Oh, that was . . .'

He started to explain the whole thing: 'That's these drums and . . .'

And I only went there looking for a bass player!

As a musician I think Frank was very clever, especially at arranging, and his band was tight as shit.

When I went to see them once in Birmingham, he said: 'I've got a surprise for you tonight.'

'Ah?'

They played 'Iron Man'. I was in the bar and I heard them play it and I thought, bloody hell! I went back out and I thought, I'll thank him after the show. But he had such a bad night that he stormed off stage, really pissed off. So I thought, hmm, I don't think I'm going to go back. Even so, it was a nice surprise.

It was on this Technical Ecstasy tour that the mysterious 'Tony's twin' was lurking about. This bloke plagued me for many years. Tony's twin dressed up like me, he had a moustache and he was a guitar player as well. He made his own thimbles and even started marketing them and selling them. He turned up at our hotel all the time and people would think he was me. Eventually it fizzled out, although I heard from this guy again not too long ago through my website. He sent a picture of him playing, but he doesn't look the same now; he shaved his moustache off and every-thing. Very peculiar.

There was another bloke who plagued me later on. He claimed to be my son. He was about fifty, so I don't know how he could possibly be my son, but he insisted he was. He used to find out where I was and phone up. My second wife, Melinda, answered the phone one day and it was him saying: 'It's Tony's son.'

Of course it threw her altogether; she thought I had a son then.

'What do you mean, you've got a son!'

'I haven't got a son!'

'I just spoke to him!'

This guy actually changed his name to Iommi. Some band even made a record about him. It was titled something like 'Practising To Be Tony Iommi'.

42

We Never Say Die

Preparing for the recording of *Never Say Die!* we were trying to write songs, but it was hard. While we were touring America, punk happened. We even had The Ramones supporting us. I wouldn't want to put them down at all, but I think that was a wrong match. They didn't go down well and were getting things thrown at them all the time, so we had to take them off the tour.

I didn't know whether I liked this punk stuff. Aggression is one thing in the music, but when it comes to spitting and cutting yourself, it just seemed a little bit far off to me. But I liked some of the songs, certainly later. And some credited Black Sabbath as an influence.

I thought, oh, I can't see that somehow.

Punk coming in threw us a bit. The Stranglers were at No. 1 at that time. I remember Geezer saying: 'We're a bit old hat now with all these riffs and stuff.'

I almost felt like, God, what am I going to come up with then?! And again the other guys used to go down to the pub and then they'd come back asking: 'Have you got anything?'

'No, can't think of anything . . .'

Writing became very difficult, especially after Geezer saying that. It felt like we didn't believe in what we were doing any more. I felt hurt. I kept thinking, if I'm going to come up with a riff, then they'll probably say: 'Oh, can't we do something else?'

The guys didn't say that, but I felt like they would. All this when I had already booked a recording studio in Toronto, so the pressure was mounting.

Then Ozzy left. He just didn't want to do it any more. It was a really difficult period for us, but we never considered packing it in. We asked ourselves, will he come back? He might change his mind, we don't know. But we also said: 'We can't just sit here, we have to do something.'

Me and Bill knew this singer from old, Dave Walker, from the time when he was in a local Birmingham band called The Red Caps. He later sang with Savoy Brown and Fleetwood Mac and had moved to San Francisco. I remembered him having a good voice, so we got in touch with him. We were grasping at straws really, thinking, we're here to write an album, we have a studio booked and we have no singer! We rehearsed with Dave for a while and wrote two or three songs with him. Word got out to the press and we even did a local Birmingham TV show with him, but we just didn't feel it was right. Then Ozzy said: 'I'm sorry' and all that, and he came back. We told Dave and he went. However, Ozzy didn't return until two or three days before we were due to go into the studio in Toronto. We couldn't cancel that because we'd paid a lot of money up front. But we still had no songs apart from the three we'd done with Dave, and Ozzy wouldn't sing those.

We went to Toronto and it was absolutely freezing. We each hired apartments close to the Sounds Interchange Studios. We also hired a cinema with a stage in it, to write and rehearse new songs. We worked here from nine o'clock in the morning in the freezing cold, because the place had hardly any heating, and then at night we went to the studio to record. It was just totally wrong for us.

Up to that point we'd write something and then live with it for a bit, giving the songs time to grow: 'Do we like it? Let's change this bit, or let's change that.'

In Toronto we never had that luxury. That's why to me *Never Say Die!* is very much off the wall. There are some tracks I liked on it, but it's hard to relate to that album because of the way it was done. It was a bitter time for us.

Accidents never come singly. The studio turned out to be crap. I had booked the place, so it was my fault. I just chose it based on the list of the names of people who had used it before. It was really expensive, but the sound was as dead as a doornail, so me and the engineer tried to get a bit of live sound in there by pulling all the carpet up. The owner of the studio heard what we were doing, so he came down barking: 'What's going on!'

I said: 'We just can't get a good sound. It's dead.'

'You can't pull the carpet up!'

'Well, we did. It's rolled up!'

It was a nightmare. They said The Rolling Stones had used the studio, but maybe they just did some overdubs or something. I actually bought a stereo that had been left behind by Keith Richards, because I wanted to play music in my apartment. It had all these marks on the top of the speakers, where somebody had been chopping up drugs. We just smoked a lot of dope at the time. One day I smoked a little too much and I said: 'I've got to go to my room.' My apartment was three floors up. I used the stairs as I didn't want to bump into anybody in the elevator. I walked up, put my key in the door, went into the room, put the light on and thought, strange, it looks different. It's all been decorated. It's got wallpaper and everything in here!

I don't know why I didn't stop there. I walked into the bedroom and there was a guy and his wife in bed and they shot up and I had the shock of my life. They screamed and I went: 'Aaaah!', screaming right back at them. I just couldn't get my head together at all.

So I said: 'I'm sorry, I'm sorry, I must be in the wrong room!' and shot out of there.

I had walked up one floor too many. My key had fitted in their door, which was really peculiar. I got to my own apartment and the next day the super came by, because my upstairs neighbours had made a complaint. I said: 'Well, my key shouldn't have fitted their door!'

I told them what happened, conveniently forgetting about the fact that I was stoned.

Despite the cold and the dope and the studio, we did manage to record an album. I actually sang backing vocals on 'A Hard Road'. It was the first time I ever did that. And the last, because the other guys couldn't keep a straight face. I was singing away, looking at them and Geezer was cracking up. I had to keep singing and he kept laughing. It was really embarrassing. Never again!

'Swinging The Chain' was a track that we originally did with Dave Walker. Ozzy refused to sing it, but we had to record it anyway, because otherwise we wouldn't have enough to fill an album. Bill said: 'Well, I'll sing it then.'

And so he did. We kept the music and Bill just rewrote the lyrics.

It's not like Ozzy didn't want to do 'Over To You' either, but he couldn't think of anything to sing on it, so we ended up bringing in these sax players instead. It was real funny period for us, what with Ozzy leaving and coming back. Going into the studio to record this album, it was very iffy. And, of course, Ozzy didn't last much longer anyway after that. He actually did end up doing one song we did with Dave Walker earlier, whether he knew it or not. Geezer wrote the lyrics for it and we called it 'Junior's Eyes'.

The title track, 'Never Say Die', was released as a single, the first one since 'Paranoid'. We'd said we would never do another single, because we were attracting a lot of screaming kids. But it had been a few years, so what the hell. It got in the English charts and we even did *Top of the Pops* with it. Again, that was a weird show to do. Bob Marley was on the programme with us. Bill at that time had his hair braided and everybody thought he was taking the mickey out of Bob. It wasn't like that at all; it was just the way he happened to have his hair in those days.

All in all, it took us quite a while to record *Never Say Die!*. We plodded on I suppose. We didn't *not* get along – we always got along – but it was hard work, much harder than it had ever been before. In the circumstances we'd put ourselves in, it was really difficult to make an album and I felt a lot of pressure doing it. It was expensive as well. It wasn't just the studio, but we also had to live there. We all became shoppers, going to the supermarket with our trolleys getting our groceries and coming back in thick snow. Shopping was also a reason to get out of the apartment, to go somewhere different for a change. And we went to this club on the corner of the road we lived on, called the Gasworks. The supermarket and the club down the street . . . so much for entertainment.

Never Say Die! was doomed from start to finish. Ozzy leaving, trying out Dave Walker – it threw the whole thing out of whack. The album was just done day-by-day, so there was no format to it. You couldn't sit back and think, oh, I can see that leads into the other. The songs didn't relate to each other, it was so off the wall. The audience must've thought this as well: what's going on here?

Again it was: 'We don't need a producer, we can do it ourselves.'

That wasn't just me saying it, that was all of us. But it would have been far better if we had used a producer. We certainly realised that when we did our next album, *Heaven and Hell*. Having a producer involved takes the strain off.

Starting May 1978 the Never Say Die tour bounced back and forth between the UK, Europe and the States, with Van Halen opening for us all the way through until the end in December. Even though they still were relatively new, they were really good. They watched us play almost every night and we became close friends. I'd see Eddie a lot. I always had a bit of coke and he'd come around to my room and we'd talk till the death. As you do.

To me Eddie Van Halen was so different from all the other guitar players who were around back then. The finger tapping – although he doesn't call it that – was a great technique. They were a really energetic band and they were going down great. They made us look a bit drab really, as they did all this acrobatic stuff, what with David Lee Roth doing somersaults on stage and Christ knows what else. Good showmanship, great players, you could see that they were really going to take off.

It was a great tour, but in our camp there were signs of cracking. Ozzy wasn't happy. Possibly his father's death had something to do with that. Jack Osbourne had died of cancer in the autumn of 1977, just before Ozzy left the first time. Ozzy's dad was a great, lovely guy and I attended his funeral. But we never really spoke about it. Maybe Ozzy just wanted to get away from it all for a while, to deal with whatever hang-ups he had. But we didn't have that luxury, we couldn't take time off. It got to the point where we just plodded on. We had achieved quite a lot, we all had enjoyed success, we all owned homes and cars, everybody was comfortable. Perhaps we got too comfortable and we lost our drive, the aggression of wanting to go out and fight for it.

We also thought, we're getting too old for this, because we saw younger kids coming up, like Van Halen. We actually weren't even that old, but we were in comparison to most of the new bands. When we did interviews, the question always was: 'How long are you going to be doing this? Don't you think it's about time to pack it in?'

We were only thirty, thirty-five years old and they started talking about us retiring. We were becoming old hat and I think the spark had gone. Everybody was thinking, we're just going through the motions of it really. And we were playing an album we didn't even like ourselves.

We played the Hammersmith Odeon on 10 and 11 June 1978 and that was our ten-year anniversary. Ten years was a long time. Van Halen with David Lee Roth didn't last ten years! We recorded those shows and released that recording as a live home video cassette at that time. It was called *Never Say Die!*, but the band was not at all well, and even though the patient was still up and about, the illness ultimately proved to be terminal.

Well before Ozzy left us for the second time, he went missing. In November he disappeared before a show in Nashville. Supposedly he had a bad throat. We checked into this hotel and he drank a bottle of Night Nurse cold and flu medicine. You're supposed to have just a few spoons, but he downed the whole bloody bottle. He went to his room but ended up in the wrong one. He saw this room open, there was a maid in there, she came out and he went into that room, passed out on the bed and that was it. Meanwhile, his bags had been sent up to his own room. We were doing a show on the night, but no Ozzy.

'Oh, blimey!'

We phoned his room: nothing. So we got the guy to go and open the door. His suitcase was still there, all packed, and the bed was made.

'God, what's happened?'

We started worrying then.

'What's going on! I wonder if he's gone down to the gig already . . .'

'Why would he do that?'

We went to the gig first, to see if he was there: no sign of him. We didn't know what to think. Then the rumour started that he had been kidnapped. We even got it advertised on TV, radio and everything that he was missing. It was just unbelievable. And it was getting closer and closer to show time.

No show.

We had to pull the gig, which really went down well. We left it to the last minute, thinking he might turn up. He had disappeared in the past and then just ended up in somebody's house, out of it, but never on a gig day. So we were half worried to death, and half pissed off, thinking, we have a hall full of people, they are never going to believe us if we go on and say: 'We can't find Ozzy.'

We then really started to panic. Even though Van Halen played, the audience was going mad and we had to get out of there quick. We got in touch with radio stations and every fifteen minutes they'd do a bulletin: 'Has anybody seen Ozzy?'

This went on and on and we were awake all bloody night wondering what the hell was going on. Then Ozzy phoned my room: 'What's happening?'

'Fucking hell, what do you mean, what's happening. Where the hell are you!'

'I'm in my room.'

'You're not in your room!'

'Yes, I am!'

'No, you're not!'

One of those.

'I took this Night Nurse, I don't know what happened, I fucking passed out.'

So that was the story. We were convinced he had been kidnapped and that there was going to be some ransom note. But he was in the hotel. We felt like killing him. But Ozzy's disappearing act was only light entertainment in comparison with what would happen over the next couple of months.

Things would only get worse . . .

43

Ozzy goes

After the world tour, the whole band moved to LA for eleven months. Again it was a tax thing, so we thought we'd ship out there, write the next album and record it. But it turned into a highly frustrating, never-ending process.

Don Arden was managing us by then, with his daughter Sharon assisting him. I did a lot of the dealings for the band, so I was in contact a lot with her, talking about where we were going to live, rehearse, record and whatever else.

We all moved into this great house, where we turned the garage into a rehearsal studio. The next move would be to come up with ideas, but that didn't happen. Again we were doing a lot of coke. Going out partying, and further partying at the house, and then trying to write this stuff; it was hard. But what made it next to impossible was that Ozzy wasn't into it. He was on another planet. We'd try and motivate him, saying: 'Any ideas?'

'No, I can't think of anything.'

And then he'd pass out on the couch. It was frustrating, because it was going on and on and we were getting nowhere. I'd be going to Warner Bros. Records because they'd want to see the progress, and they'd go: 'How's it going?'

'Oh, great!'

But we had done nothing.

'How are the tracks sounding?'

'Oh, really good!'

Bloody hell, what was I supposed to say? 'We've been here for six months and we haven't done shit'? They didn't want to hear that. It got more embarrassing every time I went down there.

We'd been there for months and Ozzy hadn't really sung much at all. We couldn't have a good conversation with him, because he took more booze and drugs and was pretty much out of it. We'd all be at times, but he was on a totally different level altogether. We could still create, but drugs and drink affect certain people differently. I think Ozzy just lost interest in it all. We had about three ideas down, musically, but we didn't know where to go next without Ozzy's input. We'd write a song and then he'd go: 'I don't want to sing on it.' He sang a bit on 'Children Of The Sea', and then he sort of fizzled away. It finally got to a point where we said: 'If Ozzy can't do it, we're going to have to either break up or we are going to have to bring somebody else in.'

Ozzy wasn't yet involved with Sharon then. As a matter of fact, I was involved with her first, but we only had a friend-like relationship. It never was a love relationship. I had to deal with her all the time and I liked her as a person. I said to Sharon: 'We are having such a problem with Ozzy.'

She went: 'Oh, give him time.'

I said: 'We've got to get going. The record company is asking us where the music is.'

It got to the crunch and we had to give Ozzy an ultimatum: 'You have to do something, otherwise we are going to have to replace you.'

And that's what happened. Bill spoke to him and said: 'Look, we're going to have to move on.'

It was sad. We had been together for a decade, but it got to a point where we couldn't relate to each other any more. There were so many drugs flying around, coke and Quaaludes and Mandrax, and there was booze and late nights and women and everything else. And then you get more paranoid and you think, they hate me. We never fought, but it's hard to get through to people, to communicate and solve things when everybody's out of it. For some reason I became the asshole in it all. Ozzy seems to think it was me who pushed it, but I was only speaking on behalf of the band and trying to get the thing going. Somebody had to make a move, somebody had to do something otherwise we'd still be there now and we'd all be out of it. So that was it.

I thought, maybe we should break up and I'll do something else. It was at that point that Sharon introduced me to Ronnie James Dio at a party. She suggested I should do a separate project and do that with Ronnie. I approached him and said: 'I'm in a terrible situation. I don't think it's going to work out any more with what we got. Would you be interested in doing something else?'

44

Susan's Scottish sect

Ozzy wasn't the only nearest and dearest leaving me. My marriage to Susan ended around the time I moved with the band to LA. In some ways I can understand why. Sue was left alone at this huge house while I was on tour and as soon as I came back I'd be in the studio. It must have been very lonely for her. She also saw the other guys going on holiday with their wives while I stayed behind, working in the studio. I didn't see that I needed to look after the relationship more. With me it was all work, work, work. I got blinded by it. You've got to do what you've got to do, haven't you? But because of that our relationship went astray.

She wanted a divorce and went ahead with the papers. It was a shock. I got bitter about it all and as a reaction to it I went a bit mad. I went to LA and I was going for it. I had so many girls come in that I booked them at different times: I'd have one girl come at two o'clock and then another a couple of hours later, telling her: 'We don't finish rehearsals till three, so if you come in at four . . .'

One time I was with this girl and I heard the buzzer going at the gate. I looked out of the window and it was this other girl. I said: 'Quick! You got to go, it's my wife!'

She freaked out: 'Aah!'

I said: 'Go across the roof and get down the wall there!'

I got her out of the window and she climbed across the roof which sloped down, so she could jump off it easy. As she was crawling along, the maid and my guitar tech were outside looking up, shaking their heads.

I gave up the Kilworth house. When I came back home from LA I moved in with my folks for a while. In the meantime, Susan joined this sect in the UK where you give your money and all your possessions away, and you move in with them and live off the land. It was really awkward. I spoke to her parents about it all and they were in shock. They said to me: 'You've got to come back and live in the house.'

But I said: 'No, I can't. I can't see me coming back there now.'

I had somebody value the furniture. I put what belonged to me in storage, sold some of the other stuff and gave Susan the money. She didn't really want it, as she had moved into this sect and she'd given them all the money she was going to give them. I never understood exactly who they were, this sect, and neither did her folks.

Well after the marriage had ended, she phoned me out of the blue and said: 'Please come and get me. I'm in trouble.'

She was up in Inverness, in Scotland. I was with a friend in a club in Birmingham and I'd had a few drinks. I panicked and said: 'She's having problems, I've got to go over there!'

Me and this friend went up in my Rolls-Royce. Because it was a long way I'd drive a hundred miles and then he'd drive the next hundred. We finally got there, all stubbly and tired and shattered, and she went: 'Why have you come up?'

'Because you were having problems!'

'Oh, well, I think it's sorted out now.'

I said: 'You're coming with us!'

'No, I'm not.'

'Yes, you are!'

One of those. She didn't, so we got in the car and went. Drove back another 300 miles.

I saw her again just one more time, when I was in a relationship with Lita Ford. Lita was in LA while I was back home in Birmingham and Susan came to my house. She wanted to get back together. I said to her: 'Look, I don't feel the same way about you any more and I've got a girlfriend now.'

It's hard to rekindle something like that. And that was the end of it. She moved to Australia and I haven't seen her since.

45

Dio does but Don don't

Ronnie was up for doing something together, but I didn't get in touch with him for a while because we were still in a state of confusion about Ozzy. After he left I finally said to Bill and Geezer: 'Why don't we try Ronnie?'

I called him and said: 'We're having another type of situation; would you be interested in having a go?'

We invited him over to the house and played him 'Children Of The Sea'. Just like that Ronnie came up with this vocal melody for it. We were really impressed, because within a day we'd gone from nothing happening for ages to being able to come up with a song immediately. We played a bit of 'Lady Evil', and Ronnie immediately sang to that as well. We thought, bloody hell, we're on to a winner! It gave us a bit of a lift. We were still feeling sad about Ozzy going, but it had run its course. Now we were pleased that we were actually able to do something.

Ozzy had left the house by then, but Don Arden was trying desperately to get him back into the band. Don finally had this band that he had always wanted ... and we broke up! He couldn't accept that, he had to have the original line-up, so he insisted: 'It's never going to work with Ronnie.'

I said: 'But it is working! We've got some good stuff and we are rolling. And Ozzy is not capable at the moment of doing this, he's not into it at all.'

He kept going: 'Give him another chance.'

We had lived all those ten months at the house and nothing was happening with Ozzy, so how come it would suddenly be happening in another couple of weeks? We also hadn't forgotten the fact that Ozzy had already left once, before *Never Say Die!*. It cost us a fortune, we weren't creating any more, everybody got depressed and pissed off with everything, so we didn't see how we could go on with him any more. Don still carried on: 'We've got to get Ozzy back, we've got to get Ozzy back!'

We said: 'Don, he's not into it. It's not going to work.'

And Don, of course, came back with: 'You can't have a midget singing for Black Sabbath!'

As he would. But we had to draw the line. We were to go on with Ronnie.

Then Geezer left. He had marital problems, so he had to go home to sort it out and basically leave the band for a while. Ronnie played the bass for a bit, so suddenly we were a three-piece: Bill, Ronnie and me. We came up with a couple of things, but that's when I flew Geoff Nicholls over. I said: 'We'll just get somebody in temporarily, who can help out while we are here.'

The first song the four of us came up with was 'Heaven And Hell'. I played this riff and Ronnie just sang away to it. It was that instantaneous. And we said to each other: 'Oh man, do we like this!'

Ronnie always drove up in his Cadillac. He had to raise the seat up, the car was that big. There were a lot of snakes where we lived. We found out that Ronnie was afraid of them, so I got this dead snake and I tied a piece of fishing line to its head and fixed it to the handle of the car door. I put the snake on the passenger's side and closed the door, so when Ronnie opened the driver's

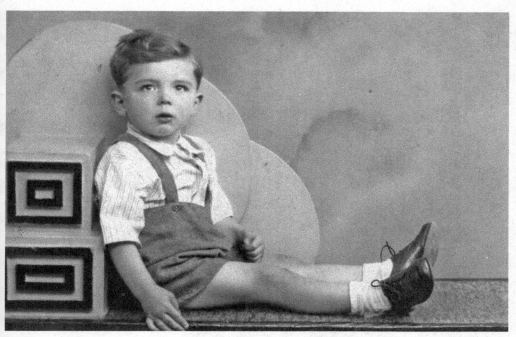

What an angel!

Out with Mum;
I'm not amused

It'll never catch on. Playing
the accordion, like my dad
before me, in our backyard
in Park Lane

Spot the hooligans: me on the back row top right, and Albert Chapman at the left end of
the middle row

My first Strat, before I painted it!

My first proper band, the Rockin' Chevrolets, in 1964

The Rest, my first band with Bill Ward

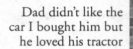

Dad didn't like the
car I bought him but
he loved his tractor

The Lamborghini is worth about five times more than my parents' house

Photo shoot for a Rolls Royce calendar. Did it ever come out?

Inside the famous Kilworth conservatory with the first of my many dogs

My first wedding, with
Best Man John Bonham
(far right of picture), 1973

Kilworth House, where I lived with my first wife, Susan

Dodgy characters

We seem happy!

Love the beard, Ozzy. Circustheater Scheveningen, Holland, October 1975

Before I found black

My baby

US success for Paranoid with both Patrick Meehans

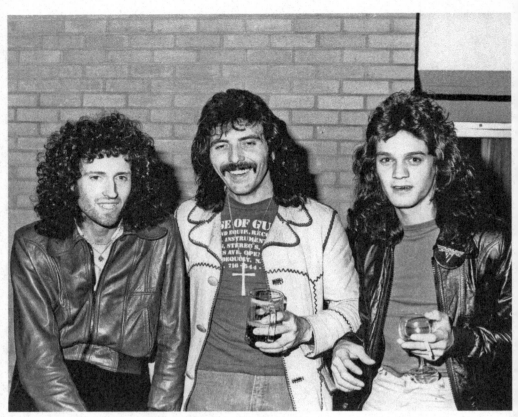

Brian May, me and Eddie Van Halen in 1978

Ronnie, Vinny, me and Geezer, somewhere strange. Buffalo, NY, December 1981

Geezer, Ronnie and me –
Mob Rules! Toledo, Ohio,
November 1981

Vinny, the first time round. Vinny followed Bill on drums, starting in Hawaii in 1980

Geezer, me and Brian May at
Hammersmith Odeon, 1989

With long-time collaborator,
Geoff Nicholls

Mum and I at
Helford House

Outside the Manor Studios. Yes, it's a black cat!

Cozy and Neil Murray in Mexico before we ran for our lives

Got ya! Hi-jinks with Vinny at Rockfield Studios while recording The Devil You Know in 2008

With Toni-Marie, my aunt Pauline and Maria

My Birmingham star on the city's Walk of Fame

A press conference with Ian Gillan in Armenia, 2009. We received the Order Of Honour award for the charity single we made 25 years earlier

Grown up baby: Toni-Marie

Maria and I at the Classic Rock Awards

Nijmegen, Holland, June 2005

Man at work. Donington Festival, June 2005

door he'd pull the snake towards him. It worked: he almost shat himself.

It came back at me, because I went to the loo one day in my bedroom and lifted the lid up, and, bloody hell, there was a snake there. Dead one again. Shat myself before I could reach the toilet seat.

We played jokes on each other all the time. Joking around like that makes people get along better. It's also a test I suppose, to see if somebody is going to be able to put up with it.

Things were going very well, but we still had Don going: 'It's never going to work. If you don't get Ozzy back, that's it.'

We were at work at the house and all of a sudden some guys turned up to take the furniture away that Sharon had rented for us. Gradually we were seeing things going missing. We warned each other: 'Don't let them in. They'll take the couch!'

It was absolutely awful, so we decided to sever our relationship with Don completely. He had wanted to manage us for such a long time, and now he had looked after us for only a short while. Sandy Pearlman, an American guy who managed Blue Öyster Cult, then wanted to take us on. We kept that on the back burner, because we went back to doing it ourselves, just like we had done before Don took over. We still had Mark Forster working for us, who had helped out with the day-to-day stuff since the *Sabbath Bloody Sabbath* days. He was like an assistant, travelling around with us, organising the hotels and transportation and whatnot.

Mark had some physical problem, an elephantiasis-type of thing in his groin. The silly thing was, he'd be standing there and he'd have this big bulge and instead of trying to hide it, he'd put a stage pass on it, so the first place you'd look was down there.

I got a call one day after the Ronnie line-up had broken up, to be told that Mark had died. They couldn't find any family, so they asked: 'Do you want his belongings?'

I said: 'No, I don't want anything.'

I felt really bad. Mark was English, but he must have married an American, because I think he had a son somewhere. I told them this, but I didn't know where he was.

Anyway, with Mark still being very much alive and assisting us at the time, we decided we had no option but to move out of the house. The Ardens had virtually emptied the place and the lease was up. We thought, let's move away from LA altogether. It was the wrong place for us then.

So we shipped out to Miami.

46

Bill goes to shits

We looked around the plane flying to Miami and said: 'Why is there nobody on this flight?'

It turned out we were flying into a hurricane and everybody was leaving the place. We thought, everybody's going out and we are coming in!

We got there and everything was boarded up. We had rented Barry Gibb's house, but we stayed at a hotel first for three days, because it was dangerous everywhere else. They boarded the building up completely. Getting ready for this storm you had to fill your bathtub and you couldn't leave the hotel. They had sandwiches there, but of course they ran out of food in the end. One day me and Geoff stood on my balcony like two idiots and we saw all the trees swaying. Then we heard: 'You! Hey you! Get back in the room! Get off that balcony!'

It was this policeman.

'You idiots, get in the room!'

It was frightening. It got to a point where they said: 'Now it's too late to leave so you got to stay. Get to shelters!'

We went: 'Oh Christ. Here it comes.'

We only caught the edge of the storm. There were lampposts

blowing over, traffic lights flying around and trees being uprooted, but it didn't hit with the full force. Still, it was bad enough to frighten the shit out of us.

We stayed at Barry Gibb's house for months. He'd moved into another place. We did the same as we did in LA: we created a rehearsal studio where we set all the gear up. We had Craig Gruber come in, a bass player who used to be with Rainbow, just like Ronnie. We kept Geoff because we got on so well with him that we tried him on the keyboards. He was fairly new to it, but he was good enough for what we wanted: play the chords and come up with some ideas as far as what to play behind the chords.

We wrote more stuff, without Geezer this time. It was awkward for me and Bill, because we were so used to working with him. Everything felt like it was on a temporary basis, because we were still hoping that Geezer would come back. It was hard, but we carried on. Writing actually went really smoothly and we soon finished an album's worth of songs.

Bill was really boozing a lot. He had his wife with him there and she was drinking heavily as well. Bill would wake up in the morning, all bright, and he'd have a beer from the fridge, and another beer and another beer. I'd go: 'Bill, how many beers have you had now?'

'Oh, I've only had two.'

But it would be about ten by then. It became known as 'he's only had two'.

Throughout the day he'd go from this pleasant phase to being really dismal, changing as he was drinking more. We'd avoid him by nine or ten o'clock at night, because he would get into a real down state of mind and become aggressive. Meanwhile, his playing was fine. He'd drink in the mornings but he was playing all right if he'd only had a few. It was afterwards, at night, that he'd slip into the next stage. And if we decided to have a day off, bloody hell, he'd go for it all the way.

As ever, Bill was the one we'd play jokes on. On one occasion, I got this number of Alcoholics Anonymous and the name of the guy in charge. I said to Bill: 'Some fucking bloke's called up. You've got an interview.'

'Huh?'

'You've got an interview. Phone him up and ask for this guy's name, and just say: "Can you help me, it's Bill Ward."'

And he did. Bill went: 'Hello? I'm Bill Ward. Can you help me, I've been told to call you.'

They started going on about the problems of alcohol. We were in the back listening in, and he freaked out completely. I'd never seen him like that. The phone went up in the air and crashed to the floor. We all fucked off as fast as we could. He didn't take it as a joke at all and was in a terrible mood for ages. We just kept out of the way for a good day.

Still, in spite of his boozing we gave him the job of going down to the bank to collect the money for the wages for everybody. We wanted to give him a purpose: 'Don't get pissed in the morning, Bill, you've got to go to the bank!'

'Oh, all right, yeah, okay.'

He really took it seriously. He'd be up in the morning and fucking shave and dress up. He bought himself a briefcase and suddenly he became this business guy, going down to the bank and becoming all responsible. It was funny the way you saw the change in him every Friday, when he had to go to collect the money.

Ronnie really liked Bill. However, having Ronnie join changed the dynamics of the band and that affected Bill. He wasn't 100 per cent happy with the situation. He was accustomed to having Ozzy around, as we all were, but Bill just couldn't get used to him not being there any more. Also I think the drinking didn't help. As a matter of fact, things got so bad that he wouldn't stay for very much longer. Bill might have missed Ozzy, but this certainly didn't mean we could have gone for somebody that sounded like him. Then there would have been criticism all over the place, and besides, there's only one Ozzy. We went with Ronnie because we liked the way he worked and we liked his voice. The music took a different turn after he joined us. For *Heaven and Hell* we were writing for a singer who was so different that it opened more doors. When you work with Ozzy for ten years you know roughly what he's going to sing and how he is going to do that. You're familiar with his capabilities. We didn't know what Ronnie's capabilities were and it was a matter of pushing all the time, to see what he could do. It was new blood in the band, I could play different chords, it gave me other places to go music-wise. And Ronnie really encouraged me to play solos, to break out a bit more. It wasn't like I had a lack of solos in the old days, but Ozzy would never say: 'Why don't you put a solo there?'

He wasn't that involved in it. Or maybe he was for a bit and then his attention span would go and he'd be off. He didn't put much in the pot. That wasn't his fault. He just wasn't that musical. He couldn't play an instrument so he wouldn't know what chords to go to, whereas with Ronnie we were working more like a band, because if you sat down with him, he'd have a guitar as well, or a bass, and he'd go: 'What about this chord?'

'Oh yeah . . . yeah!'

And then we'd improve on that. Ronnie had this huge involvement, which was great.

Ozzy would sing with the riff. Just listen to 'Iron Man' and you'll catch my drift: his vocal melody line copies the melody of the music. There was nothing wrong with that, but Ronnie liked singing across the riff instead of with it, come up with a melody that was different from that of the music, which musically opens a lot more doors. I don't want to sound like I'm knocking Ozzy, but Ronnie's approach opened up a new way for me to think, oh yeah, I can go here from that.

Ronnie brought quite a lot as far as the sound of his voice goes as well. He knew what he wanted and he could tell us in music terms: 'Why don't we try an A there?'

Ozzy couldn't; he wouldn't know what an A or a D was. At best he might go: 'We'll need something else there.'

'Any ideas?'

'Not really. What about, erm . . .'

We also became more professional. Ronnie always wanted to make everything better, he always pushed, both on stage as well as off. It was good for us, because it pushed all of us. Over the years we probably got a little bit lazy and relied too much on the things we knew, but Ronnie challenged us. That way we became more of a band again: we got tighter, trying to protect the band, protect what we had. And we believed in what we had.

47

Heaven and Hell

We recorded *Heaven and Hell* at the Criteria Studios in Miami, the same place where we had recorded *Technical Ecstasy* a couple of years earlier. For the first time since *Master of Reality* we had somebody else producing it, which was a great help. Martin Birch took a lot of the strain off me. He had done a few good albums by big name bands already, like Rainbow. Ronnie recommended him, so we thought we'd try him.

We were back in Florida, which meant there were drugs galore. A neighbour next to Barry Gibb's house had constant supplies of coke like you wouldn't believe. I'd visit him and he would have pounds of it in a big pile on the table.

'Here, help yourself.'

It was unbelievable. Here we were at four o'clock in the morning: 'Can we just pop around for a bit?'

And he would be up!

'Yeah, just pop around.'

We just went over the top because it was there, on our doorstep. It didn't stop our creative juices flowing. We've always had a fifth member, a presence, a guiding light if you like, that led us in the right direction. It was there when we were in Miami at Barry's house and we wrote 'Die Young'. In that song there's a break. In the part where Ronnie sings 'die young', it drops down to a quiet passage. At that time Ronnie had never done stuff like that, with a drop-down, it was always out and out, go! I said to him: 'We've done it for years in a lot of the Sabbath stuff, we put a quiet bit in the middle of it.'

And Ronnie said: 'Oh, yeah, it works!'

It was another learning experience for him, seeing how we wrote and what you can do, somewhere else to go, a different area. I felt I knew where to go on these things. I think we all did, we all felt: this is the fifth member guiding us. 'Die Young' is a well-structured song. It was the second single, after 'Neon Knights', and to this day it goes down really well.

'Children Of The Sea' was the one that we had already done when Ozzy was still there. I still have a version with him singing on it somewhere, with a different lyric and a totally different vocal melody to what Ronnie did with it. When we recorded the new version, I wanted it to sound like galley slaves rowing a big ship. In my head I could hear this monk-type chant, so we said to the guy at the studio: 'Anywhere we can hire some monks?'

He phoned around, trying to find some monks. It was a bit of a joke, really. But he came back all serious and said: 'Well, we can only get one monk . . . but he can overdub!'

'Ah!'

I got him to come in and, 'oo-oooo-ooo', let him do his chant. We were in stitches. We had imagined this whole choir and we got one monk.

But he could overdub.

When we were in LA we had these JVC tape machines that had built-in microphones so we could record whatever we were doing, wherever. We were in the house and we just jammed around. I had this little amp, just a few watts, and we had a little drum kit, and we must have played 'Heaven And Hell' for ages. We really liked

it. Ronnie was playing bits of bass on it at first and then we had
Geoff take over. Ronnie would sing something and that would
give you an idea where to go next. We just built the song up, jamming like that.

In Miami, recording went well, but we wanted Geezer back, so
I called him. He had sorted his stuff out by then, so we arranged
for him to come in and play the bass on the album. Craig Gruber
had put the bass parts down, but we took all that off without letting Geezer listen to them first. I was pretty confident that he
would like the new music, because we often felt the same about
stuff and I really liked our new songs. As a matter of fact, he was
knocked out when he heard them. As soon as Geezer played his
parts on it, it all came back to 'this is the wall of sound' thing, it
made the music come back in shape again. Other bass players will
just play something like 'doom doom doom', while Geezer will
bend his strings and go 'do-ommm', to put more aggression into
it. He's just different from any other bass player I've ever heard. It
worked out really good.

Having Martin Birch there prevented me from being there all
the time and getting over-involved in everything. Doing it all by
myself in the past, I could go on endlessly and just play on and on,
until I didn't know what was good and what wasn't any more. But
with Martin it was: 'Fine! We've got it!'

'Ah. Well, I'll just do one more take.'

'No. It's all right. We've got it.'

Him drawing the line was good. And we probably saved a little
money that way, too.

We managed to frighten the life out of Martin. He was tough
guy, but at the same time he was a little bit nervous. He did karate
and had a black belt in this and that, but he could be got to.

And we knew how to get to him.

We discovered that he was really frightened of black magic, so
we made it worse for him. I got a twelve-inch piece of balsa wood

and I carved it into the effigy of a man. I wrapped it in black cloth
and put it in my briefcase. I got my case out pretending to look for
something, and I pulled this thing out so he could see the little
figure.

'What's that!'

I went: 'Oh.'

I covered it up quickly and closed the case.

'What is it?'

'It's nothing. Don't worry about it.'

But he did worry. He said to Ronnie: 'Tony, he's got something
in his case. It looks like a little voodoo doll or something!'

Of course Ronnie was in on it, so he played him up some more.

After the others had gone, Martin would start asking questions.
I would go: 'Martin, really . . . It's my own personal thing.'

'Yeah yeah, what . . . What is that thing in your case?'

'I don't want to talk about it.'

He really got worked up about this thing. Then eventually he
thought it was a voodoo doll to stick pins in and the doll was him.
He said: 'I'm feeling really strange lately. You haven't sort of . . .?'

He thought that I was doing something to him and I wound
him up some more. I said: 'You're not feeling . . . Are you feeling
a bit weird today, Martin?'

'Why! Why? Why should I? What's happened! What are you
doing?'

He built the whole thing up himself, and I just encouraged him.
I would've let it go but he just kept prodding me.

'Are you into this black magic thing?'

'I don't want to talk about it!'

And then we'd make stuff up. I'd say to Geezer, just loud
enough so he'd hear: 'Are you going to go to the . . . meeting,
tomorrow?'

Martin: 'What meeting?'

'Nothing, Martin, it's just . . . just . . . you know . . .'

He took the whole scam hook, line and sinker. We pissed ourselves laughing but he was in a terrible state. 'Just tell me a couple
of little things.'

'Why, what . . .?'

'Just tell me what happens. What do you do at these meetings?'

'Oh, Martin, we can't . . . it's secret, it's all very hush hush, we
can't talk about it.'

I loved it. I really lived on it. I was looking forward to going in
the next day, just to wind him up some more. Martin changed
from being this confident chap to being a nervous wreck, going:
'What's happening, what's going on?'

'Nothing . . . nothing.'

I got the doll out again and he said: 'You're sticking pins in it!
It's me, isn't it? That's me!'

'What?'

'That doll! That's me, I've seen it!'

Fantastic, it was a real gem and it lasted the entire recording session. We never told him. He'll read this book and go: 'The bastard!'

We used Martin on the next album, *Mob Rules*, as well.

And carried on . . .

At a certain point our time was up at Criteria Studios. We
needed a break anyway. Martin certainly did, because we had
driven him loony. So we came back home to England.

I was doing a tax thing, where I needed to stay out of England
for a year. I miscalculated and came back a couple of days too
early. My accountant said: 'Get out, get out!'

'What do you mean, get out?'

'Just get on a plane somewhere. Go to Jersey!'

I went to Jersey and Geoff came with me. I booked this Grand
Hotel because it was the biggest hotel there, so I thought that was
the place for us. We went down to the bar for a drink and I got
pissed as a parrot. I was talking to the barman and he said: 'How
are the rooms?'

I warbled: 'Ah don't like mah room.'

He said: 'Why don't you change it then? Talk to the manager.'

He got the manager in.

'Ahh don' like mah roommm.'

He was going on about changing my room and I was sitting there drinking and eating all these olives. I ate so many olives they made me throw up right there in the bar. Good thing I didn't get sick all over this manager before he agreed to give me another room. He said: 'Yeah, no problem. We've got a great room.'

I didn't even get what he had said.

He went: 'It's got electric curtains.'

And he carried on about it having this and that, but I couldn't take it all in. I just heard: 'It's a big plush room.'

So I said: 'Yeah, I'll have that!'

I didn't feel very well then and went to bed. At eight o'clock in the morning the phone rang and they told me my new room was ready. I felt dreadful and really didn't fancy changing rooms at that point, but I felt obliged to because of the olive thing the previous evening, so I did. I went to this other room and it was really nice. It had this big, round waterbed and electric curtains and everything: really plush. I phoned Geoff and said: 'Come down and we'll have breakfast in my new room together.'

So he did. We stepped out of the door afterwards and there were five maids outside, all laughing.

'Fucking hell. What's the matter with them?'

I didn't realise they had put me in the bridal suite. They thought we were a couple of gays.

'Ah, no!'

From then on I'd say to Geoff: 'I'll meet you downstairs. Don't come to my room. We'll have breakfast downstairs.'

From Jersey it was on to Paris, as I still couldn't go back to England. The rest of the band flew in as well. We booked Studio Ferber over there and we came up with the last song of the album,

'Neon Knights'. We felt that we needed a fast number like this to balance out the slower songs on the album. I find that writing fast songs is difficult. I can write slow songs or mid-tempo ones until they're coming out of my ears, but fast songs I really have to think a little bit more about. I suppose that's because of the way I've always done stuff with Sabbath: most of the things were ploddy.

After Paris we finally went to London. We did overdubs and the final mix at the Town House Studios. That's where I set Bill on fire. We made *Heaven and Hell* and for a few horrible moments Bill got a little too close to hell there . . .

48

Ignition

I had set Bill Ward on fire before, but this time things got out of hand. While he was rolling around the studio howling, I was laughing my head off. But when he continued screaming and writhing the horrible truth sank in: my drummer was going up in flames!

It all started as a party bit. Bill and I had joked around a few times before, where I would hold a lighter to his beard and the thing would burn for maybe a second. It was always good for a laugh, so when we were doing some work on the *Heaven and Hell* album at the Town House Studios and he walked in, I said to him: 'Bill, can I set fire to you again?'

'Not just now, I'm busy.'

'Oh, okay.'

And I completely forgot about it. A couple of hours later Bill came over while I was doing things on my guitar and he said: 'Look, I'm going back to the hotel, so do you still want to set fire to me or what?'

Martin Birch, the producer, couldn't believe it. He went: 'Oh, blimey.'

As Bill seemed so keen on doing this, I decided to make a bit of a production of it and dosed him in this stuff with which studio technicians clean their tape heads. His clothes just absorbed it. I lit him and he went up like a bomb.

'Whoosh!'

He fell to the floor and I kept pouring on the tape-head cleaner. I thought he was joking, but he was actually ablaze. The flames consumed his trousers and they melted his socks. He ended up with third-degree burns to his legs.

Birch rushed him to the hospital. And then Bill's mother phoned me up: 'You barmy bastard . . .'

What she called me over the phone practically singed my ear. Finally she said: 'Bill might have to have his leg off!'

Bloody hell, I felt so bad I didn't know what to do. But he was okay, although he actually did get burn marks down his legs. Not too long ago I said to him: 'You still got those scars on you, Bill?'

'Yeah, I've still got them, yeah.'

I might have killed him, which is a little over the top for an innocent party bit. So I've not set fire to Bill since then.

49

Vinny says Aloha

Bill was drinking in total excess, even on the gigs, which he never used to do. You didn't notice it too much while he was playing. He was just getting more aggressive and angry, and physically he was getting in a bad way as well. He was constantly having little problems, panic attacks and stuff. It got to all of us, but we didn't have to say anything to him, because one day he just disappeared. It was 21 August, 1980. We were due to do a gig in Denver, but he got absolutely legless, got in his bus with his brother Jim driving, and just cleared off. We didn't even know he'd gone until somebody told us: 'Bill has left.'

'Pardon?'

'Bill has left!'

'No!'

He never said goodbye, nothing, he was just gone. I had talked to Bill a lot, but it shocked me when he left. That really caught me by surprise. And we were in shit street. We had to cancel the gig. Ronnie was concerned because he really liked Bill: 'We've got to get him back!'

When we finally reached Bill, we heard that he didn't want to do it any more. When we recorded the album he liked it, but the

touring side really got to him. We had to go out and prove ourselves again; he couldn't handle that and he didn't want to know
any more.

Finished!

So we had to find somebody to replace him. For me that was
awful because I hadn't worked with another drummer since well
before Black Sabbath had even started. I relied on Bill a lot. We
had played together for a hundred years!

We had a huge open-air festival in Hawaii coming up which we
were headlining, so we were panicking: 'Christ, what are we going
to do?'

We had got some tapes from different drummers, and one of
them was Vinny Appice's. Ronnie had heard about Vinny, so he
said: 'Let's get in touch with him.'

We literally had a day and a half to try Vinny out and agree
whether he was going to be the one or not. If he was good, he was
going to play in Hawaii with us, if not, we had to cancel the gig.
And he was good.

He came with this tiny little kit and he was playing away, but I
was used to Bill with his huge kit. I thought, oh, he's only using
that right now for the rehearsal. We went to Hawaii and I walked
on stage where we had this big drum riser for Bill to use, and on
it was this same tiny little kit. It was like a kid's set. I thought,
bloody hell, you are never going to be able to hear him! I really
went to bits backstage, pacing up and down, and Ronnie said: 'It'll
be all right.'

I said: 'No! I've never played with another drummer for all these
years!'

I was absolutely terrified. We went on stage and it just looked
funny, with a big wall of amps, a big drum riser, and then this
puny little kit. But, blimey, he played them great!

Vinny wasn't 100 per cent sure of all the songs, so he had written out all these notes. It started raining and all the writing got

smudged, so he couldn't read it any more. He didn't know where we were. But he did really good.

And, yes, we heard him as well.

That gig was real panic stations to me. Some idiot fired a real mortar bomb. We heard this 'shhhhhhhhhh, boom!' It exploded backstage. Luckily it was a real big area. None of us got hurt and I don't think anybody else did either, but it created a big bloody hole. I still can't believe somebody would do that. And where did they get one of them from? Pretty serious stuff!

It might've been Ozzy actually.

Missed!

There's quite a difference between the way Vinny and Bill play drums. Vinny came in with all these fast rolls, which Bill didn't play at all. Bill was from the John Bonham and Cozy Powell camp. He was good, but he had his own style, he created his unique thing. Very unorthodox. Bill wouldn't play a straightforward beat, he always put some little bits in, like a percussionist. He would hear these symphonies in his head and try to play like he had eight hands. We'd say: 'Bill, you know, you've only got two arms.'

But that was Bill. He'd listen to the songs and see all this dramatic stuff in them, timpanis and all that, so he'd think more percussion-wise. Vinny is just an out and out drummer, he'll play the beat forever. He'll also do these little odd rolls, but Vinny is a really precise drummer, whereas with Bill it was touch and go. Bill would do things and sometimes they would come off and sometimes they wouldn't.

Vinny's drumming brought something else to the music. It made it tighter, it made it more precise, probably even more mainstream. Where Bill did something like 'boom-tsj-pa-pa-pa', Vinny would simply go 'boom-tsj-boom-tsj-boom-tsj'. Less playful, but more precise. And probably with less character, because Bill had developed his own style and it was – Bill. You either like it or you don't. And I like it.

In playing with Vinny I had to retrain my mind as well. I thought, Christ, he's really good, but he cannot be too precise on the old songs, he's got to be a bit laid back. Black Sabbath was never exact on the timing. With Bill we would start off in one tempo and end up in another; it was a natural feel and Bill had that feel. I had to go through everything with Vinny, as I later have with every drummer, trying to coax him into playing the old songs as they were. But first things first. I said to him: 'You've got to get a bigger kit if you're going to be with this band!'

He never forgot that. He has this huge kit now, with drums all over the place. I said to him: 'Fucking hell, Vinny, have you got enough drums there?'

And he said: 'Well, you started it!'

There was no answer to that!

50

Getting Black and Blue

We started our Heaven and Hell tour in Germany in April 1980. We would ping-pong between Germany and the UK for a while, before making our way to the States in July. Ronnie flashed his Devil sign all over the place, the one with the outstretched first and fourth fingers, while holding the second and third down with the thumb. He gets credited for inventing it, but I've got a picture of Geezer from many years before doing just that. But Ronnie brought it more to light and, in so doing, made it his own.

Our production featured a cross. We had this thing built that worked electronically. It flashed lights all around it and they changed in different sequences, and when we played 'Heaven And Hell' the cross was supposed to burst into flames. It hardly ever worked. One classic moment came when we were playing Madison Square Garden. Ronnie did this big build-up, saying to the audience: 'I want you all to concentrate on the cross!'

He was going on and on about it.

'Keep concentrating!'

He got to the crescendo and it was: 'One, two, three!' and the cross went: 'Pfffft.'

Like a bloody little sparkler. And Ronnie went: 'Well, I guess you're not concentrating enough!'

It looked good when it burst into flames, but that night was one of those Spinal Tap moments. And that happened more often than not.

By this time we had Sandy Pearlman managing us. He'd been after us from the time we parted ways with Don Arden. We had nowhere else to go. Sandy looked like a hiker. He had a cap on his head and a bag on his back. I've never seen him dressed up. He was all right at first, but he soon turned out to be a bloody joke.

In the States he put us on tour together with Blue Öyster Cult. Because he had managed them for a long time, he favoured them over us. That's why we did the Black and Blue tour, where they would close one night and we would close the other. We hadn't been on a co-headliner before, because we'd always had bands supporting us. It seemed strange with them headlining, also because they weren't that big. I suppose Sandy wanted to make them big by putting them in that position.

It was a disaster because they used this big bloody fibreglass Godzilla thing on stage and it took them forever to break it down. On the nights we followed them, we were backstage an hour and a half before we could go on. The kids would get bored waiting, and blame us for it. And then we'd go into overtime with the unions. It was a bit unfair.

Sandy didn't manage us for very long. We fired him. He ended up getting paid off, so he walked away with a lump of cash. We just carried on with Mark Forster again. We were doing big shows and it was difficult for Ronnie to go out and stand in front of people who had seen Ozzy in that spot for ten years. Some of the kids hated it and they'd shout: 'Ozzy, Ozzy!'

But eventually Ronnie won them over.

While we were touring *Heaven and Hell*, NEMS released *Live at Last*, an album of stuff we had recorded back in 1975. It was a

Patrick Meehan thing. We were very upset about it, but it was at No. 5 in the charts by the time we got an injunction to stop it. The sound was awful on it and it interfered with what we were doing with Ronnie. The injunction collapsed on it and things were sorted out later. In 2002 it was released again, this time under the name *Past Lives*.

On 25 September 1980, while we were touring America, John Bonham died. That hit me really hard, but I don't think anybody who knew John could see him going any other way. He loved to do everything to excess. Him and Keith Moon were much the same. A bit loony, good friends as well, and they did burn the candle at both ends as much as they could. They got a bit mad; you never knew what they'd do next. I always thought, they can't keep on doing it all the time, they've got to hit a wall somewhere, there is a downside to it. But when I heard, it made me think about the vulnerability of everybody. Christ, who's next? That could happen to us! It knocked everybody for a loop, it was really depressing. John had such a lot going for him.

About two weeks later, in the Mecca Arena in Milwaukee, somebody in the audience threw this big metal cross at Geezer and it bounced off his guitar and hit him in the face. They probably thought, oh, he'll like this, a present, I'll throw it on stage for him. People who do stuff like that are idiots. If it had hit him in the head it could've blinded or even killed him.

We walked off stage and because most of the audience had no idea about what had happened a riot broke out. They were fighting, breaking chairs up, throwing pieces about, it was mayhem. But what can you do? We could hardly walk back on, going: 'Hello, we're back again, everybody quieten down.'

In November we started our first Japanese tour with dates in Tokyo, Kyoto and Osaka. I got food poisoning big time. It must have been the sushi. I was on stage, ran around in circles and just passed out, bang! They got me to hospital and they injected this stuff into me. It was the biggest syringe I've ever seen. God knows what it was, but it really worked. I should have got a load of that, really: 'Can I have some to go?'

While I got floored by sushi, Geezer managed to do it to himself. He freaked out one night and he broke the end of his finger. It must have been the sake. Him and Ronnie used to go to the bar, have too much to drink and get into a squabble among themselves. Of course the next day they would both regret it. Geezer would often get carried away, so breaking his finger probably happened that way. I wasn't there when it happened. I just heard later that the next couple of gigs were cancelled because of that. Geezer had a splint on it for a while. For once I wasn't the only one dealing with damaged fingers . . .

51

Melinda

I met Melinda in a club in Dallas after we played there in the summer of 1980. She was an American who did a little bit of modelling. I started seeing her, we went together for quite a while and she came on the road with us. The band must have thought, what is he doing now? Because she came along to Australia, Japan, New Zealand, just everywhere.

One day when we were in LA, we decided to get married at our hotel, the Sunset Marquis. I was doing Quaaludes and all sorts of bloody stuff, so I was on another planet really. I called up a vicar and said: 'Can you come over and marry us?'

He did and it was simple: sign these forms and off you go. Then the vicar said: 'Who's the witness?'

I said: 'I haven't got a witness.'

'Well, you need a witness.'

There happened to be a big teddy bear in the room and I said: 'There's the witness right there.'

He went: 'All right.'

And that was it. He never said: 'You can't do that.'

It actually stood up in court. When it came to the divorce, I said: 'We didn't really have a witness.'

They said: 'Well, who was the witness then?'

'I had a teddy bear as a witness.'

That went down well. But it didn't seem to make a difference.

So that was it. We got married at the Sunset Marquis.

After all the tours with Dio we moved back to England. That's where Melinda gave birth to our beautiful child. Toni was born in 1983. We had some happy times, but then I found out Melinda had problems. She would go to shops and come back with all these dresses with the labels still on them. She wasn't paying for them and I still don't know why. It wasn't a lack of money, I was really embarrassed because I knew people in the shops. Perhaps she thought I would pick up all the bills. Of course it put a strain on the marriage: we had a lot of rows. She would fly off the handle and get really nasty. In the end she went back to Dallas with Toni. When we were splitting up my accountant phoned me from London and said: 'What the fuck is going on? I've got $100,000 worth of bills on your American Express Card, and I've got this other bill on your MasterCard. How much money could you be spending in a month?'

'What are you talking about? I don't spend that sort of money!'

'Well, somebody does!'

It turned out that Melinda did this deal with the limousine company, where she had a twenty-four-hour bodyguard and a twenty-four-hour limo. She must have thought I was going to murder her or something. I don't know how she did it, because she wasn't a co-signatory on my card, but I got these enormous bills and I had a huge problem: I had to pay up. And that was the end of that.

The English courts didn't want to know either, because Melinda refused to come over from America. They said: 'Maybe if you can get her back here . . .'

It took me a long time to get a divorce. Her side just made it as difficult as possible, trying to get more money. I had lawyers coming over from America and going through all my accounts. Strange as it may seem, it was my responsibility to put all these people up when they came over, and they wanted to stay at, like, the fucking Ritz in London. The bills these people ran up were unbelievable. And it was just dragging on and on, because they were convinced I was hiding a lot of money. They were thinking, he's got billions tucked away. As they do. It was a bloody nightmare. It was a terrible relationship for our daughter, Toni, as well.

Melinda had her mum in Dallas looking after her much of the time.

A really weird situation. I never actually met Melinda's mother, but she was apparently a nice woman and she didn't agree with any of what was going on.

I wasn't allowed to see my daughter, because for some reason I was the asshole in this whole thing. After a long while they finally said it was okay for me to see her, but only in Dallas or Los Angeles. I couldn't take her anywhere. That door was closed shut.

Years later I got a phone call from the children's protection thing in America, saying that Toni had been removed from home. The neighbours had complained and the people from child welfare had gone around there and found that she was basically living in a slum. I thought, what am I going to do? I want to get her here! But I wasn't allowed to take Toni out. I had to go through a court case over there again to get her.

It broke my heart, but it would be years before Toni was allowed to come home.

52

Friends forever

In September 1980, Ozzy Osbourne's *Blizzard of Ozz* album was released on Don Arden's Jet Records label. After he left, we hoped that everything was going to be okay, but what do you do? Before we came to the end we tried to help Ozzy as much as we could to get him on the road, to pull himself together and do something. But it was such an uphill battle.

His being away from the band probably helped him, because he could finally do everything he wanted and get it all out of his system. For him it was either just fizzle out or get on with it, so it was good that he put a band together. And he had Sharon there; she was really taking care of him.

I didn't listen to *Blizzard of Ozz* at the time, because we were so wrapped up with what we were doing ourselves. Not that I wasn't interested; I certainly followed how he was doing on the tours and stuff, as we all did. I suppose there was a bit of a competition going on between us as well, but good luck to him. I was pleased to see that he'd got himself together and was doing the things that he wanted to do. He was probably very happy, because with us everything was built around the band, whereas now everything was built around him and he and Sharon had total control.

Ozzy did come around once to see me when I was in LA at the Le Parc hotel with my wife, Melinda, working on songs for *Mob Rules*. He had been going through a lot of stuff and shaved his head again at that time. At two thirty or three o'clock in the morning there was a knock on the door. There he was, bald, and wearing a long coat.

'Can I talk to you?'

I let him in and he talked and talked, going through all these different phases of his life. It was just too overpowering for me. I hadn't seen him for ages and suddenly here he was, opening up to me. He talked about everything, his last wife and Sharon and this and that and the other and whatever else. And then he went. It was really peculiar. He probably just needed a friend, somebody to talk to. But it was great that he came around.

Throughout the years we remained friends, despite of a lot of bullshit that went on. As soon as it got to the business again, it was a problem. But no matter what, Ozzy and me, we are still friends. And we always will be.

53

The Mob Rules

In December 1980 we went to Tittenhurst Park in Ascot to record a song for the movie *Heavy Metal*. It was John Lennon's old house. Ringo Starr had taken it over and rented it out to people like us, who could go there to write, rehearse and record. We got there right after Lennon was murdered, so it felt really, really strange. We were there for a week and had lots of time to check the place out. We looked around in the cupboards: 'Oh, what's in there? Ah, more gold discs!'

In the bedroom we saw 'John' written on one light switch and 'Yoko' on the other by each side of the bed. That was quite weird; you could just imagine them going: 'Which one is mine now?'

The room we rehearsed in was the white room that you always see in those old films about John and Yoko. They had a little studio in the back part of the house and we just used their gear. We set Vinny up in the hallway and I had my amp in the studio. We used Lennon's engineer as well, so we heard all these stories. It was quite a nice few days. It had a great atmosphere and we got some good vibes from there.

Heavy Metal was an animated film. They asked us to write a song for its soundtrack, but the movie wasn't finished yet so they just sent us some black and white sketches of it and the storyboard. It was difficult to write to that, as you don't have an idea of the timing of the scene. They just told us the length of the music they needed for this bit, and I suppose they animated more around what we came up with. We did an intro to go with this scene of these people before they turn into monsters. We made these effects, bubbling sounds and bass sounds and God knows what else, and then we went into the track 'The Mob Rules'. We recorded it right there and sent it off to the movie people, who put it on the soundtrack as it was. We wanted to use it for our own new album as well, but our producer Martin Birch said: 'Oh no, it won't match up sound-wise', so we ended up re-recording it. As a matter of fact, we re-recorded it twice, because first we had another great scheme of ours go wrong.

Martin said: 'You know how much it costs to do an album? Why don't you buy your own studio? Because then we could be in there for two months or three months or whatever, without worrying about the cost of it all!'

It was a great idea. We sent Martin over to LA to have a look at a studio he'd found, to see what it was like. He said: 'It's good. It just needs a new desk.'

We bought it and a bloody quarter of a million dollar sound desk, put that in, put the tape machines in and off we went to go and record in it.

It was crap.

We just couldn't get a guitar sound. We tried it in the studio. We tried it in the hallway. We tried it everywhere but it just wasn't happening. We'd bought a studio and it wasn't working! We re-recorded a new version of 'The Mob Rules' but abandoned it. We finally just walked out and went to the Record Plant, where we had to pay again, so it cost us twice as much. Nobody could believe it: 'I hear you bought a studio. So why are you in the Record Plant?'

'Eh ... well ...'

We ended up selling the desk. We sent this crew to pick it up and somebody thought they were burgling the place and called the cops on them. While they were doing their job a squad team was outside, ready to arrest them. But it was all explained and all sorted out. And then we sold the studio. Can Am it was called. It's actually a thriving studio now. I don't know what they've done to it, but now it's working somehow.

We wrote the rest of the songs for the *Mob Rules* album when we were in LA. We got a rehearsal room in the Valley somewhere, where we tried stuff and got ideas that we'd tape and take back to the house. I rented a place in Toluca Lake. After the rehearsals with the band, me and Geoff used to come back there, do a little bit of coke and work on some of the ideas. We'd put new bits to it, change stuff, add to it, try a few other ideas, and then the next day all of us got back together in the rehearsal room and tried it again.

Geoff wasn't my only visitor in Toluca Lake. Glenn Hughes came over one night with this guitar player, Pat Thrall. Of course I had some coke. Glenn went: 'Erm ... You don't have a bit of ... would you?'

I'd say: 'Yeah, I just have a little.'

I went into the bedroom, took a bit out of my stash, came back out again and said:

'I've got this.'

'Oh, good!'

And it was gone in no time at all.

Glenn went: 'You haven't got any more, have you, have you?'

Pat Thrall was absolutely shocked, because he had never seen Glenn in that state. They stayed until four or five o'clock in the morning, so I said: 'Glenn, I've got to go to bed, I've got to be in a studio in the morning.'

'Oh, just one more, just one more!'

I said to Pat: 'You've got to get him home.'

He said: 'I'm sorry. I don't know how to handle him. What do I do?'

'Just get him in the car and get him home!'

I hated doing it to Glenn, but I finally had to throw him out of the house: 'Out!'

They would have been there to the death if I hadn't done that. They did this project together: Hughes/Thrall. It didn't last. I wonder why.

That house was a horrible place anyway. It was hot in Toluca Lake and when I moved in there was no air conditioning. I had already wondered why I got it at such a good price. It was like a sauna in there. The neighbours probably thought I was weird, because I put all this tinfoil up against the bedroom windows, trying to reflect the heat. It was dreadful. I couldn't wait to get out.

I then moved into a hotel on Sunset Boulevard for a while. Ronnie came over and we put some ideas down in the hotel room. We found it was better to sometimes sit together swapping ideas, instead of working with everybody else around, because then they're all waiting for you to come up with something.

Heaven and Hell had done extremely well and the tour was a great success. The band members were getting along fine, but it took some effort on everybody's part to keep it that way, because the whole thing felt like it could blow up any minute. After the record became such a great success, Warner Brothers extended the contract at the same time, offering Ronnie a solo deal. That felt a bit odd to us, because we were a band and we didn't want to separate anybody. I'm not saying he shouldn't have a solo deal, but it just seemed like the wrong thing to do at the time. We talked about it and Ronnie was fine. And we just carried on.

By then Ronnie did come over a little more . . . I suppose, bossy. The way he conducted himself, the way he talked, it might have given that impression to the outside world, but he usually didn't mean anything by it. Ronnie was just very outspoken. On the other hand Geezer and myself hated to be confronted with stuff. We have always been that way, trying not to offend each other, or anybody else. That backfired in the long run, because we wouldn't say what we felt straight away. Instead we talked about it at first, and then it looked like we talked behind somebody's back, which in turn caused all sorts of problems. Of course we wouldn't respond to those immediately either, because we'd talk about it first, which in turn would cause some more problems, that we, of course, wouldn't ... Well, you know what I mean. It would ultimately lead to something that couldn't be solved any more, no matter how much everybody did or didn't talk about it.

Be that as it may, the recording of *Mob Rules* went smoothly. 'Turn Up The Night' was a fast song and a good way to start the album. Working with Ronnie, somehow the faster ones came easier than before. Another stand-out track was 'The Sign Of The Southern Cross'. We wanted a real power track on the album, just like 'Heaven And Hell' was on the previous one, and that was it: another huge, long song.

The album was released 4 November 1981. When we originally looked at the cover with a picture by Greg Hildebrandt we said: 'Wow, we really like this.'

The only thing we took out was the faces in the masks of the figures. There was a little controversy about some stains on the floor in the picture. According to some people it spelled out 'Ozzy'. Somebody mentioned it to us and we went: 'What?'

It was total rubbish. I never noticed anything and still wouldn't know where to find it.

Although I seem to remember that most reviews of *Mob Rules* were positive, some critics wrote: 'It's just *Heaven and Hell* part two.'

You can't please everybody.

'It's just a continuation of what you have done before.'

'Well, yeah, it's the band!'

'I know, but it sounds like a continuation from your previous album.'

'Yeah, it is. It's the next album!'

Or if it's not, then they're going: 'Oh, it doesn't sound anything like the last album.'

'No, it's a different album!'

What are you supposed to do?

54

The Mob tours

The Mob Rules tour started in November 1981 in Canada, followed by the States. Then we went back home for four dates at the Hammersmith Odeon starting on New Year's Eve. We used lots of pyro with fire and bombs, and we had this bloke working for us who dealt with all that stuff. Before the shows we rehearsed in London in a big room behind an Irish pub. At the time there were a lot of IRA bombings in the city. Our pyro guy decided to test a bomb in the rehearsal room. It exploded and everybody left the Irish pub in a panic. It was chaos, absolute chaos. One of our guys was in the pub and he said: 'I couldn't believe it, everybody just shot out. Left all the drinks and everything, whoosh, gone!'

Those bombs were really loud. They must have thought, hell, somebody is trying to blow us up! Mad, it was.

My good friend Brian May came down to see me while we were rehearsing. I said to him: 'Bring your guitar down and we'll have a little bash.'

He did and when we finished our set me and Brian just carried on playing. We were jamming away and meanwhile the crew gradually removed all the gear. We turned around and there was just one of my speaker cabinets and his amp, and we went: 'Fucking hell, everything has gone!'

We were totally oblivious to it, because we were enjoying ourselves so much. The pyro guy could've set one of his bombs off and Brian and me wouldn't have noticed!

We played the Hammersmith and the same pyro guy put his bombs underneath the stage. He tested one of them, it went bang and it blew a two-foot-wide hole in the floor on my side. If I'd been there, I would have been blown up. Christ, it was dangerous. The guy was becoming a liability, so in the end we told him: 'You're fired!'

No pun intended.

A couple of months later we were doing a show in Madison Square Garden. The guy who worked for me doing all my amps had built these big thick pipes. He maintained that he could put the pyro in these and it would give a real thud. He showed us and it really did. He then put them under the stage at Madison Square Garden and he set them off during 'War Pigs'. On the first note: 'Daa . . .' it was: 'Bang!'

The stage leaped and because of the concussion all the tubes went out on my amps and on Geezer's stack as well. It was just disastrous. We had only done the first note and the lot had gone. We were all right, but we had to stop.

Boom! That was it, the end, thank you and good night!

After a couple of weeks of touring the UK following the Hammersmith shows, we were supposed to go back to America in February.

Then Dad died.

He hadn't been well for some time. He had emphysema, because he'd been a heavy smoker all his life. I was back at home in England. One night I got a call from my mother. Dad had fallen out of bed. I got on the phone to his doctor and I screamed at him, telling him to get over there. I shot over there myself with

Melinda and found Dad on the floor, unconscious and breathing heavily. And then he just gave up and died.

I witnessed him die. It was horrible.

It was a difficult time. We postponed the start of the American tour, but soon I was playing away again, night after night, and travelling all over the place. Working hard ... just like Dad had done all his life.

55

A Munster in the mix

The Mob Rules tour went smoothly and we all got along well, although there was all this talk about Ronnie planning to do a solo album. That didn't really sit well with Geezer and me. We heard he was doing rehearsals with a solo band and we thought, what the hell is going on?

We recorded a lot of the American dates for what was to become Black Sabbath's first official live album, but the whole project turned into a bloody nightmare. We were in LA at the Record Plant again. We had this bloke called Lee De Carlo doing the engineering and the mixing for us. His sister was Yvonne De Carlo, the actress who played Lily Munster in *The Munsters*. We went ahead mixing this live album and then it started: me, Geezer and Ronnie would leave the studio and when we came back the next day it would sound different. Lee would never say anything. We would put it right, come back the next day and it would be different again! Lee eventually broke down. It was driving him mad, he was drinking more and more Scotch, and he finally said: 'I've got to tell you, you're going away at night and then Ronnie comes in and alters everything.'

'You're kidding!'

'No. I don't know what to say. I'm in a terrible position here.'

'Why didn't you tell us all this was going on?'

'I didn't know what to do!'

Ronnie has always denied that he did this, but that's what Lee said. How true that was I don't know – it's only his word – but we believed it at that time. We hit the roof and we had a big blow-up in the studio. We stopped Ronnie coming down there and that was the end of it. Ronnie said: 'I'm off.'

He went, and Vinny went with him. We broke up there and then.

Me and Geezer carried on and finished the record. *Live Evil* was released at the end of 1982, beginning of 1983. It did pretty well, considering everything and the fact that the band had broken up by then.

Amazingly, Ozzy put out a live album as well around the same time. Where *Live Evil* had songs from *Heaven and Hell* and *Mob Rules*, with some older Black Sabbath stuff, *Speak of the Devil*, Ozzy's album, was all re-recorded Sabbath songs with none of his solo stuff. I was unpleasantly surprised that he just did the old set. It still surprises me to this day: he goes out and does 'Iron Man' and 'Paranoid' all the time, even though he's got a great repertoire of all of the songs he's done on his own. I think putting out the live album like that was down to Sharon, trying to put the cat among the pigeons.

After Ronnie and Vinny left, I called up David Coverdale and Cozy Powell to see if they would be interested in joining us. Coverdale's words were: 'Ah, bollocks, I just signed a deal with Geffen Records to do a Whitesnake album.'

Cozy was with Whitesnake as well, so that was those two taken care of.

Me and Geezer had to rethink the whole thing. We had a million tapes sent in from different singers and most of them were horrible. One of them was from Michael Bolton. I didn't know him at the time. We had Michael come in and we had him sing 'Heaven and Hell', 'War Pigs' and 'Neon Knights'. He was quite good, but he wasn't exactly what we were looking for then. We dropped a bollock there, didn't we? Michael Bolton! A little bit of a mistake.

It was hard to find somebody who was going to fit the bill, to sing the Ozzy and the Ronnie stuff. But an unlikely lad was lurking around the corner, and soon we'd be reborn . . .

56

To The Manor Born Again

By the time Ronnie and Vinny left, we switched management again to none other than Don Arden. He hadn't been interested in managing us without Ozzy, but he changed his mind, maybe also because he'd had a big blow-up with Sharon after she took off with Ozzy. And after the Sandy Pearlman disaster we welcomed Don back with open arms.

Don came up with the idea of us meeting Ian Gillan, of Deep Purple fame. He said: 'See how you get on!'

I didn't know Ian. We arranged to meet him at lunchtime in a pub in Woodstock, Oxfordshire, called The Bear. We had a drink, then another drink, and another drink, and another drink. The pub opened and closed and opened again and closed, and we were still there. And at the end of the night we had a band together.

The next day Ian apparently didn't remember that very well, because his manager, Phil Banfield, said to him: 'Next time you decide to put a band together, will you inform me? I just got this call from Don Arden about the band and I said: "What band?" And Don said to me: "Well, he just joined Black Sabbath!"'

There certainly was a buzz around the business. They were going mad about us teaming up. And even in the pub in

Woodstock some fans came up to us who couldn't believe they were seeing the three of us together. It was unusual, guys from two big bands getting together to start a new group.

Phil Banfield managed Ian and Don managed us (Phil would later introduce me to Ralph Baker and Ernest Chapman, who in 1988 took over my management). Back then we let Don handle it, because Phil didn't want to get involved too much with him. Phil and Ian looked at him like: 'Don Arden, he'll cut your hands off!'

We weren't going to call the band Black Sabbath. The idea was to have a supergroup of different names in one band and call it something else. But Don thought we should carry on with the name Black Sabbath, and so we finally went: 'Well, all right then.'

Me and Bill Ward had stayed in touch and when we put the new band together I thought, let's see what Bill is up to. We asked him to come over and he soon did. We thought it would be good for Bill to be playing, because that's what he is, a player. He was doing well at that time. He was living in LA, where he had stopped drinking. He came over to England with this guy from Alcoholics Anonymous, a sponsor, so as far as we were concerned he was getting clean.

We went to The Manor, a studio in the Oxfordshire country-side owned by Richard Branson, to record *Born Again*. Ian said to me: 'When we record I'm going to stay outside.'

I said: 'Outside? What do you mean?'

'Well, I'm going to have a marquee outside the house and I'm going to stay in there.'

'Why is that then?'

'It would probably be better for my voice.'

'Okay.'

I thought he was joking, but when I arrived at The Manor I saw this marquee outside and I thought, fucking hell, he's serious. Ian had put up this big, huge tent. It had a cooking area and a bed-room and whatever else.

We had all the pyro left over from the tour, so one night we put it all around the tent. After Ian had gone to bed, up it went: Boom! The whole thing just flew up in the air and he was on the ground, all bewildered, going: 'What happened!?'

The worst of it was, he'd put his tent right next to the lake and Richard Branson had all sorts of prize three-foot-long fish in it. The concussion went all through the lake and killed some of the fish and stunned the rest, so they were all floating on the surface. Concussed carp: when Branson heard about it he was not happy at all.

While we were up at The Manor we thought that in the long run it would probably be cheaper to buy our own cars instead of hiring them for our upcoming tour, so we bought four new Fords. Bill especially was very pleased with his new wheels. One night we all went down to the pub and Ian went home to The Manor a little before us. There was a go-kart track that went around the swimming pool, and he decided to take one of the cars to race it around there. He lost control of it and, bang!, the car flipped upside down. He got out, but the car caught fire and he just left it. He got back in the house, threw the keys on the table and said he was going to bed. The next morning Bill got up and he said: 'What happened to my car?'

We found it down the go-kart track, upside down and burned out. Bill hit the roof: 'Who did this!'

Ian had his boat out on the Cherwell, the river that runs along the back of The Manor. Bill found out it was Ian who had flipped his car, so he got a chisel, went out to the river, smashed holes in the bottom of the boat and sank it. Then Ian came out: 'Fucking hell, somebody's stolen my boat!'

He drove up and down the river to see whether it had drifted off or if somebody had stolen it. He couldn't find it and went completely potty. He reported his boat missing, but then found out that it was in the river, underwater. He had these two gigantic new engines on them and they were ruined. So Bill got his own back.

Ian had walked away from Bill's crashed car unscathed, but he did injure himself when he tried to get into my room through the window. He climbed up a ladder, stepped over the window sill, got his foot stuck in the radiator, fell into the room and twisted his ankle. All because he wanted to put a fish under my bed.

Absolutely mad.

Richard Branson came to stay for a few days and him and Ian were smoking these huge joints. A right one he was. Don Arden and his son, David, came to see us at The Manor as well. To welcome them properly we put some bombs on the entrance gate. As Don and David drove in the bombs went up: Boom!

It was an unusual match, that line-up, but we did have a lot of laughs. We produced the album ourselves. Ian had nodules on his vocal cords at the time. When we first met him, he said: 'I'm not going to be able to sing too much because I have a problem with my voice.'

'Oh?'

But we put down the songs without too many hitches. Ian's lyrics were about sexual things or true facts, even about stuff that happened at The Manor there and then. They were good, but quite a departure from Geezer's and Ronnie's lyrics. There was a brick building at the back of The Manor, and it was close to a church. I had some gear set up in there because I wanted to try to get another guitar sound. The noise was deafening and all the locals complained. They drew up a petition against us and the priest brought it around. And that's why one of the tracks from the album is called 'Disturbing The Priest'. It's a good example of how Ian wrote about real events.

In those days you had to make your own effects. Bill made this particular 'tingngng!' sound on 'Disturbing The Priest'. He got this by hitting an anvil and then dipping it into a bathtub full of water, so the 'tingngng!' sound slowly changed and faded away. It took us all day to do that, because trying to lower the anvil gradually into the water was a nightmare. It took two people on one end and two more on the other to lower it, with somebody else hitting it. It was so heavy that we couldn't speak or anything, just sort of nod to each other. It was a sight to see: if somebody had made a film of it, it would have looked absolutely ridiculous. But it worked. All this to create this one 'tingngng!', which nowadays you can get from a computer in seconds.

I thought 'Zero The Hero' was a good track, and apparently I'm not the only one who likes it. When I heard 'Paradise City' by Guns N' Roses I thought, fucking hell, that sounds like one of ours! Somebody also suggested that the Beastie Boys might have borrowed the riff for '(You Gotta) Fight For Your Right (To Party!)' from our song 'Hot Line'. If it's true let's sue them. We won't play any more; we'll just make money from lawsuits! But needless to say we didn't sue! 'Keep It Warm' was a riff that I'd had floating about since *Mob Rules* and I thought it was about time we used it. I have a habit of keeping my riffs; I've got thousands of them. You know a riff is good when you play it and it gets to you. You just feel a good riff. The one that might be the beginning of a new song is the one that jumps out and you think, that's it, I like that! I found that while I'm still able to keep writing them, I usually don't go back to the old ones, so I'm only getting more and more. Maybe I should sell riffs!

When it came to doing the mix, Ian played the stuff back really fucking loud. Supposedly he blew a couple of tweeters in the studio speakers this way. We did the mix not knowing that they had gone, and nobody noticed. We just thought it was a bit of a funny sound, but it went very wrong somewhere between the mix and the mastering and pressing of that album. We didn't follow that through, and apparently when they tested the lacquers the sound was really dull and muffly. I didn't know about it, because we were already out on tour in Europe. By the time we heard the album, it was out and in the charts, but the sound was awful. It sold really well, but we were very disappointed that it hadn't come out as we all wanted it to. The original tapes sounded so much better.

Born Again was very different from anything we'd done before. Lyrically, because Ian's points of view on things were different from those of Ronnie and Geezer. And sound-wise, because that got all pear-shaped somewhere along the line. But there're some very good, heavy tracks on it. The cover was another matter. Ian couldn't believe it when he saw it. He went: 'You can't do that. You can't have a baby on the front with claws and horns!'

He absolutely detested it. Somebody had presented this thing to Don Arden: 'I've got this idea for you . . .'

And Don went: 'That's great!'

He really pushed it on us: 'I think it will cause a lot of problems, a lot of interest, people will talk about it!'

People talked about it all right.

I was in stitches when I first saw it, but then we ended up actually having it.

'Who would have that?'

'We would!'

During the recording Bill had some problem with his ex-wife. I think it had something to do with getting custody of his son. One day I bought Bill a plaque, because he'd been a year off alcohol. I went to give it to him and he was pissed as a parrot. It was such a downer, because it was all going so well and then, bang!, off the wagon and depressed again. I said to Geezer: 'What's happened? What's going on?'

He said: 'Oh, he's had some bad news from LA.'

The sponsor from AA had gone by that point. We caught him stealing stuff off Bill, so we sent him packing. We tried to bring Bill around, but he went through a weird stage. Over the next few days he sat in the kitchen at The Manor. This lovely old house had all these original leaded windows and in a fit of rage Bill threw all these plates and crockery and everything through them. We had people come over to redo them all, put in other windows and lead them, and, would you believe it, the next day Bill did the same again. He was just really angry about it all and he wanted to go back to LA, to get himself into recovery again.

It was real disappointing for us. He had recorded the album, but . . . now what?

57

Size matters

We wondered who we should get to replace Bill. I called Bev Bevan, who played with The Move and ELO, to see if he'd come along for a while. Bev was an old mate. He said to me: 'I don't know whether I can play it.'

I said: 'Come and have a go.'

We rehearsed, he got used to the songs and he played better and better as it went on, and in the end he toured with us for as long as this line-up lasted. It was nice to have another old friend on tour. At first we didn't even know how long Bev was going to be needed. We thought Bill would come back, but he just wasn't capable.

When we were thinking about the stage set for our Born Again tour, Geezer said: 'Why don't we have something that looks like Stonehenge, you know, with stones and all that stuff?'

'Hmm, that's a good idea.'

Geezer jotted down what it should look like and gave it to the designers. Two or three months later we saw it. We rehearsed for the tour at the Birmingham NEC and we said: 'Oh great, the stage set is going to come today!'

It came in and we couldn't believe it. It was as big as the real

Stonehenge. They had taken Geezer's measurements the wrong way and thought it was meant to be life-size. I said: 'How the bloody hell did that happen?'

'Well, I put down the height in centimetres, but they must have thought it was in inches.'

We were in shock. This stuff was coming in and in and in. It had all these huge columns in the back that were as wide as your average bedroom, the columns in the front were about 13 feet high, and we had all the monitors and the side fills as well as all this rock. It was made of fibreglass and wood, and bloody heavy.

The tour continued throughout Europe. I suggested we play 'Smoke On The Water', because Ian was known for it and it seemed like a bum deal for him not to do any of his stuff while he was doing all of ours. I don't know whether we played it properly, but the audience loved it. The critics moaned; it was something out of the bag and they didn't want to know then.

Ian had all the lyrics written out as he had a hard time remembering them. He got to a point where he had them all over the stage. One time during 'Black Sabbath' they blew too much dry ice our way. Ian was standing there with his head down, hair in front of his face, huffing and puffing, furiously trying to blow the dry ice away from his lyric sheets.

I went: 'You can't have all those lyrics lying around, it looks a bit obvious.'

He said: 'I've nearly got them. I'll have them soon!'

But he never did, he just couldn't remember them. Ian wasn't very sure-footed either. He once fell over my pedal board. He was waving at the people, stepped back and, bang!, he went arse over head big time. He jumped up and tried to make believe it was part of the show. Ian was very funny. As a matter of fact, off stage Ian was a bloody lunatic. On stage he was quieter. Instead of being a lunatic on stage and quiet off!

Ian had these two big bongos on a stand when he joined us, like Edmundo Ross. I said: 'You can't use those!'

He said: 'I always used them when I was with Purple.'

'It won't look right in Black Sabbath, having a set of bongos stuck right in front of you.'

'Well, I don't know what to do with my hands if I don't have them. I'm so used to hitting them.'

'It will look terrible, these bloody bongos in the middle of the stage.'

'What if I put them on the side, by Geezer?'

So he put them by Geezer then. Him tapping his bongos.

One time the crew put some string on them. The idea was to pull them away while he was playing them, so he'd have to follow them. Unfortunately it didn't work out very well. When they pulled on them, the bongos wobbled, nearly falling over. But he was still trying to hit them. We managed to get rid of them in the end, thankfully.

When Ian first joined us he said: 'I don't know what to wear.'

I said: 'Everybody wears black or maybe leather.'

'I don't really wear leather.'

It's a bit difficult singing in Black Sabbath with flowery shirts on, so we asked him to darken down a bit. Had about five or six waistcoats made, all black leather, and in the end he had some leather pants as well. We were actually getting him there bit by bit.

On 13 September we were due to play a bullring in Barcelona. We were invited to this really nice club the night before. The drinks were flowing and then Ian decided that he was going to set the waiter's arse on fire. He got his lighter going while the guy was serving somebody else, burning him on the backside. I thought, here we go, and said to Bev: 'I'm going to go back to the hotel now.'

He said: 'I'll come with you.'

But Ian went: 'Just hang on, we're all coming with you in a minute.'

'Oh, fucking hell. Well, okay, all right.'

We had another drink and then the place closed, so we went. Ian walked out with his pint of beer and they said: 'You can't take that outside.'

He did anyway and then it was: 'Don't push me!'

And bang! A fight started and it was an awful one. They came from everywhere, all the kitchen staff, the waiters, the bloody lot, with knives and martial arts nunchucks and everything. We were just the band and two security blokes. We were fighting for our lives and Ian Gillan was nowhere to be seen. He later claimed he fell in a ditch, but I reckon he legged it. Geezer hit somebody with a glass and it cut his hand open. The police came and they arrested him and one of our security guys. They put them in jail and threw two people from the club in with them, who proceeded to beat our security guy up right there.

How on earth we got back to the hotel I don't know. Then we tried to get a call out to Don Arden, but the hotel had been phoned by the club and they blocked our calls. We all went: 'Oh, God. Now what?'

They threw us out of the hotel, because they had ties with this club. The Mafia were involved in that; it was a heavy scene. We got on the tour bus and tried to find somewhere to stay, but nobody would have us. We drove for ages and ages and somehow we ended up staying about a hundred yards from where we were originally. We managed to get Don on the phone and he said: 'I'll send somebody over.'

He arranged this team of eight German heavies to come over. And, sure enough, in the middle of the night, straight away, boom, there they were. The head guy was older, grey hair, glasses, very well dressed, and he said: 'Just stay in the rooms and don't move. I'll go and see them.'

Don had told me: 'This man is very serious.'

Supposedly he had killed such and such a number of people and I thought, oh fuck, we don't want to get into that! So I said to him: 'God, sort it out but don't go there. Please don't make it any worse than it already is.'

He said: 'They'll listen to me.'

He was a lovely guy and I got along fine with him, but it was like something you'd see in a movie. We played the bullring on the night and I thought, oh dear, we're in the open air, we messed with the wrong people, we're going to get murdered! But the Germans went around all the entrances and all the dressing rooms and secured the whole place. They were real professionals.

The worst of it was, we had a guy from the *Daily Mail* travelling around with us. He saw all this and reported it all in the paper. He came in to do some photographs and a little story about playing in the bullring, but he got a lot more than that.

In October we took the whole Stonehenge thing to America. We had carpenters on it and a big crew to set it all up, but on most gigs it just wouldn't work. The columns at the back were too high and we ended up just using the ones that held my and Geezer's cabinets, but even those were massive. At the end of the tour we tried to give it all away to the people who had bought London Bridge and reassembled it in Arizona, but they didn't want it. We couldn't take it back to England, so the crew dumped it off at the docks somewhere and left it. Just ridiculous. We abandoned Stonehenge right there in America.

I didn't see the movie *Spinal Tap* until later. Don Arden said to me: 'We've got a front cover to do tomorrow.'

I said: 'Okay. Me and Geezer?'

'With Spinal Tap.'

'Spinal Tap? Who the bloody hell is Spinal Tap?'

I don't think even he knew at the time.

'I think it's some up-and-coming band and they have a movie coming out.'

'And we are doing a front cover with them? We've never heard of them!'

Me and Geezer did the shoot with them anyway, which was funny, but I still didn't have the faintest idea who they were. It was only later when I saw the movie that I realised what it was all about and where they got the idea for the scene with the tiny Stonehenge from.

And they had a midget as well.

Because the *Born Again* album cover had a picture of this red baby with claws and little devil's horns, Don Arden's idea was to recreate this baby on stage. So one night at a gig he said: 'I want to show you something.'

'Okay.'

He made Ian and me wait outside this room and finally said: 'Okay, you can come in now.'

We went in, it was dark and we just saw these red eyes, peering at us.

'Blimey!'

We put the light on and there was this midget in a rubber outfit who looked like the baby on the cover. We thought, fucking hell, Don's gone over the top! He said: 'It's going to be a great addition to the show!'

The idea was that the midget would climb up the 13-foot-high columns, run across them, and then jump off them on to the drum riser, which was about halfway down the stage. And then he'd jump off the riser to the front of the stage, look at the audience, cry, and his eyes would light up and the show would start.

The midget was a bit of a pop star, because he'd been one of the little bears in *Star Wars*. Ozzy at the time also took a midget out on the road; I think he called him Ronnie. I don't know who had the first one, really. It became a thing. Midgets were in demand. But we had the most famous midget because ours was in *Star Wars*.

'Who's got the most famous midget?'

'We have!'

He kept ribbing the crew with it: 'I've been in the movies!'

They really didn't care about that at all, so they did all manner of things to this poor guy. One night they locked him in a flight case.

'What's happened to the midget?'

Nobody could find him. The little guy nearly suffocated.

Then another day I went down for a sound check and I could hear: 'Help! Help!'

I looked up and they had him hanging over the stage on a chain, upside down. The poor bugger, he really took some stick. It was becoming a real thing for the crew: 'What can we do to him next?'

We finally decided it was best for all parties concerned if he left, especially after the crew decided to put the lights out on him at the very moment that he jumped from the columns on to the drum riser. He went: 'Aaaaaah!'

Splat!

He caught the edge of the drum riser and nearly broke his neck. Meanwhile, we were backstage waiting to come on and it just blew the show. We said: 'That's it, he's gone!'

They would have killed him if we hadn't fired him.

Up until that point I had always worked with people who were completely committed. Looking back at it now, it doesn't look as if Ian was. I think he had a ball and did his best, but he knew all along that he was going to get out. And we never thought, oh, he's going to be here for ten years. With this line-up we just set out to see where it was going. We did one album, toured for a year and that was it. We didn't know until the very end that Ian was going back to Deep Purple, but it had run its course by that point. Being with Purple, that was his gig. We didn't really think about doing another album together, we never had fights, we got on great and we still do. We had a fantastic time and more laughs than ever. We just took it day by day. And the last of those days came in March 1984, when we had our final gig together in Massachusetts.

That was the end for Ian, and for Bev as well.

58

Last man standing

Right after Ian Gillan left, we met up with Ozzy to talk about getting the old band back together again. We've had one or two times like that, where we discussed him coming back. If it had been up to us, it would have happened. But Don wouldn't have anything to do with Sharon and Sharon wouldn't have anything to do with Don. It was always these stupid managements beefing on about something that stopped us from doing what we wanted to do.

We still needed a new singer, so out in LA me and Geezer listened to tapes again, boxes and boxes of them, sent to us by all these young guys who were dreaming about joining Black Sabbath. This one guy called Ron Keel sent a tape in and I said to Geezer: 'This lad's pretty good. Have a listen to him.'

He played it and said: 'Oh, yeah!'

We went out for dinner and drinks with him. In the course of the evening I said to Ron: 'I really like the stuff you sent.'

'Oh, thanks.'

I said: 'I like that third track, so-and-so . . .'

And he went: 'That's not me.'

'What do you mean it's not you? It's on your tape!'

He said: 'I'm on the other side.'

He'd sent the tape with him on one side and another, different singer on the other. So we made a right boo-boo there. Ron actually did have a career later, because he's a good singer as well. He just wasn't what we were looking for at the time. We never figured out who the other guy was, but after this happened we'd had enough, so we got a producer to try out the singers who had sent in good tapes. It's like doing *The X Factor*: you go through all these kids who sing in the bathroom and think they are great. Most of them were rubbish.

We wanted somebody who looked right, had a good voice and could sing the old songs, because that's what people wanted to hear as well. When Ronnie James Dio came into it, he was so different from Ozzy, but he could still sing those old songs in his way and it sounded right. Most of the people we tried just didn't sound right. A lot of them couldn't reach the high notes. Come to think of it, that was one of the things Michael Bolton actually could do.

We gave the most promising ones we auditioned a little extra time. Like David Donato, who we allowed a couple of weeks to settle in. We also recorded a couple of tracks with him. One of the songs was 'No Way Out', which, after many changes, turned into 'The Shining' off the *Eternal Idol* album. Different vocals, different lyrics, different arrangement, but still the initial riff. Dave looked right and he was a nice enough lad, but he had a bit of a strange, high voice. Before we knew it, Don Arden already had *Kerrang!* magazine doing photos, even though we were going: 'We don't want to release these yet, he's not a definite yet!'

And, sure enough, bang, he was out. After millions of tapes and countless auditions, we still hadn't found ourselves a singer. But our drummer problem had been sorted, because Bill had come back. Or so we thought. In the summer of 1984 he left again. In and out like a yo-yo he was. Bill is one of those people who is difficult to understand sometimes. Even after all the years I've known him, I still never know what it is that makes him tick. And right after Bill, Geezer went as well.

But I didn't leave. The only person left standing was me.

Mug!

59

The mysterious case of
the lofty lodgers

After finishing the Born Again tour I rented a house in Bel Air. It was a wonderful place, but I heard these noises all the time, people talking and bumps in the night. I'd look around the house but nobody would be there.

'Blimey, where does that come from?'

Weird things happened. I came back one night from rehearsal, walked into the kitchen and found a plait of hair on the kitchen table, a couple of feet long. Like a ponytail.

'How did that get there?'

Another night I came home and found the same sort of thing wrapped around the handle of the front door. I couldn't explain it.

I could never figure out the sound of people talking in the house. I called the Bel Air police every time I heard it. At first they'd go around the house: nothing. But they never checked the loft. And after a while they'd come around and go: 'Oh, it's him again.'

I got so concerned about it that I even stayed down at my friend's house a couple of times. He had a bloody armoury there.

He had revolvers and pump-action shotguns and, just like in the movies, a little gun in a book. He said: 'I'll come up with you and we'll have a look. I'll bring my gun.'

And so he did. He sat there in the lounge all night. Nothing happened. I thought, he thinks I am loony now. He left and the next day it started again.

I then hired a security guard. The sauna overlooked the swimming pool, so I put him in there. I said: 'If you see anything, let me know.'

After a while he got fed up and said: 'Hey, man, I can't stay here all night!'

I whispered: 'Shhhh, we're trying to catch somebody!'

I was going to extremes to find out who these people were. After the security guy left, I had one of the crew stay with me, but he would be snoring away so loudly that he couldn't hear anything. Finally, Mark gave me a Magnum. I slept with this huge gun in my hand. One night I heard this horrendous noise. I grabbed Mark's gun and I dashed to the car with no shirt on and as I drove out I looked back and I saw all these faces in the kitchen window, looking out at me. It freaked me out. I drove straight down to the police, they came up and: nothing. Gone!

Then I found out that the wires of the burglar alarm had been cut inside the house. I should have moved out really, but then I had Geoff Nicholls to stay with me. I just wanted somebody to see something, if only to prove that I was not crazy. I really thought I was going loopy and so did everybody else.

One night Geoff and me were in the lounge at two o'clock in the morning and we saw this bloke running across the lawn.

Fucking hell, finally!

I got my gun and we opened the door slowly. We slipped out and crawled across the grass. The house was built on a hill and we could hear talking down below. I whispered to Geoff: 'All right, we've got a gun and when they come up . . .'

We must have been lying there for about an hour waiting for these people to appear, and then the sprinklers came on. It was like a Laurel and Hardy skit, both of us going: 'Waah!'

We were soaked and, of course, after that we never found them. But at least Geoff had seen somebody as well. It wasn't just me any more.

One night a guy from the crew built this trap in the garden. He made all these zigzags of wire all across the yard and it took him all day to do it. The idea was that if somebody came across he'd get stuck in it and I would be able to see him.

I heard a noise. I called the police. They came over. And then they got stuck in it.

I went out with my gun and the police were going: 'Drop the gun, drop the gun!'

'No, no, I live here!'

'Drop the gun!'

They could have shot me. I could have shot them as well, come to think of it.

This thing went on for months. Eventually we found a trap-door. Upstairs there was a cinema room with a big screen. In the wall there was a cutout, and because it was all papered you couldn't really see it. We opened this thing, stepped through it, and we could walk all around the house. It was quite a big area; you could virtually stand up there. We found all these piles of cigarette butts and beer cans outside the vents, through which you could look into the rooms. They had obviously been sitting there, seeing everything I did. Fucking hell, they could probably tell a few stories.

I was relieved that we found that somebody had been there and that the police could finally see that as well. They never found out who it was. They said afterwards that the easiest thing for me would have been to get a dog. With a dog I'd have found them in no time. Now why the hell didn't I think of that?

It made me so paranoid that I eventually moved into a hotel. The first thing I did there was tape all the vents up. I just had a terrible fear of it, so there I was, roasting at the hotel. Even now I've got cameras around my house everywhere; I've got the gates and the dogs. And it's all down to that experience.

60

Lovely Lita

Lita Ford opened for us on the Born Again tour. We got together after a show to have a chat, and we hit it off. It developed into a relationship and when I lived in Bel Air, in the house with the people in the loft, she came to visit me there. After I moved out of there and got a penthouse at Crescent Heights and Sunset in LA, she moved in with me. I was still married to Melinda at the time. We had split up, but it took me a long time to get a divorce, so I suppose technically I was committing adultery. Lita and I even got engaged, but we couldn't do any more than that until I got divorced.

Lita helped us look for a new singer. She knew a couple of people we could try, but after Bill and Geezer left I was in need of a whole new band. It was her idea to let me use the drummer and the bass player of her band, Eric Singer and Gordon Copley. Eric wanted to play in my band more than he did in Lita's, so he said to me: 'If you want a drummer, I would be interested.'

He ended up working with me for quite a while. Lita then looked at it as, oh, he's nicked my drummer. She got the hump about it so bad, that our break-up came mainly from that.

At the time I was doing a lot of drugs again, which was also hard for her. Me and Geoff Nicholls would be at the penthouse a lot, trying to write something and doing coke at the same time. Every time Lita came home, Geoff would be there. It looked like I was more involved with him than I was with her.

Me and Geoff were in the penthouse one day and I put the chains on the door and something up against it, because you get paranoid when you do a lot of coke. We were working on a song when we heard this loud bang. It was Lita. She couldn't open the door and pushed it so hard that the whole rim of the door came off, with the chains and everything. And then she got pissed off, because we were at it again.

It was a shame, really, because I messed up the relationship by being constantly out of it. She was a nice girl and we got on well. It just started coming apart, certainly when the Eric thing happened. We were together for about two years. Then we went our separate ways. Lita was later managed by Sharon Arden. She phoned me and said: 'I'm looking for a manager. What about Sharon?'

I said: 'I don't know. It's up to you.'

Sharon got Lita to do a song with Ozzy that went to No. 1, so she did all right for her. For a while. Until she dropped her.

61

Together again, for a day

I was in the middle of doing my album when they asked us to perform at a huge show. All these people were doing it and it was for a very good cause. I said: 'Sounds good. Let's do it.'

So, in July 1985, the original Black Sabbath line-up got back together for a one-off gig at Live Aid in Philadelphia. We probably thought that it might be the first step towards getting back together again. We got on well when we saw each other there and I think we all hoped it would happen, but the powers that be have to allow you to do it. It has to be in aid of charity, otherwise management would think somebody was making money out of it and it wouldn't happen. And there was no greater charity cause than Live Aid.

The organisation offered us a time slot in a rehearsal facility. We got to the space and were supposed to rehearse three songs. Instead of doing that we ended up talking about old times. We were there chatting away, then we played for a bit and then stopped when somebody would say: 'Oh, remember so-and-so?'

Not much of a rehearsal, really.

This girl came in and stood at the back, watching. I mentioned this to somebody: 'Can you tell her this is a closed session?'

I didn't know who it was. She had dyed her hair dark and looked nothing like Madonna, but it was Madonna and she wasn't very happy about being tossed out.

We went back to the bar afterwards, had a great time together and got solidly sloshed. The next day we were on at something like ten o'clock in the morning. I had a dreadful hangover so I put my dark glasses on, and then we played 'Children Of The Grave', 'Iron Man' and 'Paranoid' in the bright sunlight. It was a great thing to do and we were certainly aware of the importance of the occasion, but it was over very quickly.

Meanwhile, Don had issued Ozzy with a writ, because he thought we were going to get together again and that Sharon was going to manage us. Don wanted to stop anything happening, because he made his point that he managed me and that there was no way we were going to do anything without him. Don and Sharon – they were both as paranoid as each other. Don sent a writ to Ozzy; the guy who presented it right there at Live Aid looked like a fan, so Ozzy thought he wanted his autograph and signed it. I didn't actually see the writ, as Sharon whipped that away right quick.

It put a little bit of a dampener on the occasion.

I don't know whether Live Aid made a difference. You do the thing, they raise the money and what happens then? They buy the food or whatever they need, but you're never 100 per cent sure who gets what. But I think it was a good thing to do anyway.

We got to Philly, had a drunken night, got hung over, did the gig and disappeared. The subject of getting back together didn't even come up. I got on the plane back home and didn't see them again for years.

62

Twinkle twinkle Seventh Star

I was now the only guy left in Black Sabbath. Without a band, I got the idea of doing a solo album with all different singers. I made a list of people I wanted, like Robert Plant, Rob Halford, David Coverdale and Glenn Hughes, but it opened a huge can of worms trying to get somebody to sing. I ran into all sorts of contractual stuff, the record companies didn't let them, so it was: 'Oh no, we are doing an album, I can't sing on yours.'

Eventually the idea was dropped. We then tried this guy called Jeff Fenholt. He was another one who had played the lead in *Jesus Christ Superstar*, in the Broadway version of that musical. So we had had Ian Gillan, who was the original Jesus Christ Superstar, and here we had the Broadway Jesus wanting to join Black Sabbath. We tried Jeff out and he had a good voice. I cut a couple of demos with him in Los Angeles. One of the tracks was 'Star Of India', which later turned into 'Seventh Star'. Another one was 'Eye Of The Storm', which ended up on the album as 'Turn To Stone'. And we had a track that eventually turned into 'Danger Zone'. Of course these demos got out and found their way on to a bootleg album. Again. They called it *Eighth Star* or something like that.

Jeff seemed a nice enough guy. It might have worked with him, even though I wasn't 100 per cent convinced that he'd be able to do our older stuff. But then Jeff Glixman came in to produce the album and he didn't think Fenholt was working out, recording-wise. And that was that.

A little later Jeff Fenholt suddenly became this big TV evangelist. I couldn't believe it, because when we met him he was saying things like: 'Oh yeah, I fucked that chick.'

The *New York Times* did a thing about him being with Black Sabbath and they wrote that he saw the light, rejected evil and all this bollocks. We were right back in the satanism thing because Fenholt was going on about it. I was getting phone calls to do *Larry King Live* about him. I thought, I'm not getting involved in that! You try and talk religion on TV in America and you have no chance. Especially him being an evangelist now; they're all going to side with him and I won't have a leg to stand on!

Around the time we did some demos I thought Geezer was going to return. His wife and manager, Gloria, said he wanted to come back as well. But the next thing I knew, he had joined Ozzy.

'Bloody hell, what happened!?'

Glenn Hughes was, as I've said, one of the singers on my wish list. He came in and sang, and I thought, bloody hell, he's good! He was so impressive that I thought it would be great to use Glenn on all the songs of what was to become the *Seventh Star* album. But it was difficult to work with him. Fucking hell, he did ten times more coke than me!

It just turned into a nightmare. He'd go: 'I've got this idea, I've got this idea!'

He'd snort a big line and say, all hyper: 'Listen to this, listen to this!'

'Yeah, okay. Good.'

'Yeah, but I've got this other one, listen to this!'

He drove you up the wall. Even he himself now says: 'I don't know how you put up with it.'

What made it even worse was that he had all these hangers-on coming down to the studio as well. I tried to get rid of them, because I could see that they were just leeches. I guess he could afford this big entourage at the time, as he'd just come off the Deep Purple thing, but it didn't last. He lost a lot of money and ended up selling all his stuff.

When we were doing *Seventh Star*, we recorded the album with Glenn Hughes and Eric Singer, and we had Dave Spitz on bass, a good player we'd found through Jeff Glixman. It was a first for me to play with musicians that young. I was thirty-seven at the time, and Dave and Eric were about ten years younger than me. It felt funny because, when I talked about old times, they didn't know what I was on about. They would ask me stuff and I'd start talking away and then I'd find out, hang on, they haven't got a clue, I can't go back that far because they can't relate to that.

'Remember so-and-so?'

'No, we don't.'

'Oh ... you forgot.'

And then I'd realise, bloody hell, they weren't even born then!

We started recording in LA, but we finalised the album in Atlanta, Georgia, because Jeff Glixman could get a good deal on a studio there. The basic tracks had been done already, so only me and Glenn went down there. I had taken this big stereo to Atlanta with me. Glenn had nothing to play his stuff on, so I lent it to him. I had just bought it and he swapped it for some coke. I said to Glenn: 'What happened to my stereo?'

'I lent it to somebody.'

'Oh ...'

Then I saw this coke dealer with my stereo and put two and two together. Glenn was uncontrollable, but he sang like a dream and absolutely effortlessly. He'd sit in the studio, slouching, with a mic, and . . . sing! Just incredible, a God-given voice.

We didn't take a long time recording the album: some tracks were actually done in the first or second take. We also tried to finish quickly because I paid for it all. The record company came up with a good advance later, but I fronted everything myself.

We finished *Seventh Star* in August 1985. Gordon Copley's original bass playing is on 'No Stranger To Love'. We kept that from the very first sessions. It just seemed to go well with that track. I thought it was a great song, but what I didn't like was doing the video for it. The first day they took some footage of me and Glenn playing away. The next day I had to be there at something like 5.30 a.m. to do this shoot with the girl from *Star Trek*, Denise Crosby, Bing's granddaughter. I'm not very good at videos anyway, but I had to do this love scene with her, which was very embarrassing. They put this black eyeliner on me and everything else. It wasn't what we were all about at all, and I hated it. To make matters even worse, they had me walk into Los Angeles canals at seven o'clock in the morning, in the freezing cold with mist rising. I had just bought these new boots so they were well and truly knackered after that.

Seventh Star was released in January 1986. It was supposed to be a solo album. I certainly didn't want to release it as a Black Sabbath album, because I hadn't written it as a Black Sabbath album. I wanted the freedom for it to sound as it did and tour without calling the band Black Sabbath, also because Glenn was uncomfortable about that. But when the question of the name came up, Don said to me: 'The record company says that you owe them a Black Sabbath album, so they want this one.'

'Ah . . .'

In the end it was billed as 'Black Sabbath featuring Tony Iommi'. Neither I nor Glenn was pleased with it, because we felt we weren't doing the record justice presenting it this way. And to go out and play 'War Pigs' and 'Iron Man' – it just wasn't right.

Seventh Star reached No. 27 in May 1986 and it dropped off the charts after five weeks. Not really a big seller. I don't think I even noticed it, because of all the aggro we had within the band.

We had a tour coming up, but somebody was about to choke on it.

63

Glenn falls, but there is
a Ray of hope

The Seventh Star tour kicked off in Cleveland, Ohio, in March 1986. We had a big stage set with lasers and everything. Don Arden's idea again, but I had to pay for it all. Of course. To say the tour got off to a bad start is an understatement, because it went disastrous with Glenn. I had hired this bodyguard called Doug Goldstein, who later managed Guns N' Roses, to watch him and to keep all the hangers-on away from him. But no sooner did the tour start than Glenn disappeared back to Atlanta. Doug brought him back just in time for the show. We were at the side of the stage and he went: 'I can't go on, I can't go on.'

So I literally threw him on: 'Get out there!'

I hated being like that but I had to do it.

Doug Goldstein ended up doing all sorts of things to pin Glenn down. While staying in rooms with adjoining doors, he actually attached a string to his toe and tied it to Glenn's hotel room door, so as soon as Glenn moved Doug would know about it. It was a bloody nightmare. But Glenn was cunning; he managed to get drug dealers in somehow.

I wasn't there when it all happened. I just know that our stage manager, John Downing, ended up thumping Glenn on the day before the first show. John was tough, very forceful, and he could handle himself. He was good at what he did. He had worked for Jimi Hendrix and The Move in the past. John said that he couldn't control Glenn and that he took a swing at him, so he clocked him. That was John Downing's side of it, but he is dead now so we can't ask him about it any more. He drowned. While he was on tour in Europe, John had had a row with some bootleggers and when he was coming back to England on the ferry, they were on the same boat. The story goes that those bootleggers lobbed him overboard and his body was washed up a couple of days later.

John broke Glenn's nose. Don Arden apparently said to John: 'He had to go on stage, why didn't you thump him in the back of the head?'

Typical!

Glenn claimed that the blow caused a blood clot in his throat. Sure: of course it wasn't the coke. It obviously affected his voice. It does sometimes, it dries your throat up. Glenn is such a great singer but he was just unable to perform. On top of that, he was getting extremely paranoid. I spoke to Don about it, and I said: 'We are going to have to pull the shows.'

'We can't pull the shows. If we do, they'll sue us!'

'Oh . . . fucking hell!'

I simply couldn't afford to run that risk, so what we had to do was locate another singer and bring him in a couple of days before we actually fired Glenn. This way we'd be able to get him to see the show and see how it all worked, before taking over. We'd go down to the gig in the afternoon to rehearse with him, to get him into the role of it. Then, when it all happened with Glenn, the new singer would be able to go on stage to continue with the rest of the shows.

Dave Spitz knew this young singer called Ray Gillen from a

band in New York. He was a good-looking guy with a great voice. The girls loved him, and when he was with us there were suddenly lots of women coming to the shows. We brought Ray in during the afternoon of our third show. We ran through the songs and Glenn was wondering what was going on: 'Who is that guy I keep seeing?'

It was really awkward, but it was the only thing left for us to do. It was either that or cancel shows. We had to go on with Glenn and then slot Ray in straight away. It was also difficult for me, because Glenn had always been a mate and I felt really underhand doing it. We've talked about it since and Glenn understands. We gave him all these chances and he just buggered them up.

That third gig went great from our side, but Glenn was so bad that night that I had a row with him after the show. I got angry because he was letting everybody down, including himself. He could hardly sing at all any more and Geoff had to take over on some of the vocals. Of course he sounded nothing like Glenn, but he just tried to finish the songs.

A lot of people underestimate how tough you have to be when you're leading a band. You always become the arsehole. People don't understand, they're not there and they don't see all the things that are happening, why you end up kicking somebody out. But there's a reason why they're not there any more. Either they leave of their own accord, or they are not pulling their weight and you get rid of them, because the band has to carry on.

The gig in Worcester, Massachusetts, on 26 March was Glenn's last. When he discovered he was out, he banged on my door, screaming: 'I know about this fucking singer!'

I thought, I'm not going to answer it now. He was raging!

Fate would have it that our next gig in upstate New York was cancelled thanks to another Christian protest, one of the many times that happened to us. And the irony of it was that the cancelled gig was in a town with the fitting name of Glens Falls.

Luckily for both of us, ten years later and the drugs consigned to history, we'd hook up again for the DEP studios sessions.

Three days after Worcester, Ray Gillen did his first show with us. He was thrown in at the deep end, but he did really good. Finally we had somebody again who really wanted to do it and had the right attitude. Even so, ticket sales weren't very good. With Glenn we did big gigs and we did good business. Now we were touring with an unknown guy, so the interest went off. It took all that time to build it up, and then it all came crashing down right quick. It was appalling. We had to pull the tour in the end, because we were losing too much money.

But we soldiered on, starting our UK tour in May, doing twelve dates ending with two shows at the Hammersmith Odeon in London. The halls weren't that big, but ticket sales were all right. Of course, there was a bit of confusion about who was in the band as well: Ian Gillan, Ray Gillen, it was hard. Ray was really a good find, but nobody knew him. We had to break him in, people had to come and see him. It would take time to build it up.

The big question was, did we have that time?

64

The quest for The Eternal Idol

While we were trying to get back on our feet with Ray Gillen, I got into a real hole. Don Arden stopped being my manager. He got done for fraud or something to do with tax evasion. They arrested him and put him behind bars for a while. I was asked to help him out, just like the other band that he managed, Air Supply. His lawyer said to me: 'Look, Don's in a lot of trouble. We need to help him out otherwise he's going to die in that jail, he's never going to be able to stand it. We've got three hundred grand off Air Supply. Could you put some money in as well? You'll get it back. We'll draw up these papers and everything will be sorted.'

So I did. I put about fifty or sixty grand in. Never got it back, of course, and neither did Air Supply as far I know. And suddenly all the papers we had signed got lost. What a mess. In the end somebody had to go to jail and Don's son, David, got incarcerated instead of his father. David basically covered for Don and did the time.

At that point it was really difficult to find somebody who could manage us. Then Wilf Pine approached me. He said: 'Patrick Meehan can help you out.'

Same old thing. It's ridiculous and I know it was a stupid thing to do, but I got back with Meehan. The people who surrounded me were trying to rip me off anyway, so my thought was, it might as well be someone I know and who might do something for me while he's about it. The devil you know. It's all a bit vague now because it was a period when I was back into doing a lot of coke again. And so was Meehan.

So I got involved with Meehan and, of course, bang!, it went pear-shaped immediately. He got into too much of that playboy thing again. I went to a couple of places with him and he introduced me to some dodgy people. Nice people, but dodgy people. And I thought, here we go again.

We were writing songs for what was to become the *The Eternal Idol* album in London and I stayed in this hotel in Mayfair. I was there for six weeks and I thought, Christ, this must cost a fortune. But Meehan went: 'It's all right, because I'm buying the hotel.'

There was champagne and dinner and God knows what else. The whole band was staying there and Ray Gillen was in this apartment next door. As time went on the owner of the hotel kept saying to me: 'When is Meehan going to sort out this hotel and all? When is he going to pay me any money?'

I'd go: 'I don't know. That's got nothing to do with me.'

Meehan never came up with the money. Not long after that this bloke turned up dead: burned to death! The executors of his will went through all the books and they figured out how much I owed. I got a bill from the hotel which I had to pay in the end. Another Meehan special.

When we jammed at our rehearsals and writing sessions for *The Eternal Idol*, Ray would always sing just anything, but when it came to doing the actual songs, he didn't come up with many lyrics. It's difficult if the singer can't come up with his own stuff, but I think the biggest problem with Ray was that he got carried away with the stardom. He went a bit wild. He stayed in a nice apartment in Mayfair; all of a sudden he had all these women around him and he got into this playboy lifestyle. He was up all night drinking and he became this other person.

Ray was a really nice guy, though. They were all nice guys, Eric Singer and Dave Spitz as well. Eric had this eighties hairstyle which made him look a little bit like a woman, and so we started calling him Shirley. He is a good drummer and he has done well for himself, playing with Alice Cooper and Kiss and the like. When we had Dave and Eric in the band, they were a great little team. They loved to play and would try stuff all through the night. They were always energetic and that was good for me as well.

Even so, something didn't sit well with me. Geoff and me were older than the rest of the people in the band, so I felt ancient. Ray was only twenty-five. It was like he and Eric and Dave were novices; they hadn't worked for it like everybody else who has been in the game a long time. They had come along and just like that they could go out and say: 'I'm in Black Sabbath.'

It was great they were there and I liked them as players and as people. But it didn't feel the same any more.

Meehan's idea was to go to Montserrat to record the album, but first we went to Antigua for a short break. We stayed at this resort that Meehan had bought in the seventies. He said: 'This is my hotel.'

I couldn't believe it! I met people there who used to work for us and who I hadn't seen for years. Even our old accountant was out there, still apparently friends with Meehan. Bloody hell, it was like our manager was the king of the town out there. I asked him about food and where I could go. He said: 'Oh, go to any restaurant on the beach and just sign for it.'

'How are they going to know who I am?'

'Oh, they know who you are.'

And that's what we did. We had lobster and this and that, no questions asked, and signed for everything. We lived pretty well and had a great time.

The other lads went on to Montserrat a bit earlier than me, because I decided to sail over there with Meehan on his boat. He had a skipper and the bloke's wife worked on the boat as well. It was great during the day when we set off. We sat on the deck and sunbathed, it was lovely. We had all these coconuts and the captain made cocktails with rum and coconut milk. We drank these all day so I got absolutely rat-arsed. Then this big storm came in. It was pitch-black out there and the boat was flying all over the place, literally going up in the air. Water was pouring in and my suitcases were floating around in the bottom of the boat. I was inside, feeling sick and throwing up. Then all the cupboards burst open and all these things fell out, canned food and this and that. I was terrified because the captain's wife came down saying: 'Cor, this is one of the worst storms I've ever been in!'

'Great! Thanks for telling me that!'

I survived, but I swore I'd never get on a boat like that again.

Meehan had rented a house in Montserrat for the two of us. We got to this five- or six-bedroom place and I thought, this is nice. My bags had all been underwater and everything in them was sodden. I had a leather briefcase that had gone completely green because of the saltwater. It had my stereo in it and my passport, and all the stuff was just trashed.

When we arrived it was still light, but after nightfall it was completely dark out there. Meehan had to shoot off and do something, so I was in this bloody house by myself for the first few days. No sooner had he left than there was a power cut. Because I'd only just arrived I didn't know my way around the house. I didn't have a torch or anything, and I couldn't go next door because there wasn't a next door. I was sitting there on my own and I shat myself. I started thinking, somebody might have cut the power so that they could come and stab me and cut my throat! I was praying for the morning.

Everything returned to normal, but I hated staying in that house on my own, stuck in the middle of nowhere.

Jeff Glixman, who had also done *Seventh Star*, came over to produce this album, but he wanted to change Ray Gillen and he didn't like Dave Spitz, so we ended up replacing Jeff Glixman instead and got Chris Tsangarides to finish the album. In all this confusion Dave left because he had some problem at home. Bob Daisley, who'd done all the lyrics and written songs for Ozzy, was taken on to finish the album with us. He put all his bass bits down on the tracks we had done already and then we wrote another song with him. He was a good player and we got on really well.

Meehan would sort out advances for everybody, and I'd sign the cheques for the guys in the band. The money came from an account that contained the advance from the record company. Meehan would say: 'We owe the band this much money, sign these cheques and I'll do the rest, I'll sort that out.'

The old con. I would have had enough coke or drink to go: 'Oh yeah, that's a good idea!'

I was in a terrible state. I always felt like I was going mad, because all these different things were happening and I didn't have anybody to turn to. The band would go: 'What is going on?' And I'd say: 'I have no idea. I don't know what's happened here.'

I didn't know how this was done or how that got out of hand or how the other thing went wrong. Meehan promised everything to everybody and then, of course, when that all went out of the window it was down to me. It was a really, really difficult time for me. We were just going from day to day, surviving as best we could. Meehan was supposed to pay everybody. I later heard he didn't, but I never knew that at the time. I was signing the cheques, but they weren't getting them. I think that was the reason why Ray eventually left, and Eric as well. Ray ended up joining John Sykes's band Blue Murder, and Bob Daisley took Eric Singer with him to Gary Moore.

It was the same all over again, until it got cut off, bang, just like that one day. I complained to Meehan about some cheque that had bounced, and he just said: 'Well, if that's the way it is, I don't want to do it any more.'

And that was it. I thought, fuck!

He probably didn't see enough money coming in. Of course, flying everybody to Antigua and Montserrat and keeping everybody alive for all that time must have been expensive, so it might well have cost Meehan more than he made off us.

Finally!

We recorded a fair bit in Montserrat, but what with Dave leaving, Glixman going as well and the troubles with Meehan, we decided to go back to London. We finished the album there with Chris Tsangarides. I knew Chris from old; he was the assistant engineer on some of the early Sabbath records. He was really keen on music and he loved our stuff. Geoff Nicholls, me and Chris even had a little joke band at the time. We called it TIN: Tsangarides, Iommi and Nicholls. We were just jamming around in the studio. I still have some tapes of that lying around somewhere.

By the time we got to the Battery Studios, Ray Gillen had left. My friend Albert Chapman managed this guy called Tony Martin. He said: 'Try him, he's got a good voice.'

Tony came into the studio without having had any warning or anything to sing on some of the tracks we'd written with Ray in mind. He sang some of the stuff similar to Ray, following some of the melody lines that we had already recorded. He did really well, so we replaced Ray's vocals with Tony's voice.

Years later, in 2010, Ray's vocals surfaced on the Deluxe Edition re-release of *The Eternal Idol.* We decided to release it because fans had been asking for it for years, and after all this time it served as a nice hats off to Ray as well.

'The Shining' was the first single off the album. It was like a faster 'Heaven And Hell', it had a similar sort of tempo. We needed to do a video for it, but with Bob and Eric gone we didn't have a bass player or a drummer. We brought this guitar player who I didn't know from Adam, and he ended up miming playing bass on the video. Bloody hell, it was getting ridiculous. Terry Chimes of The Clash played drums in that video. He was a great guy and we ended up doing some shows in South Africa later with him.

The song 'Nightmare' came from me being asked to do the music for *A Nightmare on Elm Street*. A guy from the movie phoned me in Montserrat and said: 'Will you come to LA tomorrow?'

'I'm in the middle of doing an album. I can't just pack up and leave everybody to come to LA.'

They sent me the script and I spoke to the producer a few times. I was all set to do it, but then Meehan started to put his oar in. He asked for so much money that they backed out. I would've loved to have done that. It didn't happen, but I had already written a song and we called it 'Nightmare'.

Bev Bevan came up to London to see me and ended up playing on 'Scarlet Pimpernel'. He tried a few things, like maracas. With the old band we always used maracas and bits of wood, tambourines and anything. You were making up your own sounds. We always ordered a percussion box and used different things on every album, 'doing!' or 'ping!' or whatever. But the art of that disappeared with the more modern players. In the eighties and onwards nobody seemed to use that any more.

It was Meehan's suggestion to use an idea based on a Rodin sculpture on the cover. I had no clue who Rodin was at that time. He told me about it and I said: 'Oh, yeah, that sounds good.'

We went to this photo shoot where we had two people done in bronze paint. They stood there for bloody hours having their photos taken, to duplicate the idea of the original Rodin statue. They may well have ended up in hospital, because that's what had happened with Bill when we painted him. You just can't cover parts of the body up like that.

The Eternal Idol was released in November 1987. We started recording it with one band and ended up finishing it with another. You don't want the band to break up, but when it does you bring somebody else in and that changes it again, and yet another person and it changes it some more, and you're gradually pulling away from what you once were. I lost track of it all in the end, because there were that many people in and out in such a short time. How I've always looked on it is that you replace somebody when they leave. It's like if you have a factory; if somebody leaves, you don't close down the factory, you replace him. It wasn't as cold as that, actually: I always looked to find somebody who could replicate a friendship as well, but I never found that. I was certainly never able to replicate the friendship the original four guys in Black Sabbath had. It was the same with the line-up of Heaven & Hell, with Ronnie. You can't find that again. You think you can, but you never do.

The album didn't sell very well at all, which was really disheartening. It was nice to finally get the thing done and get it out, but it was in the lap of the gods as to what was going to happen with it then. It must have been hard for fans to accept all the changes in the band. I remember when I was a kid and The Shadows got a new line-up it didn't feel the same to me. Now kids saw us with yet another line-up. I can understand that they were thinking, oh, what's going on? It always takes years for something like that to get accepted.

During the recording everything had fallen apart, everybody just left. But I couldn't leave. I had to hold the fort and put it all together again.

65

Taxman!

I tried on a few occasions to get Geezer back. It was a bit of an up-and-down thing where one minute he wanted to do it and the next he didn't. He came to London one time while we were recording there and we all went out to Trader Vic's, the restaurant below the Hilton. We didn't eat anything, we just drank. We had all these exotic bloody rums and while I was trying to talk Geezer into coming back we got paralytic. Geezer's wife, Gloria, came to pick him up and, as we walked out of Trader Vic's, Geezer gave the guy at the door a £50 note as a tip. Gloria came flying past, and whoosh, she snatched the £50 out of the guy's hand, put Geezer in the car and off they went.

He didn't want to come back. Management would certainly be one reason for Geezer saying no, because he didn't want to have anything to do with Meehan. He was quite right, of course.

I was at an all-time low, but I did pull myself out of it. Once Meehan was out of the picture things started getting better. The last thing he did for us was send us off to Sun City by way of Athens, playing a couple of weeks for a lot of money. We really needed that at the time, because with the band changing constantly we hadn't done any shows.

These people came over from South Africa and they said to me: 'What can we do for you to make you believe that this is going to happen? What would make you happy?'

Out of the blue I said: 'Buy me a Rolls-Royce.'

As you do. But they said: 'Okay. Which one do you want?'

'Oh!'

It was as simple as that. They said: 'You pick it, we'll pay for it.'

I picked it, they paid for it, and then I knew they were serious about it.

Before going to South Africa we went to Greece. It was the first time we'd played there and also our first gig with Tony Martin. It was in the huge Panathinaikos football stadium, so Tony must have shat himself. While we were doing our sound check there the promoter let the kids in. I was livid. I grabbed him and pushed him up a wall, going: 'You fucking idiot!'

Afterwards he took us out to dinner anyway. I thought, oh dear, I called him all the names under the sun and threatened to kill him, and here I am, sharing a meal with him.

It was 21 July, the height of summer, so it was roasting when we did the show. Fans were climbing up the bloody lighting rig at the side of the stage. It got really dangerous, so we were told to get off the stage and we had to cut the show short. So that was a nice start for Tony Martin.

One of the first things we did when we got to South Africa was go to Johannesburg to do some press. Right in the middle of doing that, somebody let a bomb off down the road. That was the only sign of any kind of trouble that I noticed. It wasn't connected to us, it was just one of those things. Well, I hope it wasn't to do with us.

The promoter took us out on a safari. We left at five o'clock in the morning in a couple of open-topped Land Rovers, and all I saw was the dust from the car in front. We'd stop for a bit, look into the distance and everybody would go: 'No, I can't see anything.'

We saw nothing, absolutely fuck all. Great safari!

Sun City turned out to be a good place to play. We did six shows in the three weeks, playing Saturdays and Sundays. During the week it was as dead as a doornail there, but at the weekends, when we played, it was packed. The promoter was black and we were playing to audiences just like everywhere else, black and white. They'd never seen us and we did a couple of great shows. To me it was another gig. Why not branch out? I never thought about the political side of it. I was a bit blind to all that, I didn't really know how bad it was. I just thought, I'm a musician, I want to play and get my music around wherever I can. But, boy, did I get some stick for playing Sun City.

When I got there I saw all these pictures on the walls of all the bands that had played there before us, like Queen and Status Quo, so I wonder why it was me who got all the shit then. They really came down on me hard back in England. But I can't say I regret doing it. Fans are fans and it seemed a shame that these people shouldn't be able to hear our music.

In November and December 1987 the Eternal Idol tour went through Europe. The last gig was in Rome, where we played at the same venue as the Pope. He was appearing there the day before us and he had this light and sound system. After his thing was over we tried to get rid of his stuff, so we could get ours in.

'Can you ask the Pope to move his gear, please? For Black Sabbath?'

That didn't go down very well.

It was around this time that I started having problems with the taxman, and it was then that I got in touch with Phil Banfield, basically looking for help. As well as having his own agency, Phil continued to manage Ian Gillan and he told me about Ernest Chapman, who was Jeff Beck's manager. I met up with him and the first thing Ernest said was: 'You don't do drugs, do you?'

I said: 'No, no!'

'I don't want anything to do with anybody doing drugs.'

'Oh. No, I don't do them!'

Lying through my teeth. A really good start to the relationship.

I was amazed at how straight he was. We started talking about stuff and I said: 'What about commissions?'

We had nothing signed and he just said: 'Don't worry about anything like that. When we've sorted it out, I'll take a percentage. What do you need now?'

There was nothing in it for him except grief, but I think he liked a bit of a challenge. Ernest and Phil Banfield worked a lot of things out, and then Ernest said: 'Ralph works with me at the office and he does a lot of my stuff as well.'

I met Ralph Baker and then Phil gradually moved out. And Ralph and Ernest have been my managers ever since.

The first thing they helped me with was this big tax situation that I went through after the break-up with Meehan. The tax people came on to me like a ton of bricks. I didn't go bankrupt, but I did become insolvent. The taxmen said: 'You have to sell your house.'

They came to my house and looked around at everything. They saw all the guitars and all the equipment, and they jotted it all down.

'Right, how much will we get for this and how much for that?'

'Eh?'

I couldn't believe it. They were willing to rip everything from under me.

I phoned Ernest up and he got them off my back for a bit. But I still had a huge bill to pay.

They asked: 'What has happened?'

I started: 'Well, the accountant's . . .'

They said: 'This is not the accountant's problem, it's your problem.'

I thought, wait, the accountant was taking some of my money

and putting it to one side for tax! When I spoke to him he said: 'Well, I did, but you wanted this and that, so I used the tax money.'

'Oh, that's just great!'

My income was frozen during the investigation, but Ernest got it sorted out for me. He managed to work a deal out and got my royalties coming in properly as well. And he sorted the Meehan thing out.

We were back to square one. There was me, Tony Martin and Geoff Nicholls. It was time to leave all the ugly business behind and rebuild the band.

66

Headless but happy

After eighteen years our deal with Vertigo in England and Europe ended, and the one in America with Warner Bros as well. It's horrible to be dropped, but that's the way it goes I suppose. Soon after, I met Miles Copeland who owned I.R.S. Records. He came to my house and said: 'You know how to write albums, you know what people want. You do it and I'm fine with it.'

I thought that was great, so we went ahead and signed with I.R.S.

Most of 1988 I was busy sorting out a lot of rubbish from my past. When Phil, Ernest and Ralph got involved there was a mountain of shit to go through. It seemed like we were in never-ending meetings about everything, trying to clear the path before we could start afresh. Of course there were stumbling blocks along the way.

There was a guy who lived near me, a wrestler, who wanted to put a charity thing on to raise money for Children In Need. He asked me: 'Could we put a gig on?'

I said: 'Yes, we can play there, but I don't want it announced as a Black Sabbath thing.'

It was just a one-off with me, Geoff playing bass, Tony Martin and Terry Chimes, but it got blown out of all proportion. The gig was on 29 May 1988 in the Top Spot Club in Oldbury, one of those working men's clubs where they have a comedian, a juggler and all that sort of stuff. And here it was: 'Top of the bill tonight: Black Sabbath!'

I just wanted to help raise some money for kids. It was all done as a kind gesture but it became a bloody thorn in the side. We got lots of flack for it, with people going: 'Look at Black Sabbath playing a little club like that.' To make things even worse, apparently the bloke made money out of it and kept most of it.

By that time we had already made steps to put the band back together again and regain some credibility. I met with Phil Banfield, we talked about drummers and Cozy Powell's name came up. He had played with Jeff Beck, Rainbow and Whitesnake and I had been threatening to work with him for years but it never happened. Me and Cozy met and he was on board. That was a great start; it gave us the credibility we were looking for.

Cozy was really helpful. He stayed for two or three weeks at my house and we'd sit in a room, get a bottle of wine and off we'd go. I had all these ideas, Cozy would tap along and come up with ideas as well. We had the tape player going and just jammed around. If nothing came up we'd chuck it and go for the next one. Maybe we'd go for a walk, come back and have another go. It really worked well. We'd get Tony Martin over and then get into a rehearsal room and try it with everybody. We felt inspired. We were coming up with stuff and we were really pleased with it.

Around that time I heard again from Gloria Butler that Geezer might want to come back. I was telling Cozy about that and he was going: 'What's happening? Is he going to do it or not?'

'I don't know. Gloria said he will.'

But the return of Geezer never happened. We recorded our next album, *Headless Cross*, with this session guy called Larry Cottle. He was a jazz player and a bloody good one at that. We had him on the video of *Headless Cross*, but he didn't look like the sort of guy to be in a rock band. We weren't even sure he'd be the sort of person who would go on tours, because he was used to doing Ronnie Scott's and little jazz clubs like that. But he was such a good bass player. He'd come to the studio and say: 'What sort of thing do you want? What about this? Or that?'

And he'd play all these different kinds of things.

'Yeah! That's it!'

He did a great job and that was it. He played everything on *Headless Cross* and left after the recording.

We recorded the album from August through to November in the Woodcray Studios, a little farm place in Berkshire, not far from London. They had a studio there and two or three bedrooms. Cozy would come on his motorbike and then go home, because he lived not that far from there. Me and Cozy produced the album ourselves. Of course, I couldn't tell Cozy what his drums sound should be. He knew what he wanted and before we started recording he'd test his drums for however long it took to get them right. And then I'd do the guitar and all the rest of it.

We were really determined to make a good album. We were excited because we were playing together and we brought out the best in each other.

Tony Martin wrote the lyrics to all the songs. *Headless Cross* is a little village in the vicinity of Birmingham and Tony made it famous. We did a video for the title track at a place called Battle Abbey in Battle, near Hastings, in Sussex. It was the exact spot where William the Conqueror had defeated King Harold at the Battle of Hastings about a thousand years ago.

Working in this dilapidated old abbey was all right during the day, but they didn't start the actual filming until something like midnight. They wanted to capture the light coming back up in the morning out of these ruins while we were playing there. By that time it was hellishly cold and we were frozen stiff. Cozy was drinking brandy just to keep warm, but he got pissed as a parrot. He nearly fell off his drum stool. I had a big red nose and couldn't feel my hands. We did catch the morning light, but we caught flu as well.

I got Brian May to play the solo on 'When Death Calls'. He came down a lot when we were recording, sat in the studio and talked away. And I said: 'Do you want to . . . play on the album?'

'Ah, can I?'

'Yeah!'

'What do you want me to play?'

So I'd get a track out.

'Play on that?'

'Yeah, okay!'

He just improvised, because he'd only heard it for the first time right then and there. I left him in the studio for an hour and came back: 'How are you getting on?'

It was great; he was really good. We've played together many times because we enjoy it so much. We've even talked about making an album together. One day.

On 'Nightwing' we used Tony Martin's guide vocals, because he never sang it quite the same after that. He tried it a couple of times, but we went: 'No, we'll keep the original because it's got that feel to it!'

Things like that also happened a lot with my guitar parts. I'd just play it a certain way and that was it. You try it again, and then you try to get too precise. So I've kept guitar parts that were on the original demo for the track. The same with solos. That's why I always try and do the solos in the first few takes, because otherwise it gets too robotic. I prefer to do a solo instinctively, to just go and play. When I record a track in the studio I'll usually play six solos in a row. Then I'll ask myself, is it getting better or worse? Usually they get worse as I go on. If I don't capture it in so many tries, I'll leave it for a while. It's better to try again later, with a fresh outlook on things.

I play solos off the cuff. I'm not good at sitting down and working the solos out, so when I play different tries for a solo, they vary a lot. I can never play them exactly the same. That was really embarrassing when I did one of the first instructional videos. They said: 'We want to play 'Neon Knights', 'Black Sabbath' and 'Heaven And Hell'. Can you play the solos to them?'

'Well, I'll play *a* solo.'

So I did and then they said: 'Can you play it slow now?'

I went: 'Oh, fuck. I don't know what I played!'

Brian May can play his stuff note for note, but I can't. I just played the solo that went with the thing, similar but not quite the same. And it certainly was impossible for me to play it slowly so that people could learn it. I started thinking about it then: what do I play? How did I play that? And once I started thinking about it, forget it. So when you watch that video, you'll see that I played it different on the slow version. I can remember riffs until they come out of my ears. I remember riffs from years ago that I haven't even recorded. But when it comes to playing a solo note for note, and trying to play that version slow, forget about it.

Headless Cross was released in April 1989. It did much better than *The Eternal Idol*, but we were very unhappy about the way I.R.S. promoted it in the States. Off we went to America to do a tour and, as you do, we went round the record shops and there wasn't a fucking album in sight. There wasn't even a poster up, nothing. Cozy blew his top: 'What the fuck's going on, there's no advertising, there are no albums in the shops!'

In Europe the way they worked that album was fantastic. In fact, *Headless Cross* did better there than the original Sabbath albums with the old line-ups had done. We went: 'Bloody hell, finally!'

So it's safe to say that it wasn't down to the quality of the music that it didn't do all that well in America.

67

Oh no, not caviar again!

When it was time to do some shows, we approached a bass player Cozy knew. He said: 'Shall we get a meeting together with Neil Murray and see how you get on with him?'

Neil turned out to be a great player. Finally, we had a real, credible and very good band together.

We toured America in June 1989, me and Cozy, Tony Martin, Neil Murray and Geoff Nicholls, but we went home after about two weeks. There was a stark lack of promotion, not only for the album but for the shows as well. We were meeting people in town: 'What are you doing here?'

'Oh . . . We're playing here tonight.'

'Eh?'

It was all very Spinal Tap-ish.

At the end of August we started our UK tour. We ended the old-fashioned way, with two Hammersmith shows. Brian May came up and did 'Heaven And Hell', 'Paranoid' and 'Children Of The Grave'. He hadn't played that last one with us before and so he shouted: 'What key is it in?'

'It's just in E!'

It went very well. At another gig on that tour I brought Ian

Gillan up to do 'Smoke On The Water' and 'Paranoid', which was great for the fans. It went down a storm. We could never do things like get Brian or Ian up with the original line-up, because that was too set.

We had a good time on these tours because there wasn't much pressure, apart from the usual financial worries. We stayed in lesser hotels, travelled all together on the bus and cut down in all sorts of ways, but we had a great time together. We did what we were supposed to be doing: play.

We'd had a lot of trouble in the early years with religious nut-cases but it came as quite a surprise when in 1989 it started again. We were in Mexico having just toured Japan, and the visit began well in a lovely hotel supplied by the promoter. We were told that there had been a bit of a campaign against us orchestrated by the Catholic Church and backed by the local mayor but were assured it was all okay. We didn't realise how big a deal it was; all we'd come to do was play a show. We also subsequently learnt that the football stadium we were due to play in was the third choice after the promoter was refused permission in other towns – not sure we'd have gone if we'd known that!

Anyway we tried to relax for a couple of days but the crew were nervous as there were a lot of heavy security guys hanging around with guns and the facilities at the stadium were extremely basic. And as the crew went to set the gear up they were suddenly arrested at the site. These security guys wouldn't allow the show to go on purely because the police were worried about riots and God knows what else.

We were told that fans were coming from all over Mexico by train, it was really a big deal, so we thought maybe if we went down and had a look at the stadium for ourselves it would help.

But before we could get going instructions came through to us saying 'pack-up, we're leaving', as the mayor had now banned the show and thousands of disappointed kids were likely to blame us. You don't argue with a man with a machine gun and by then the first of the trains had arrived and the fans were pouring out. The station was right next door to our hotel so we had to lie-down on the floor of a minibus while the driver abandoned the road and nearly turned us over trying a short cut through a huge drainage ditch! Escape made, we sped on to Mexico City where we made sure we were on the next plane back to the UK!

We did go back to Mexico with Heaven & Hell in 2007. Maybe they've forgiven us or simply not associated the band with Black Sabbath.

After Mexico, we went on to Russia, another exotic country. We did ten nights in Moscow at the Olympic Stadium, a massive place, and it was sold out. On Saturdays we did an afternoon show as well. The audience would go out after that show and then they'd all come back in again for the evening one.

We were supported by Girlschool. The first night at the hotel in Moscow we went to the bar and one of the girls was there as well. Then their bass player came in and, just like that, punched her in the face. We went: 'Bloody hell! What was all that about? Christ, we haven't even started the tour yet and they are fighting already!'

Really peculiar. But they turned out to be all right. They could drink a bit as well. And Cozy had a little romance with their singer and guitar player, Kim McAuliffe, that went on for a short while after the tour. She was a really nice girl.

Playing in Russia was weird because in the hall in Moscow the first rows of seats were set back, away from the stage, and all of them were taken up by officials, with all these men dressed up in suits and women in ballroom-type dresses. They obviously had something to do with the government, and looked so out of place, as if they should have been at a different gig altogether. The rowdy kids were behind them, except that they couldn't be rowdy. The security guys wouldn't stand for that. They were pretty heavy with the kids.

It was winter and freezing cold. Every day they'd pick us up in a van and drive us to the gig, together with this big metal container in the back full of soup. We took all our own catering with us. The food was locked up in one of the rooms and we had a guard on it, but it still went missing. It was just at the time when they were pulling down all the statues of Lenin. The country hadn't opened up yet; there wasn't a McDonald's or anything at that point. Our caterers went down to the market to buy fresh food and often they'd be in trouble. If they bought up all the chickens and vegetables and whatever else, the locals would be up in arms. It was bloody hard for them.

We stayed at this hotel called the Ukraine. It was a bit like Grand Central Station, because it had a big open lobby and it was really cold in there. We had two KGB people travelling with us all the time and we were very aware of them keeping an eye on us. I wondered if our rooms were bugged. It was so behind the times that if you wanted to make a phone call you had to book it well in advance. My room was very depressing. It was big but it only had a bed and a china cabinet in it, with pieces of the china going missing every other day. It was obviously the maids taking cups and saucers and whatnot, but I got the blame.

The hotel was very dodgy as well. When you looked under the balcony, you saw all these credit cards lying there. People had obviously been robbed and the thieves had thrown out the stuff they couldn't use. Some of our crew actually did get robbed. Two of them were sharing a room and one of them took his clothes off and went to bed. He heard somebody come in and he thought it was the other bloke. It wasn't. It was a thief, who nicked all his clothes, his wallet and everything.

After Moscow we did another ten days in Leningrad. The crowd was different there, much more like a regular crowd and right up the front as well. It was really good.

But we came back with loads of caviar, especially Cozy, who was a big wheeler-dealer. He got in with the manager of the Olympic Stadium. We went up to his office and this bloke had all these tins of caviar and hand-painted lacquered boxes and so on lying about. We gave him a couple of T-shirts for this, a pair of sneakers or whatever for that. They loved the T-shirts with the band's name on them, so Cozy ended up with a suitcase full of Beluga caviar. God knows what that would be worth.

I came back with bloody uniforms, military hats and all sorts of shit, which seemed like a great idea at the time. But as soon as I got them home it was, well, what do I do with them? And now they are in the loft. But I also brought caviar back and that lasted for quite a while.

We ate a lot of it out there, because there was nothing else. The first time we went to the restaurant in the hotel we sat down and it was: 'What would you like?'

'Would you have some of . . .?'

'No.'

'Have you got . . .?'

'No.'

'What about . . .?'

'No.'

'Or . . .?'

'No.'

'Well, what have you got?'

'Ice cream.'

'Ice cream!?'

Really peculiar.

'Well, we'll have that then!'

Everybody would be dying to get out to the gig so that they could get something from our catering. But we had so much caviar to the point where we went: 'Oh no, not caviar again!'

Europe had been great, Germany was sensational and Russia was good for us as well. The album was doing good and the gigs were sold out. To me it felt as if we had turned a corner.

It felt real again.

68

TYR and tired

For our next album, *TYR*, we went back to the Woodcray Studios in February 1990, with me and Cozy producing it again. On *Headless Cross*, Tony had just come into the band and he assumed, oh, Black Sabbath, it's all about the Devil, so his lyrics were full of the Devil and Satan. It was too much in your face. We told him to be bit more subtle about it, so for *TYR* he did all these lyrics about Nordic gods and whatnot. It took me a while to get my head around that.

I particularly liked 'Anno Mundi'. It starts with a choir singing in Latin 'Anno Mundi' and 'The Sabbath Stones' are really powerful, slow, pounding tracks. I like those heavy riff-type things, and 'The Sabbath Stones' is particularly heavy.

We did a video for 'Feels Good To Me', a ballad. It was a love story about some girl on a motorcycle and some boy who cheats on her and falls out with her and all that stuff. It also had footage of us playing on stage somewhere. It was a bit of a sloppy video, over the top for the sort of stuff we did.

You could compare *TYR* to *Headless Cross* like you could compare *Mob Rules* to *Heaven and Hell*. If anything, *TYR* had a heavier feel than *Headless Cross*. There's the Ozzy thing and the Ronnie thing, and then there's this. It's like these albums belong to a lost era. I am even struggling to remember stuff from that time, because in a way it's wiped from my mind. Geezer came to the show at the Hammersmith Odeon and we got him up to do 'Iron Man' and 'Children Of The Grave'. It was the first time we played together since Live Aid, five years earlier. The reaction from the fans was great. I think whenever somebody from the original line-up gets up, they love it. I know I certainly enjoyed it.

After the Hammersmith gig we went to Europe. In the Jaap Edenhal in Amsterdam Cozy used CO_2 gas that was like a pressure cooker blowing its top with steam shooting up from the stage. When that happened it blew a couple of tiles out of the ceiling, which then came down on his head. So Cozy literally brought the roof down!

69

It's Heaven and Hell again

In December 1990, after the final dates of the TYR tour, Geezer came back. He had enjoyed getting up on stage with us at the Hammersmith Odeon in September. Neil Murray said at the time that he thought it was really good when Geezer played. Neil was the sort of person who would go: 'You should try it again with Geezer.'

We did, Geezer came back and Neil was never vindictive about it.

After Ronnie departed back in 1982, we didn't speak for many years. It wasn't like there was a lot of bad blood, but it was just a little uncomfortable. And he and Vinny were off doing the Dio stuff and they were doing quite well with it, so it was highly unlikely that we were going to team up again. But one day Geezer got on stage at one of Ronnie's shows and played on 'Neon Knights' with them. They hadn't seen each other for ages and really got on well. Geezer said to me: 'It was really good. It felt great to play with Ronnie again.'

When I saw Ronnie again we started talking about doing a line-up. Vinny wasn't playing with him any more at the time and Ronnie went: 'I've got a really good drummer, Simon Wright.'

I went: 'Well, we are thinking of using Cozy.'

That was a bit awkward because Ronnie and Cozy had played in Rainbow together and didn't really get on that well. Eventually we went with Cozy anyway and started writing for what was to become *Dehumanizer*. It was a difficult time because we had already rehearsed with Tony Martin, who now had to leave the band. It wasn't really fair on him. We had made a few great albums with Tony, but everybody was excited about the idea of getting Ronnie back, certainly the people at the record company and our managements as well. In a way we got the old line-up back, except for the fact that we now had Cozy on drums.

But it was just awful. There was real friction between our singer and our drummer. Ronnie wasn't mad about having Cozy in the band and I remember Cozy going: 'If that little cunt says anything to me, I'm going to smash him in the face!'

Ronnie went back to LA and so we brought Tony Martin in and rehearsed a bit with him. Ronnie returned once again, replacing Tony; it was just one big mix-up between these rehearsals. Then Cozy's horse had a heart attack and fell on him, breaking his hip and knocking him out of action for a long time. If it wasn't such a horrible thing to say, you could call his accident a blessing in disguise. I loved Cozy and he was a great friend, but you have to have the right combination in a band. We already had enough friction going on with everything anyway, so we needed to have something stable. Getting Vinny back was the obvious answer to all our problems.

Having Ronnie in the band was a good musical move, because the two of us worked well together. Even so, writing *Dehumanizer* took some doing, because we changed it around and analysed it too much. There was a lot of pressure because everybody was expecting so much from us. First of all we put Ronnie in a bit of a corner because we didn't want him to sing anything about dungeons and dragons and rainbows. It was a difficult thing to say to him, because he'd sung about rainbows on every album he ever did and here, all of a sudden, he was faced with us going: 'Can you not sing anything about rainbows, please?'

He had to rethink the whole thing.

'I've always used rainbows!'

'Well, you know, we think it's a bit much.'

It got a little uncomfortable, and there were tense moments. We rented a house in Henley-in-Arden and Vinny and Ronnie lived there while the rest of us drove down to rehearsals from our homes. We jammed a lot together and came up with loads of stuff. Vinny taped everything. He'd give us a copy and then we'd live with it a bit. We analysed and pulled them apart a lot, but in the end we came up with some good songs.

Ronnie knew this German producer called Reinhold Mack, and we decided to use him. He had done Queen and ELO and Brian May said to me: 'Are you definitely sure you are going to work with Mack?'

I said: 'Why?'

He went: 'Mwoah, hmm.'

In other words, we've used him and I'm not sure if you should use him. It didn't sound like his experiences with Mack were altogether positive. He did produce it, but I think that album suffered from too much of a live drum sound. We recorded the album at the Rockfield Studios. Vinny played in this room that had glass all around and when I hear the album now I just hear the brightness in that room. Vinny liked it – drummers love that big sound.

Recording went well, though; it took us no more than six weeks. The album opened with 'Computer God'. Geezer wrote the lyrics for that and since that album his input has gone from strength to strength. I've always wanted to get him involved musically as well: 'Come on, show us one of your riffs.'

His immediate reaction was always: 'Oh, you won't like it. You're going to laugh.'

But he's never actually played me anything for me to laugh at.

'After All (The Dead)' was an amalgamation of Geezer's stuff and mine. Geezer put one of the riffs in that song, which I thought was really good. He played a bit of guitar on it as well, just the little filly bit. When he played this idea to me, I couldn't quite grasp what he was doing. He started playing it to show me, and I said: 'I can't get this, but you know it. Why don't you play it?', so he did.

'Time Machine' was a song that we've played throughout the years. We wrote it for the *Wayne's World* soundtrack, and recorded it well before we went in with Reinhold Mack. Leif Mases had produced Jeff Beck's album, and Ernest Chapman managed Jeff, so that's how we got him in just to do that song. Leif had done the ABBA stuff in the early days. From ABBA to Sabbath – quite a stretch!

The final track of the album was 'Buried Alive', a mid-tempo song that had an almost grungy sound. If I say it like that, it sounds like we were influenced by grunge, but of course we weren't. The grunge bands had obviously been influenced by us, and I heard a lot of them say that umpteen times as well. Even so, it wasn't a particularly good time for our sort of music. *Dehumanizer* was very well received and it charted fairly high in the UK and the States, but we thought it would do even better than that, because we hadn't been together for ten years.

Apart from all that, I was not pleased with everything that happened when we recorded it. This band wasn't fitting like a glove, it was a bit volatile. We were about to go on tour, but at the same time I felt the thing could blow up at any minute.

70

Bound and shackled

The modestly sized venues we played during the Dehumanizer tour reflected the changing times, but we started off with a bang. In June 1992 we did huge shows in São Paulo, Porto Alegre and Rio de Janeiro. That was a bit wild. There was one show where we shat ourselves. We were in the dressing room and we heard that the crowd was rioting. We weren't supposed to be on until a certain time, but they wanted us on there and then. They were getting all overexcited and started invading the stage. We thought, Christ, if they storm it, we've got no chance backstage! Eventually they got them to move back and we went on, but that was a bit hairy.

To be honest, we were more of a hazard to ourselves than the crowd was. One night in São Paulo I went to bed and left Ronnie and Geezer in the bar. They got drunk and had a disagreement. Geezer walked out all worked up about it and there was this big bronze statue in the centre of the lobby, which he decided to head-butt. Guess who came off worse?

I didn't know about it until the next day, when I saw him in dark glasses. I said: 'You all right?'

He mumbled: 'Yeah . . .'

'Well, blimey, what happened to you?'

'Weuhh ... long story ... I dunno ...'

If he drinks too much, Geezer can get a bit violent. But he picked on the wrong bloke then. I couldn't believe it; his eye came up like a balloon.

On the last Black Sabbath and Heaven & Hell tours we had individual dressing rooms. We did that to give each other space. If I wanted to run over stuff and practise for a while, the others didn't have to sit there and listen to me. And if they wanted to start chatting with friends, I didn't want to listen to them. I prefer not to see anybody before a show, because I like to get my head around what we are going to do, while Ronnie would sometimes see people. And Geezer likes to lock himself away and sleep. But on the Dehumanizer tour we couldn't have our own dressing rooms because of the size of the venues. It was me and Geezer in one dressing room and Ronnie and Vinny in another.

This also came about because there was a bit of tension between both parties. We didn't hate each other – it was just down to the different ways different people talk, what with Ronnie still being very outspoken and me and Geezer avoiding any kind of direct confrontation. But despite the downsized venues and the tension we were playing well and we pushed on.

At the same time Ozzy announced his retirement. About two months before he was to do the supposedly last gigs of his life, on 13 and 14 November 1992, at the Pacific Amphitheater in Costa Mesa, California, we were asked to perform there with him. It was Ozzy's first farewell tour, so we genuinely believed that he was going to retire. So when they asked us to do it, we said: 'Yeah, okay, of course we'll be there.'

We were going to open for Ozzy with the current band and then do three songs with the original line-up at the end of his show, to round it all off. We thought it would be a nice gesture to do it. We asked Ronnie and he said: 'I'm not doing that.'

In no uncertain terms.

'I'm not supporting a clown.'

He was adamant he wouldn't do it, but we were used to him being very direct, so we put it in our tour schedule anyway. We thought, well, he might settle down and change his mind. Of course Ronnie didn't, so that was the nail in the coffin. Fair dues to him: he did say from the outset that he wasn't going to do it.

We had agreed to come and play and it was all going ahead so we couldn't really pull out. We needed to replace Ronnie for the two Costa Mesa shows and we thought, well, Tony Martin knows the songs. So we asked him first, but there was some problem with that. Then Rob Halford got in touch and he said: 'I can do it if you want me to.'

We got a rehearsal room for one or two days in Phoenix, where Rob lived, and we went through a new set to play on this show. We did some Ronnie-era songs and Rob even suggested doing some of the Tony Martin stuff. We also rehearsed some of the old Sabbath songs that we knew Ozzy would never do, like 'Symptom Of The Universe'. Rob still had the range to be able to do that. In the end we had a tight set of eleven songs. It was one after the other, bang, bang, bang.

We had managed to find a singer for the Costa Mesa gigs, but then somebody else threw a spanner in the works. Two nights before it was all supposed to happen, I suddenly found myself in jail.

We had finished a gig in Sacramento. I came off stage, got into the tour bus and somebody knocked on the door: 'Is Mr Iommi on board?'

'Who wants to know?'

'We're with the District Attorney's office and we've got a warrant for his arrest.'

I thought, oh, no! What the fuck is this about?

They said: 'Can we come on board and take Mr Iommi?'

'No.'

'Well, we can either come on board now, or keep the bus here until the proper papers arrive and come on board then and take him.'

So I said: 'Just let them come on.'

My ex-wife Melinda had tried to do me for child support. She had claimed that I wasn't paying it. Instead of checking that first, they just came out to arrest me. You're immediately guilty until you've proven your innocence. They pulled cars behind and in front of the bus and that was it. They took me off the bus and said: 'We're not going to handcuff you now. We'll take you in a car and we'll go out around a corner where there're no fans.'

As soon as we were out of view they handcuffed me and put chains on my legs. I was sitting in the back of this car and we travelled for an hour to Modesto. That's where Melinda lived, so that's where they were going to put me in jail. I was wondering what the hell was going on.

They put me in the holding cell with a guy with no shirt on, who kept saying: 'You don't want to be in this jail, man, they'll kill you.'

I was in Modesto County Jail all night and I couldn't sleep because of the noise and the worry. I probably lost about ten pounds overnight. I kept thinking, does anybody even know I'm in here? I'm very grateful to Gloria Butler, because she kept phoning the cops up every fifteen minutes, saying: 'Don't put him in a cell with anybody else, you've got to put him on his own!'

Eventually they did, they put me in a cell by myself. The guy next door to me was convinced I had come to kill him. He said: 'I know you want to kill me, but I'm going to get you in the shower. I know Satan sent you!'

Fucking hell.

It was a Thursday night and they wanted bail money the next day, otherwise I would be in there over the weekend, until

Monday. I had to get out to do a gig in Oakland the next night and the Costa Mesa thing with Ozzy the day after. They set bail at $75,000, an enormous sum of money because not paying child support was a big thing there. I had paid, it was all rubbish, but I didn't have a leg to stand on. Eventually a lawyer came in with a briefcase with seventy-five grand in cash. Gloria had phoned Ralph Baker and Ernest Chapman and they had provided the money.

I had to go in front of the judge all shackled and I felt as if I had committed a murder. As soon as I entered the jail, it got around like wildfire. A guy who was serving the coffee to everybody, through the bars in tin mugs, knew who I was and so pretty soon all the prisoners knew. The guards were walking me down to this chamber to see the judge and there were all these guys in these cells that I passed, going: 'Hey! Tony! What's up!'

The governor of the jail, in his suit and tie, said: 'I'm telling you now: we don't want a John Lennon incident here. We are going to walk on each side of you, you'll have one person behind you and one person in front of you, and you keep up pace with them.'

It was unreal. Me with my handcuffs on and with these shackles around my legs, just trying to walk, and in the meantime all these kids shouting all this stuff.

Unbelievable.

It was on the front page of the papers of course: 'Arrested!'

I got out on bail but they took my passport off me, as I wasn't allowed to leave America. The lawyer recommended I get out of California. He said: 'Go somewhere nice and just sit tight.'

So after doing Costa Mesa I went to Florida, as far away from California as possible without leaving the country. But I developed a complex about going out in the streets. Every time I saw a policeman, I felt guilty.

'Where's your passport?'

'I haven't got it. They took it off me.'

All I did was sit tight and keep in contact with the lawyer. That set me back a bit, as he was expensive, a top guy coming to get me out. Eventually it all got sorted out and I got my passport back and I went home. But I don't think I ever got the $75,000 back.

It was a right mess, that whole thing.

They got me out of jail in time to do the show that night in Oakland. It was Friday the 13th and it would be Ronnie's last gig with us. We broke up after that. It never actually came to a 'That's it!' We just parted company. Ronnie refused to do the Costa Mesa gig and said: 'If you go and do it, you'll be doing it without me.'

Those were the terms under which we did it, and so we did it.

The first of the two Costa Mesa nights, Rob was nervous. He walked on stage way too early and he started the song too early as well. It's bloody tough to learn somebody else's songs that quick, and then to go on and actually do them with the band, but Rob did great. He really is a great professional.

The second and last night we did the thing with Ozzy. We came off stage after our set with Rob, and then later we came on again, me and Geezer and Bill Ward, who'd joined us for the occasion as well, and we did 'Black Sabbath', 'Fairies Wear Boots', 'Iron Man' and 'Paranoid' with Ozzy. Doing those few songs together brought back a nice vibe and the crowd was great. They were in awe; they couldn't believe we were on stage together after all these years. It was a great gig.

Of course after that there were rumours all over the place about the old line-up getting together again. Everybody assumed, oh, they'll probably do it. Well, it may have come up, but we didn't do anything at all about it at that time. It was a great thing to do, but after the show we were left with nothing. We had a big finale and that was it. We didn't have a band any more.

I sat in Florida for six weeks, waiting for my passport, dying to go home.

71

In harmony with Cross Purposes

I returned home and my first thought was to get a band together again. We auditioned some British drummers, but none of them worked out. At a certain point Bobby Rondinelli, who had played with Rainbow, called me. He wanted to do it. I suppose it's the old thing: if you don't call, you don't get anywhere. Fair dues to him, he got in touch and it got him the job. He flew over and as soon as he started playing, that was it. He was a similar drummer to Vinny, very precise. He fitted in personality-wise as well.

We didn't look around for other singers, we simply asked Tony Martin back again. He got screwed around so many times by us really, but he was good enough to hang in there. As soon as Bobby came in we started writing the songs for our next album, *Cross Purposes*. So it was me, Tony, Geezer, Bobby and Geoff, and it went really well. We finished writing the new songs in the summer of 1993.

Leif Mases helping us out with 'Time Machine' for the *Wayne's World* soundtrack had been a good experience, so this time we asked him to produce the whole of *Cross Purposes*. He was good to work with and the recording went smoothly. Songs like 'Virtual Death', a heavy, powerful riff, and 'The Hand That Rocks The

Cradle' were joint efforts between me and Geezer, who came up with more and more ideas. And 'Cardinal Sin' was a song about a Catholic priest from Ireland, who hid his love child for twenty-one years. That would be a very topical song now, with all the stuff that's been going on quite recently.

'Evil Eye' was a track we were working on when Van Halen were playing the NEC in Birmingham. Eddie got in touch with me and I said: 'We're rehearsing. We're writing a new album.'

He wanted to get together, so I picked him up from the hotel in Birmingham and we drove down to Henley-in-Arden where we rehearsed. We got him a guitar from the music shop, one of his models, had a jam and he played on 'Evil Eye'. I played the riff and he played a great solo over it. Unfortunately we didn't record it properly on our little tape player so I never got a chance to hear it!

That was a funny day. Eddie said: 'Don't you want any beers? Can I pick some beers up?'

I couldn't drink because I had to drive him back to the hotel, but we picked up a case of beer, got to the rehearsal place and he was legless by the time we left. But it was great to see him, and it was great he came over to have a play. Having a jam with Eddie and letting go a bit, it gave everybody a boost.

The album was released in the beginning of 1994. In the sleeve notes I gave a big thanks to 'all at the Modesto County Jail for the kind hospitality and making me realize that there's no place like home'.

Even though *Cross Purposes* wasn't a huge seller, it did all right. For once I.R.S. were getting behind it; they were even doing advertisements for it on MTV. It was with renewed confidence that we embarked on another world tour.

Motörhead supported us in America. Their singer, Lemmy, is a real character.

Of course, there's no food on their rider at all, only booze. You walk past their dressing room and there's nothing to eat, but there is all this wine and Jack Daniel's and beer. They are the epitome of rock 'n' roll. It just goes on and on and on with them. I'll never forget seeing their guitar player, Phil Campbell, at the side of the stage once. He threw up, and the next minute he was on stage, playing away. Cor blimey, how do they do that? How do they cope with that? Their bodies must be indestructible.

Lemmy is probably going to die on stage. I certainly don't see him settling down in some old people's home. He used to go on their tour bus and he'd get off in the same clothes the next day, on stage as well, come off . . . Motörhead, they just live like gypsies really.

One funny story I heard about Lemmy: he was playing away and he said to his monitor guy: 'Can you hear this horrible sound coming out of my monitors?'

The bloke said: 'No.'

And Lemmy went: 'Neither can I. Turn me up!'

The last tour we did with Dio, we had them on one of the shows with us. Lemmy came up to me and said: 'How are you enjoying the tour?'

I said: 'Oh, I really like it. It's great that we've all known each other so long and we're all around the same age.'

And he said: 'Yeah, and we all know the same dead people as well.'

I was thinking, he's hit it on the head. Blimey, he's right!

Tony Martin had a fabulous voice, but we were always on to him about his performance. He was very amateurish as far as that was concerned. Overnight he went from working only local little venues in Birmingham to big stages everywhere. It was a difficult position to be in, to have to front a band that everybody knows from great performers like Ozzy and Ronnie. It was a bit much for him and, just like Ray Gillen when he joined us, Tony got carried away with it. His head got a bit bigger. We were playing in Europe somewhere and Tony had this portable video player. He was at the

bar of the hotel showing these people a video of himself performing with us: 'Look, that's me up there!'

Very unprofessional: you just don't do stuff like that. Albert
Chapman, who was managing him at the time, was livid. He said:
'Put that fucking thing away!'

And then he suddenly started going under the name of Tony
'Cat' Martin. Where did this 'Cat' come from all of a sudden? He
did these things that were just off the wall.

One time in America during the Cross Purposes tour, his lack of
stage presence or star quality, or whatever you want to call it,
became painfully clear. Right in the middle of the show Tony
decided to run along the audience between the stage and the bar-
riers holding the people back in the front. He jumped off the stage
to start his run and this security guy grabbed him and tossed him
out because he thought he was a fan.

'But I'm the singer!'

'Yeah, right.'

Things like that would never happen to Ozzy or Ronnie. But
you couldn't complain about Tony's voice. That was just great.
He'd get on and do the job, and he never missed a show. Tony was
a nice guy as well and he stuck with it for ten years.

In April and May we did the UK and Europe with Cathedral
and Godspeed. Those two bands travelled together, but they were
always fighting. It got worse as the tour went on. You'd see them
first with sticking plaster here and there, and next you'd see the
bandages come out and one had his arm in a sling. Really peculiar.

In April our gig at the Hammersmith Odeon was recorded and
filmed for a video and CD package called *Cross Purposes Live*,
which was released about a year later. I once heard somebody
describe it as the most underpromoted release of all time. That's
probably very true, because even I can only vaguely remember it
being released.

The final European show turned out to be Bobby Rondinelli's

last gig, because we finished the tour again with a couple of shows in South America and I was talking to Bill and I said: 'We're doing South America next.'

He went: 'I'd love to play South America!'

'Oh? You want to do it with us then?'

'Oh, yeah!'

Blimey.

He said: 'What do you want me to do? Meet you there?'

He didn't know any of the songs with Tony Martin, so I said: 'No. You've got to come to England and rehearse.'

'Oh, all right then.'

He came over, we rehearsed and he was great on the old Sabbath stuff, but he struggled a bit on newer songs like 'Headless Cross'.

It was Geezer, me and Bill, so we had almost the old line-up, plus Tony Martin. Off we went to South America, with Kiss and Slayer on the bill, as well as a few others. We got on stage in front of something like 100,000 people and the pressure was on; we got by but in the end dropped the newer material. In order to keep going we ended up only doing songs like 'Iron Man' and 'War Pigs', the stuff Bill knew. But fair dues to Tony, he sang those old songs great.

After the tour ended, Geezer went back to Ozzy. Things needed to change. I said: 'That's it! I'm getting Neil and Cozy back!' Within five minutes we were back together again. There might have been some hard feelings because of how things had worked out in the past, but we resolved that. We got back together and started work on the *Forbidden* album.

72

The one that should've
been Forbidden

The record company suggested we should use a more hip producer. They were going on about the guy who produced Ice T, the
guitar player in his band, Body Count, Ernie Cunnigan, better
known as Ernie C. They said it would give us a bit more street
cred, because they thought we'd lost that. You know what it's like:
you get these whiz-kids at the company who come up with these
great brainwaves that don't work. And that was one of them, but
I half-heartedly went along with it. Cozy wasn't mad on the idea
either and now I can see why. The production was dreadful. Here
I was working with someone from a hip hop background. Not
that there's anything wrong with that, but I just wasn't familiar
with it and it opened up a whole new can of worms for me.

The first thing Ernie C did was to get Cozy to play this ta-ta-ta-
ta bass drum stuff. It's a different style of playing altogether that
these hip hop guys do as opposed to what we do, and it caused all
sorts of ruckuses. Cozy was a respected drummer in his own field,
and here was somebody coming along, going: 'Play this.'

It really offended him. And the more Cozy tried, the more he got pissed off because he didn't want to play it. It made it very difficult for everybody, because we all felt that bad vibe. To make things worse, all this was coming from a producer who didn't know anything about us. Ernie claimed he did, but it was a total shambles. The sound wasn't very good on anything and I wasn't happy at all with that album. None of us was.

I thought, well, maybe it's me that's wrong. Maybe they can do a better job than us. So we gave them the benefit of the doubt and just kept out of it. Also, if we'd have started throwing our oar in, saying, 'We want that to sound like this', we would've been back to where we started again. What would have been the point of having somebody come in then?

Since the days of Rodger Bain I've always been involved in the production and the mixing somewhere along the line, but not at all with this album. If it had gone down a storm I would really have been worried: blimey, it must have been me all along!

It was a bad experience from start to finish. *Forbidden* was released in June 1995. I thought it was crap, even down to the cartoon cover art, so it didn't surprise me that it didn't sell. However, we did tour with it. We started the Forbidden tour off with two big festival gigs in Sweden and Denmark and then went to the States, again with Motörhead supporting us. Cozy and me got up to a lot of silly pranks; he was as bad as me. Setting people's beds up and taking the legs off things and removing the TV from the hotel room and throwing it out of the window – it was back to the old days again. I got one of those blow-up dolls and I put clothes on it and I hung it from the balcony of our hotel in Los Angeles. People were looking up and we were screaming and shouting, pretending there was an argument going on. More and more people were looking up and then I threw the doll off the balcony. Mad it was.

I've always been one for playing jokes on people in every line-up of Black Sabbath, but, of course, they got back at me as well.

In the early days I was once taking a shower when there was a knock on the hotel room door. I opened it and it was Ozzy with a full bucket of water. As I put my head out, he threw the water over me, dropped the bucket and ran. I started after him, but I had no clothes on and the door shut behind me. I thought, ah, for Christ's sake!

I knocked on the other guys' doors because I wanted to phone down to reception to get help, but of course they wouldn't let me in. I stood there in the hallway naked and, ding!, the lift door opened and all these people came out. They were all dressed up from their night out and there was me with no clothes on at all. We all stood there, staring at each other, not knowing what to do. They must have thought I was a right pervert. Eventually security came up, because someone had phoned down saying: 'There's a naked man running around in the hallway!'

I had to explain what had happened and they let me in my room again. The guys got me good that time.

My most embarrassing moment was when we came back from America after a big tour. We got to Heathrow and one of the guys said to me: 'I can't get all my suitcases on the trolley. You couldn't put one on your trolley, could you?'

I said: 'Sure.'

And so I did. We went through 'nothing to declare', and of course they stopped me.

'Excuse me, sir, are these your suitcases?'

'Yes.'

'Can we look in them?'

'Go ahead.'

They opened my suitcases and they were fine. Then they got to this other case and opened that up. I could've dropped dead on the spot, because this suitcase was full of sex toys. There were blow-up dolls, dildos, handcuffs, all the paraphernalia. I couldn't believe it and didn't know what to say. There was a queue behind me, other people waiting to have their suitcases searched. They were pulling all this stuff out and I heard all this giggling going on behind me. I was so embarrassed, especially because they knew who I was. And, of course, I couldn't suddenly go: 'It's not my suitcase.'

They really set me up and I have to say it was a great one. Of course, after I'd gone through customs there they all were, in stitches. They thought it was hilarious. That's what happens when you play jokes on people. They get you back!

We finished in the first week of August with three dates in California, carefully avoiding the city of Modesto. They were Cozy's last gigs with us. I had seen it coming as the tour progressed. He wasn't happy at all, because the situation had changed. He wasn't involved as much in the writing as before; it was down to me again. He wasn't the co-captain of the ship any more either and he didn't feel at all comfortable with that. And bloody Ernie C telling him what to play obviously turned the tables on him. So he decided to quit the band and left.

Bobby Rondinelli came back and off we went again, on a tour that was scheduled to go on until well into December. But my arm was going numb. It started to get really bad in America, so I went to a doctor there who also happened to be a surgeon. He said: 'Your problem is in your neck and it's really dangerous. You need it operated on as soon as you can. And it just so happens I can do the operation tomorrow.'

I went: 'Hang on. No!'

I thought, Christ, I've got to get home to England and get it properly seen to. I flew home and went to see two specialists. They said: 'No, the problem is in there, in your wrist.'

Thank God I didn't go with this bloke in America, or I would've had an operation on my neck. I had a carpal tunnel operation instead. They cut into my inside arm, just above the wrist, and it's almost like a plastic band that goes around there. I was awake while they operated on me and I could actually hear it go 'crack!'. It made me feel sick because I could hear the noise and it felt all cold as the blood came out. Here I was, getting nauseous, and the two surgeons were merrily talking away: 'Oh, did you see that thing on TV the other day . . .'

They were trying to involve me in the conversation as well, going: 'Oh, look how lovely this is cut away', but there was no way I could look at it. Bloody hell, I was doing my utmost not to vomit while I was being operated on.

Then they stitched it up and that was it. After a while I could play again. It cured it and I was never bothered by that again. Nowadays it's everything else that's playing up!

Carpal tunnel did cut the Forbidden tour short, as we had to cancel a couple of weeks' worth of dates. Just as well, really. I financed the tour and paying for the bus, the crew, the hotels, the musicians, this and that, and it was actually costing me money to go out and play. We just couldn't keep on doing that.

I was sitting back home with my arm all bandaged up. When the tour stopped the band broke up and it would be many years before I'd see Tony Martin again. And I had no idea that *Forbidden* was Black Sabbath's last studio album ever. Or at least for a very, very long time.

73

Flying solo with Glenn Hughes

After the *Forbidden* album the deal with I.R.S. Records expired and to all intents and purposes Black Sabbath was on hold. I talked to Phil Banfield and Ralph Baker about working with a singer when I heard Glenn Hughes was coming to England. He came over to see me, and we started writing songs really quickly. He was singing and playing bass. It was only a bit of fun really; what we did wasn't intended to be released. It was just something to see what we could do. Also I needed to work because at that point I wasn't doing a fat lot. I needed to keep myself going.

Glenn suggested getting Dave Holland, who, years ago, was the drummer with Judas Priest. Dave came over and played a bit on this electric kit. We put some ideas down and we went into UB40's studio, called DEP, so that we could demo the stuff properly, with Dave playing a real kit. We recorded all the songs and then left them because I went to do the first Black Sabbath reunion tour with Ozzy, after which I started to work on my solo album, which went in a different direction altogether. That's why these DEP sessions just got lost, forgotten about.

After a while these things came out as a bootleg. I thought, how did they get it? I asked Glenn and he said: 'I don't know.' There were only so many people who had access to the tapes. It could've been somebody at the studio, someone to do with Glenn or Dave Holland, or someone to do with me. We never did find out.

Some time at the beginning of 2004 my guitar tech, Mike Clement, was at my studio at home transferring boxes of cassettes of riffs on to CDs. He came across a couple of the tracks from the DEP sessions and said: 'Why don't you put them out, they're really good!'

These tracks coming out on bootlegs was a real pain anyway, so I said to Ralph Baker: 'We've got to do something about this. Maybe we should mix this album and finish it and put it out ourselves. Just to kill the bootleg stuff, really.'

We remixed the tracks, I added a couple of guitar bits and changed a couple of things. And I had to put a new drummer on because, in the meantime, Dave Holland had been done for molesting young kids. I was terribly shocked when I heard about that. I couldn't believe it. I was watching the news one morning, and they went: 'Dave Holland, Judas Priest . . .'

You could have knocked me over with a feather; I had no idea he was like that at all. I remember Dave playing on one of the DEP sessions one day and he brought this young lad. I never thought anything of it. He said: 'This is so-and-so, I'm teaching him to play drums, he's a student of mine.'

'Right, hello.'

He was probably about eleven or twelve years old or so, maybe a bit older. But when I found out about all that, blimey. He was sentenced to seven or eight years in prison. We thought, we can't release these with Dave on them! So I took his drum parts off. We brought in Jimmy Copley, a really good player who I knew from Paul Rodgers's solo stuff, and he did all the drums at my house. Because there were no click tracks on the tapes, he basically had to play to Dave Holland's tracks. It was a bit awkward, but Jimmy did a real good job.

They were just demos, we didn't go into the sounds and stuff, they weren't intended for release. But when the album, *The 1996 DEP Sessions*, was released in September 2004 it was received very well. And after all those years, it finally killed the bootlegs.

74

Living apart together

I met my third wife, Valery, when I was in London recording *The Eternal Idol*. I went out to a club called Tramp one night and I met Val down there. She was a model and a dancer. She danced in one of these variety-type shows, where they would have a dancing team with ten women and a bloke, like a musical. And as a model she did advertisements for face cream and hand cream.

We swapped numbers. She called me up and we started seeing each other. I didn't really want to get involved, because at the time I was too interested in doing more drugs, but eventually we did get a relationship going. We were together for six years and then we got married.

Our wedding was an extremely quick affair. I tried to do it all quietly, but Phil Banfield knew about it and he wanted to be best man. We just got married at this register office with Phil as my witness. We went back home and all my friends were there.

Blimey, what happened here? It's supposed to be a secret!

Phil had organised it and, bloody hell, that surprise party, it was really good!

We were together for about twelve years. Val helped me out a lot with getting off the drugs, because she hated all that. I really owe a lot to her for doing that. Alcohol was never a major problem, but I was doing a lot of coke and speed. I was going through a part of my life that I didn't even realise I was in, it was getting worse and worse and I didn't see it. I got more aggravated and into more arguments and I became somebody else, I suppose.

When we were married Valery wasn't going to put up with it any more. We'd have a bust-up every time I did a line. She could tell straight away if I'd done something. I used to sneak into my studio and do a line and then it was: 'You've been doing coke!'

So eventually I thought, it's not worth it, arguing every time I do some drugs. It was either stop, or that's it. And that's what I did. Well, I stopped doing it regularly, let's put it that way. I stopped doing it every day.

Val had a six-bedroom house in north London and I had my house up in the Midlands. She liked to stay in London where her friends were, and I never wanted to move to London, so we'd be in her house for a while and then come back to mine. Or she'd be in London and I'd be home. When I was on tour she wouldn't stay in the Midlands at all, so that meant I had to have somebody to look after the house there. It was a bit of a funny relationship really.

Valery had a son, Jay, a really nice kid. It was a bit strange for me, moving from not having my own daughter there and getting married and having somebody else's kid instead. I couldn't bring my daughter at first, so it was all very complicated.

I desperately wanted to bring Toni home. Melinda married again and had two kids with her new husband. Apparently this guy owned some nightclubs in Los Angeles and was deep in the Mafia, but he got caught for something and he was jailed for seven years. Melinda spent a lot of his money while he was in jail and then dumped him. This bloke got out of prison early, at which time the courts allowed him and his sister to have the kids, all three of them. So I went over to Modesto where they lived, to see

Toni at their house, because they would have to be there when I
visited. It was an awkward situation because he had the other two
kids and Toni was looking after them. She was about twelve or
thirteen by that time.

After a while, visiting rights were relaxed. Toni was allowed to
stay with me in LA and I took her with me for a week on tour. In
the hotels we'd have adjoining rooms, but she'd have to have the
door open and the light on, as she was terrified because of all the
things that were going on in her life.

After going through this whole procedure in the courts, I eventually got her out. My big problem was that they thought, oh, he's
in a band. Ah, Black Sabbath! I didn't have a leg to stand on.
They'd ask: 'When you're on tour, who is going to look after her?'

'Well, I'll have a nanny.'

It came down to a choice between an ex-con who wasn't the real
father and me. The lawyer I hired in Los Angeles said: 'Look, you
are the father and we are going to get her back for you.'

Eventually we did get her back and in 1996 I could take her
home to England. Finally!

Toni was a nervous wreck when she got here. She was thirteen,
she'd been thrown around from pillar to post and she didn't know
what the hell was going on. It took her a long time to settle down
and become normal again. For a long time she had bad dreams.
She had her own little room with the door open and the light on,
and then she'd start screaming in the night and I'd rush in. At first
I wondered, how can I help, what am I supposed to do? You give
her love, but it was also a matter of me being accepted, because she
had missed a great part of her life with me. She didn't get on with
her stepfather, so it was very difficult.

In the meantime my marriage with Valery was in trouble. She
wanted this London life and she wanted to travel the world,
whereas I didn't. I'd been all over the world umpteen times on tour
already. We both wanted different things, so were at loggerheads a

lot. But the crunch came when Toni came to England. She already had a son whom we both looked after, so she said: 'She should go to college. Put her in school and let her stay at school.'

I said: 'You can't do that. She's been thrown around everywhere; she's got to live with us.'

Valery then wanted us to live in London and we went to see a high school down there, but Toni wasn't happy. She was too young. It was difficult for her to come over from California and suddenly live in London. She didn't really know Val and then to go to this school where she knew nobody was very hard. So Toni didn't want to live there and Val said: 'If she doesn't want to, that's it, I've done my bit.'

I got really pissed off about her saying that, because Toni deserved a good life. In the end I had to hire a nanny to look after her. I thought, Christ, I'm married, she's living in London and I'm hiring somebody to look after Toni in the Midlands. I had no other option, because I was on tour. Somebody had to do what I was doing and earn the money. It was a real shambles. One of the reasons why me and Val broke up was that she just wouldn't accept Toni and I couldn't deal with all that. We gradually pulled away from each other and then the marriage came to an end. We just didn't communicate well. Instead of talking things over we were always arguing, and I hated that. I said to her: 'If we ever get into an argument, let's just say "stop". And then we'll stop.'

We started arguing one day and I said: 'Stop!'

She went: 'What do you mean, fucking "stop"!'

And she carried on again. So 'stop' never worked.

I just made my mind up: I'm not going to go any further with it. So I said: 'That's it, Val.'

And she went: 'You can't divorce me!'

I said: 'It's not working. I don't want this life any more. Do your own thing.'

I wanted to break away for her sake as well, so she could do the things she wanted to do and lead the life she wanted to live. She doesn't see it that way. She thinks I left her for Maria, but that wasn't the case. Val and me finished long before I met her, but she thinks I had been going with Maria for a while before we broke up.

Valery saw this house in Spain and I bought her that, and I bought her another house in London as well. Breaking up is always hard. But for me, the pain wouldn't last long.

Soon I'd get together with old friends and meet the love of my life.

75

The love of my life

Early in 1997 Sharon Osbourne called and said: 'Would you be interested in doing a few shows with Ozzy, or maybe a tour? I'm asking you first and if you say yes, then I'll ask Geezer.'

It was supposed to be a casual thing as opposed to involving lots of lawyers, so I said yes. Then she asked Geezer and he said yes. I think she was under the impression that Bill would want to go through lawyers and therefore it would be hard work involving him as well, so she didn't ask him. I asked her about Bill, but she said: 'No, we are going to use Mike Bordin, Ozzy's drummer.'

Geezer and me were only going to do a few songs and it didn't seem like it was a big thing, so we agreed on doing it with Mike. The plan was for Ozzy to do his own set first, and then we'd walk on and close the show, not unlike we'd done in Costa Mesa back in 1992. It was just a 'join you on stage' sort of thing. We agreed on a fee and did it. In May 1997 we started a five-week tour of America, for about twenty-five Ozzfest shows.

I liked it. It was good and things were going well between me, Ozzy and Geezer. I think it was a bit of a trial thing anyway, to see how we all got on again. Initially we didn't see a lot of each other. Ozzy would fly in later and arrive at the gigs separate from us and

Geezer and me each travelled in a bus of our own. We also stayed at the best hotels, always the Four Seasons or the Ritz-Carltons. It was okay, it was organised well.

On 17 June, Ozzy's voice gave out and he cancelled the show. Geezer and I heard Ozzy was not going to fly in, but we were in the dressing room already and the bands were playing. We had Marilyn Manson on with us, Pantera, Type O Negative, Fear Factory and a couple of others. Somebody said: 'Would you be able to play with some of the other guys, with Marilyn Manson singing?'

I said: 'No, we don't want to do that.'

'Well, we've got to do something.'

'Not with us. If you want to do that, let them do it and jam or whatever.'

It wasn't that we had anything against the other bands, but we were there to do it with Ozzy and that was that. We certainly wouldn't go up and jam, because that was the kiss of death: you could see before it happened what was going to happen. And, sure enough, it did: before they all went on to jam somebody announced that Ozzy had lost his voice, and there was uproar. They just went crazy. As they do.

These other guys went on anyway and played, which was good of them. They prevented it from getting completely out of hand. Still, the crowd turned police cars over, rioting, it got pretty bad. We left fairly sharpish afterwards and got out all right. We went back there two weeks later to do the rescheduled gig and that went fine.

One day I bumped into this girl, Martina Axén, who was the drummer in the Swedish band Drain STH, who were on the tour as well. She said: 'You've got to come and see the band.'

I went to watch them a couple of times. They were really good, so when Martina asked if I could help them with a song, I said: 'Yeah, come over to the house after we're done.'

Their singer, Maria Sjöholm, always kept to herself, so I never met her. After the tour she and Martina flew over from Sweden, just for a day. They came over to the house, where it was just me and my daughter, Toni. Valery wasn't there, because at that point we weren't an item any more, so they said: 'Can we cook for you?'

'Yeah!'

After getting groceries at the local market, we went into the studio and I played them some things. I asked them what they wanted and came up with an idea for them. That took all of twenty minutes and then they went into the house to start cooking. They had brought all this red wine over and two huge bars of Swedish chocolate. I already had this big bar of Cadbury's chocolate. They started eating that, and we had a few drinks. It was off to dinner and we had some more drinks and they also ate all the chocolate they'd brought for me as well. The pair of them just polished off these two big bars! I'll never forget that about them – it was really funny.

I had to fly off somewhere the next day to start another tour, so they drove up to London with me. I picked Ozzy up on the way and then the four of us went to the airport where they took a flight back to Stockholm.

Throughout the year I talked to Maria on the phone about how the song was going. It became a regular thing. I'd call her and we'd just be chatting away, sometimes for hours and hours. We got more and more friendly and, right before the 1999 Black Sabbath Reunion tour started, I just said: 'Why don't you come over for a few days? I'll send you a ticket. Come to the show in Phoenix.'

She thought about it and said: 'Okay.'

She flew in and she was really nervous. I didn't quite know what to do either.

Oh dear, she's turned up!

We played Phoenix on New Year's Eve and then she came with us to Las Vegas. We really enjoyed each other's company. And that was it: we started seeing each other a lot and eventually she moved to England. That was in 1999.

The track we wrote for Drain STH was called 'Black' and it appeared on their album *Freaks of Nature*. It was released in 1999, but the band broke up not long after that. As an all-girl band, it was tough for them out there. They had toured for years and Maria had had enough of the travelling. She told the other girls and gave them a tour's notice to find somebody else. They didn't, so they parted company. I probably got the blame for that.

We didn't get married until 2005. I'd been married before on 2, 3 and 6 November, so that wasn't an auspicious month for me. I said to Maria: 'No way we're getting married in November. Don't even mention November!'

We were on tour in August, a safe distance from November, and when we had a break in Los Angeles my office organised this woman to come over to the hotel and marry us right there. We got married on 19 August at the Sunset Marquis. I didn't tell anybody, not even the band. Nobody was there, so I got Eddie, who worked for me, to come up to be the witness. We wanted to do it without all the fuss, so we did it all quietly.

Best thing I ever did!

76

Reunion

We didn't want to play with Mike Bordin. We all wanted to have Bill back for the next tour. Ozzy, Geezer and me had done the initial test of how we were getting on. We were asking ourselves: is it going to work? What is the interest like? Well, we did get along and the shows went great and everybody loved it. So it seemed obvious that we should get the old, full line-up back for a next tour.

We had to make the terms so that we didn't get into big arguments, not from our side but management-wise. We each had our own management and that could be hard work, so we decided that it should be left to one person without everybody else chipping in as well, otherwise it would be chaos. And that's what happened. Because Sharon had organised the Ozzfest, she was also going to manage the reunion.

We rehearsed with Bill and worked out the show, and then we did a few gigs before going to the NEC to record the *Reunion* live album on 5 December 1997. We did the NEC too early in the tour, really. I thought we needed to play a lot more first. We had rehearsed, but we had only done two gigs and then suddenly there we were, doing two days at the NEC and recording it. We hadn't got into routines and whether to do a little solo here or build a big climax there; we were just playing the songs. It would've been nice to have loosened up more.

It was nerve-wracking, because we knew we were recording it. When you do a regular show, after the last song it's over and done with, but when it's recorded everybody can see and hear it afterwards forever and ever. Also it was a hometown gig, which made us even more nervous. Friends were coming. Brian May was there and Cozy and Neil as well. As a matter of fact, the four of us went out for dinner to a Chinese restaurant afterwards.

Even so, we were all happy to be able to play together again. I think it went better than we expected. As a matter of fact, it went great!

I went over to the A&M Studios in Hollywood to mix the live album with Bob Marlette. Then these guys from the record company came down and said: 'Why don't you write two new songs for the album?'

'Eh . . . right. Now?'

'Now!'

'Oh. What, me and Bob?'

Because we were the only ones there.

'No, we'll get Ozzy down as well.'

To write a song in the middle of a mix is not a particularly good idea. You've got your head around how everything should sound, and then you don't want to be thinking, what are we going to write, how do we start? And if you don't have the band to start jamming, and you don't even have Ozzy half the time, it's bloody difficult. We just dropped the mix and started working on the new songs. I had no ideas lying around, so I had to come up with something there and then. It was a good thing I had a guitar there! And off we went.

Blimey.

Bob Marlette used programmed drums, just so that I could put the riff ideas down. That's how we did it with 'Psycho Man': I played a riff and he put a drum to the riff, and then we'd build it up like that. Ozzy came down and disappeared and came down again and went and sat in the other room and got a sandwich and fell asleep and whatever else he did. Quite often he dozed off on the couch in the control room while we were putting the song together. One time he was spark out and then woke up to go to the toilet. He was gone for about twenty-five, thirty minutes. We thought, where the bloody hell is he? We need him now!

We sent somebody out to look for him, but the guy came back and said: 'I can't find him. He might have gone home.'

We phoned his home, but he wasn't there.

'Where the fuck is he?'

Even Tony, the guy who works for him and never leaves his side, didn't have a clue. Then we heard all this commotion in the hallway. It was another band, and they were going: 'Oh man, Ozzy Osbourne is in our studio. He's asleep on the couch!'

We thought, oh, no!

Ozzy had come out of the toilet, half asleep, and he didn't remember what studio we were in. He'd gone into their studio, right in the middle of their recording session, and he'd fallen asleep on their couch. They were out in the studio, playing away, and they came back into the control room and found him snoring away. They were in awe of him, so they weren't about to tell him to leave. We sent somebody in to get him, but in the meantime Ozzy had woken up, come back into our studio, and, hovering about, he'd knocked a full pint of water into the recording desk and the bloody thing blew up!

But when Ozzy was awake at our own session he'd be all enthusiastic: 'Oh yeah, I like this!'

It was the first time I actually saw him write lyrics down and really get involved in it. We wrote the songs and recorded Ozzy's and my bits in one day. It was too fast, we never had time to live with them, but the guy from Sony Records was standing outside, waiting to hear them. We got Geezer and Bill to come in later to put their parts down. And that was it. We had the two tracks, 'Psycho Man' and 'Selling My Soul', but I wasn't pleased with them. It could've been so much better if we'd had more time to work on them.

At the time it didn't lead to plans for a new studio album. It was only later, right before Ozzy started *The Osbournes*, that we actually went into the studio to write a new album. We were there for three or four weeks and managed to put about six ideas down. It wasn't a very full band effort. We had a go but it was a bit like pulling teeth. We'd jam for a bit and put stuff down, but then Ozzy would disappear or fall asleep on the couch again, or he'd go to make the fire and he'd come in and say: 'Would you like a cup of tea?'

'Okay.'

And then he'd disappear again for two hours.

'What happened to the tea?'

It was like it used to be in the old days. He just didn't have enough of an attention span to stand there and work a song over. But that's Ozzy, that's just how he is.

Still, we could have done an album. We got the six songs and the idea of Rick Rubin producing the album was brought up. Geezer, Ozzy and myself went to see him at his house in LA. There was a bloke who came in to greet us, he sat us down and we waited. After about ten minutes Rick Rubin came in. I'd never met him and didn't know what to expect, but he was definitely a character. He was wearing a kaftan and he was like an old hippie in some ways, like a Buddha. Very calm.

We played him the stuff and he liked about three of the tracks. And that was it: we never saw him again and we never followed it up. It fizzled out because Ozzy started with his television show *The Osbournes*. It's a shame, because if everybody had been involved and really got off their arses, we could've come up with something good.

I still have those six songs somewhere. We didn't do anything with them, but that was as close as we ever got to recording a new album.

77

Cozy's crash

In April 1998 I was in LA at the Sunset Marquis hotel when I got a call from Ralph. He said: 'I'm really sorry to tell you that Cozy has been killed in a car crash.'

It was a real shock. I was just stunned.

All the years I knew Cozy, he was a bit of a wild character. I've been with him in the car a few times and he was a very good driver, but he went so fast I was terrified. He used to drive around the track in his old Ferrari, because he liked speed. He also had a couple of big motorbikes and he really tore ass on those things. When we recorded *Headless Cross* with Cozy at Woodcray back in 1988, he'd come down on his bike and sometimes, when he'd had a right few drinks, I'd take his keys off him and hide them so that he couldn't ride home. He'd go: 'Where's my keys?'

'You're not going to drive home like that!'

'I'm all right, I'm all right.'

The old 'I'm all right' thing. But he'd have to stay.

They were fast Yamaha bikes and I thought, one of these days he's going to come off one of them. I didn't expect it in a car. And when I heard what happened, it was bloody awful.

Cozy was seeing this girl. She was married but separated, or separating, and she had problems with her husband. Cozy was at home and he'd had a few drinks, as he tended to, and she called him all upset and said: 'Can you come over quick?'

Cozy lived about thirty or forty miles away from her. He flew down the motorway in his Saab, quite a quick car. While he was driving towards her she phoned him up. 'Where are you?'

'I'm on my way.'

While they were on the phone, she heard him go: 'Oh, shit!'

And the next thing: bang!

I think it was raining at the time. Cozy wasn't wearing a seat-belt. He hit something and went straight through the windscreen. What a complete and utter waste of such a talented musician and good mate.

78

Bill, Vinny, and Bill and Vinny

With the *Reunion* album in the can, we planned a fully fledged tour with the original line-up and in May 1998 we went into rehearsals for it. It had been twenty years since the four of us had worked like that. This time we tried to communicate properly by talking things through, instead of going in like bulls in a china shop. Instead of: 'We're doing this', or even: 'Let's do this and let's do that', everybody was going: 'What do you think, shall we do this?'

We had a laugh and worked well together again. It was good because we were prepping to do something we knew. We just rehearsed through the songs. Ozzy would sing them and leave, and then we usually ran through them again on our own. On 19 May we were running through the show and, when we got to 'Paranoid', the final song, Bill said: 'Cor, I feel really strange. Is it all right if I have a lie-down?'

'Yeah, go and have a lie-down.'

I took him upstairs and he got into bed and said: 'Could you ask my assistant to come up?'

'Sure.'

'Just to give me a massage for a bit, because my arm's gone a bit numb.'

I never thought anything of it. Me and Geezer went out for a bit of fresh air and walked up the drive and then down the road. We saw this ambulance come flying past and we jokingly said: 'Bill!'

We always did; any time we saw something like that it was always: 'Ah, Bill.'

And, bloody hell, this time, sure enough, it was. Minutes later we saw the ambulance flying past again in the opposite direction, taking him to the hospital. We got back and Ozzy was going: 'Bill has had a heart attack! Bill has had a heart attack!'

'Christ, that was the ambulance then?'

'Yeah, that was Bill!'

They took him to the closest hospital about twenty miles away. He had to stay there for a while and obviously couldn't play.

We didn't cancel the tour. We asked Vinny Appice to stand in for Bill while he was convalescing. We'd been working with Vinny on and off with Ronnie and Bill always liked him, so it just seemed the way to go. Vinny was fine with it; he came in and rehearsed with us, and then we did the tour of Europe with him.

We had rehearsed songs we hadn't played for years. When we started off, we had a two and a half hour show. It killed me because it was a long set, but it was great. We were playing a lot of other songs besides the regular, routine ones.

The tour started off in June in Hungary. Certainly in the beginning it went really well. The Milton Keynes Bowl, with bands like Foo Fighters, Pantera, Slayer and Soulfly, was one of the highlights. Bill came to that gig; it was nice of him to turn up. We got him on stage and the audience loved seeing him. He was standing there in his tracky pants and I couldn't help it because they were all loose and, whoosh!, I pulled them down in front of all those people. Typical me and Bill. I used to do that all the time to him and, of course, this was an ideal opportunity. He just stood there, pulled them up and took no notice. He's a real character like that.

In October 1998 the *Reunion* album was finally released. Our label, Epic, organised a record-signing tour of eight cities in America for the four of us, including Bill Ward. They put us in the St Regis Hotel in New York. It was incredibly expensive: every room came with its own butler. We used that hotel as our base and we had a private jet to fly us out to Dallas or wherever it was we had to do the signings and radio interviews and anything else. We'd do the business and fly back to New York again.

Meanwhile, we had so many people coming to the stores where we did our album signings that it got out of hand. Sometimes security was rough on the crowds. We ended up saying to our tour manager: 'They can't do this to the kids, pushing them around and being aggressive with them like that. They are fans, they should take it easy on them!'

We did one in a mall and the whole place was packed. I'd never seen that, signings in the middle of a shopping mall. These appearances at record shops were really good, if not a little too successful.

We also did the *Late Show with David Letterman*, our first TV appearance together in twenty-three years. I was bit worried, because I wondered what it would be like to do 'Paranoid' with a live audience in a talk show like that. I thought Letterman and his people would be a bit snooty about it, but they were really nice. David was in and out, really; we saw him on the night when he came to say hello and shook our hands. We talked to him but not a lot. We saw Paul Shaffer during the sound check and had a chat with him. He might have asked if he could play, but we just did it with the four of us. And that was it. We played, it went down great, and good night.

We started off our American tour on New Year's Eve in Phoenix, Arizona. That was the one Maria came over for. It was a big gig.

We always had a big fireworks display afterwards, so we could leave without getting stuck in the traffic of people trying to get out at the same time. We always got off stage and then left immediately.

Bill was back with us for this tour, but we took Vinny along as well. We didn't want Bill to strain himself. As much as he said: 'I'm all right', we were concerned he might feel rough one night, and go: 'I don't feel well, I can't play.' Also, with Vinny there, if he got over-exhausted he could say: 'I can't play these two songs, I need a rest', and Vinny could step in. I thought this would be good for Bill's peace of mind as well, but I heard later that he was actually offended by the fact that we had Vinny up there. But none of us meant it in a bad way; we were just concerned about Bill. We never used Vinny anyway, because Bill played great and stayed healthy. As a matter of fact, I got flu and Ozzy caught a cold, but Bill was as fit as a fiddle.

Bill couldn't drink, Geezer wasn't drinking and Ozzy wasn't supposed to be drinking, so the only one drinking was me. We each had our own bus and a trailer as well, and there I had wine and champagne and whatever else. I wouldn't flaunt it in front of everybody and it was actually awkward when Ozzy came in. He'd often visit me in my trailer, and I never wanted to drink around him, so for me it also turned out to be a rather dry tour.

After the last gig of the American tour we felt it would be a shame to stop, so two months later it was announced that we'd go on, this time headlining the upcoming Ozzfest tour. From the end of May 1999 until the end of August we toured throughout the States with acts like Rob Zombie, Slayer and System Of A Down. On the second stage, among many others, was Maria's band Drain STH, so we were on the road together.

On one of our days off we were staying at the Four Seasons in Palm Beach and Rob Zombie was there as well. Me and Maria were looking out of the window and we saw Rob coming out with his wife. It was roasting out there, but like always Rob was in all his leather gear. He walked up, got on a sunbed and was lying there, sunbathing the Zombie way. Everybody else was wearing shorts and Rob was dressed to the max in leather trousers, leather top, leather hat and leather boots. Maria and me were in stitches. Rob is a lovely guy, but talk about keeping up the image!

We ended the year with two shows at the NEC in Birmingham. I remember thinking, this could well be our final date ever. I felt a bit sad, not knowing if we were going to do it again. We recorded a live video there, called *The Last Supper*.

That seemed like a perfect name for it, but we weren't done quite yet.

79

Belching after a Weenie Roast

In February 2000 we got our first Grammy, for Best Metal Performance for 'Iron Man' from 1998's *Reunion* album. I thought, bloody hell, all those years of making music and we get nothing, and when we finally do get a Grammy it's for the live thing! A year or two later we got a nomination for another one, for 'The Wizard'. I don't really remember why that was nominated, but, then again, I never knew why the first one was either.

Apart from getting a Grammy, 2000 was rather uneventful. In June we had a one-off show at the KROQ Weeny Roast Festival at Angel Stadium in Anaheim, California. Sharon got in touch with us and said it would be a great gig to do. We would be surprise guests, performing after Ozzy's show.

It was definitely a surprise. Ozzy had played his set, and then the revolving stage was supposed to turn and we'd be there and we'd start playing. Throughout the whole day I thought, this is really silly, it's going to be such a quick changeover. How are we going to pull that off?

The stage turned around and I started the riff for 'War Pigs', the big note, but nothing happened. As the stage turned all my cables were ripped out of my amps and all the power went. My guitar tech nearly had a heart attack, going: 'Ooh, what do we do, what do we do!'

It was so embarrassing standing there like a couple of dicks. The audience, who didn't expect us to be playing anyway, was probably thinking, who's that lot there then? After what seemed like an eternity, they wheeled on these two speaker cabinets and Zakk Wylde's Marshall amp, just so we could play. We were only going to do twenty minutes anyway and we spent half that time pissing around. We came off that show and we had another one like that to do in New York. I said to Sharon: 'There's no way I'm going to do that.'

She went: 'Well, no, whatever you want . . .'

I was so embarrassed I couldn't talk to anybody for days after that. I just hid at the Sunset Marquis hotel and kept out of the way.

Back home in England I found some comic relief with Bev Bevan and Jasper Carrott. We'd been friends for years and we talked about doing this band thing as a bit of a laugh. They had done a couple of things and they asked me if I'd join. I said: 'Yeah, that sounds like a lot of fun.'

Jasper came up with the name Belch. It's the B from Black Sabbath, the E and the L from ELO and the C from Carrott. Jasper is a comedian and in Belch he was the singer.

Phil Tree was our bass player and Phil Ackrill played rhythm guitar. Phil Tree now plays with Bev Bevan in The Move. It was great fun, I really enjoyed that. Belch was a pop band: we played anything from 'Blue Suede Shoes' to Tina Turner or Dire Straits to 'All Right Now'. We rehearsed at Jasper's house. The idea was just to play at one of our friend's parties, but what was supposed to be a lark turned into paying gigs. I didn't think we were good enough to be paid, but it started to become serious. We did one gig in Doncaster, a hundred miles from Birmingham, and it was just like the old days. We were all going in Jasper's estate car and we broke down on the motorway. None of us was used to that any more, because we always had people working for us to sort this stuff out. So we were looking at each other, going: 'What do we do now?'

'I don't know.'

'Christ! We've still got a long way to go!'

Jasper phoned this bloke who worked for him and he arranged for a car to come and pick us up, take us up to the gig and then bring us back afterwards. We finally got to this gig and there was wine, champagne, the works; it was a real big, flash do. We played a little set and then guzzled bottles of champagne.

On the way home we had to stop every twenty minutes because we were all throwing up as we'd drunk so much so quickly. Eventually we all got back to Jasper's drive and everybody fell out of the car going: 'Bleeehhrghgh!'

It was like forty years ago, only with grown men.

We did a few gigs and we had requests for a lot more. Jasper had a weekly TV show and we even played on that, doing 'Route 66' and a song by Status Quo. And we had Belch T-shirts as well, really naff ones. But Jasper got too busy doing his comedy shows. He owned a big part of the television production company Celador, and he went on to do *Who Wants to Be a Millionaire?*. The other band members got too busy as well. We didn't break up as such; we just didn't have the time to do it any more. But who knows? Maybe we'll do it again someday.

Just for a laugh.

80

Iommi, the album

When I told Sharon Osbourne about my idea of making an album with all different singers, she was really interested in releasing it on the Osbournes' label, Divine Records. We had some offers from other companies, but I thought, well, she's good at what she does. She offered us a good amount of money, but, more than that, she was going to get it going, give it a kick up the arse, do the promotion. So we came to an agreement. We seemed to get on well then, but I couldn't resist referring to the many disagreements we'd had in the past when I thanked her in the CD booklet, writing: 'Who'd have thought it!'

I wrote some of the stuff at my house but most of it was done at producer Bob Marlette's place in California. I didn't quite know what direction to go in after the Sabbath stuff. Follow that or just go off a bit? What we ended up doing was still riffy, but more modern. Bob directed it that way, and he did a good job at that. He's a keyboard player as well, and he had a good ear for what was needed. I wrote the riffs and he put a drum pattern and effects to them. He used a lot of effects, computerised stuff, because he was good at that.

We did what I'd wanted to do when I did *Seventh Star*. This time, there was huge enthusiasm. We had every singer we wanted and more. We actually had to turn people down. It was also a good experience for me to work with so many different artists. It was a challenge. Take, for instance, how we worked with Billy Corgan on the song 'Black Oblivion'. We went into the A&M Studios and Billy was going to play bass and sing. He came down to the studio a few days before and I played him some riffs. I recorded them on a little cassette for him to take away and listen to. He came back a couple of days later and brought drummer Kenny Aronoff down to the studio with him. Billy said it would be nice to do a track with loads of different changes in it. We ended up writing and recording it at the same time. It was that quick. There's actually a lot of stuff on the album that we played live. We were jamming and it really pushed your brain.

It helped to have Kenny Aronoff there as well, because he's really good. I'm sure he's one of the few who'd be able to play something with so many changes in it, there and then, as we were doing it.

'Oh, let's put another bit in here!'

Going through the whole song again and playing it live, it was nerve-wracking. I was working with people I'd never worked with before, writing songs I had to get my head around while normally I'd live with them a bit first, and all that in one day, writing it and recording it. 'Black Oblivion' with Billy was a tough song in particular, with all those different changes in it, but it turned out great and it was a good experience doing it this way.

'Laughing Man', with Henry Rollins, was one of the first we put down. Henry came over to Bob's studio, which was basically a small room at his house. Henry was singing away into a microphone while I was sitting on the couch only a few feet away. It's a very heavy track. We had played a couple of things to Henry and he picked that one and wrote all the lyrics to that. He really enjoyed doing it.

Another guy who was really up for it was Dave Grohl. When I had him come down to the studio to do 'Goodbye Lament', I already had Matt Cameron on drums and Dave said: 'Oh, I'd love to play this track? Can I play drums as well as sing?'

So he played drums and he was really good. With most singers, like Serj Tankian from System Of A Down, Skin of Skunk Anansie, Phil Anselmo of Pantera, Ian Astbury from The Cult and Billy Idol, we'd send them a cassette with a track we'd written beforehand. They'd put lyrics to them, come down to studios, be there for the day and sing it.

Peter Steele's 'Just Say No To Love' was very different, because he has such a unique voice. I knew him because we'd had Type O Negative on our tours so often. When he came to the studio he kept saying: 'I'm so honoured to do this, that you asked me. And I'm really nervous.'

I said: 'Don't worry. Relax.'

Before he sang he said: 'Have you got any wine?'

I got him a bottle of wine and to settle his nerves he gulped the whole thing down just like that. I felt sorry for him, really. He died in April 2010, which came as a huge shock to me. Peter was a big, tall and very, very nice guy.

Ozzy wrote the lyrics to 'Who's Fooling Who'. For Ozzy to sit down and write lyrics was unusual, but he came back with them and did it. It was much the same as when we did 'Psycho Man', one of the new tracks for the *Reunion* album. He came down and sat there and told a few jokes. It's an all-day thing with him. He then put a bit down and Bob worked with him on that: get a verse first and then build that up. He had done two verses and then I had done an up-tempo thing which I wanted him to sing on as well, but he didn't so I just played a solo in it.

The album was released in October 2000 and it was simply called *Iommi*. Sharon held a big launch party for it. She put a lot of work into it and I thought she did a good job. The album got great reviews all over the place and especially in America it received a lot of airplay. Sales were good as well, although I wasn't really bothered about that. It was much more important to me that I'd done something that I had wanted to do for a long time. It was nice working with different artists, younger and older.

81

An audience with the Queen

The year 2001 passed without much incident. Again Black Sabbath joined the Ozzfest, starting off with a couple of gigs in the UK, after which the summer was spent on the road in America. The following year after we skipped the Ozzfest, as we didn't want to headline it every single year. The same bands on the bill every time would be deadly for the fest and we didn't want to get into a situation where people would think, oh . . . them again!

Sharon Osbourne did have a big surprise in store for me that year. In May 2002 she got in touch about me and Ozzy doing a gig at Buckingham Palace for the Queen's Golden Jubilee, celebrating the fact that Queen Elizabeth II had been on the throne for fifty years. I thought, that's a strange request to get us on that show. They were used to having Cliff Richard and The Beach Boys, Tom Jones and Shirley Bassey, Paul McCartney even. But I certainly wouldn't have expected me and Ozzy. That was a real curveball.

They said: 'Would you mind having Phil Collins play drums?'

'Of course, great, fantastic!'

And we had Pino Palladino from The Who playing bass, a lovely guy. At our rehearsal we started playing 'Paranoid' and Ozzy turned around and gave Phil Collins a really weird look. I know what Ozzy's like, he just does that anyway. But Phil didn't. After a while Ozzy left and I ran through the song with Phil and Pino again. Phil said to me: 'What's the matter with Ozzy, haven't I been playing it right?'

'Yes, you've been playing it fine.'

'But he gave me such a dirty look!'

'He probably didn't even notice he did that. No, there's nothing wrong.'

'Oh, I was concerned. Tell me if I'm not playing it right.'

'You're playing it great!'

The next day we went to Buckingham Palace to do the sound check. It was like Fort Knox to get in it, which is understandable I suppose. We went on stage, outside in the grounds of the Palace. We did our sound check but had to come off stage in the middle of it, because there was a fire in one of the rooms in the Palace. Apparently they had boxes and boxes of fireworks they were going to let off on the night and were concerned we'd all blow up, so they had to go and investigate.

Brian May had called me the day before. He was to go up on the roof to play 'God Save The Queen', and he said: 'Would you do it with us?'

I said: 'Oh God, I can't do that. I would never be able to learn that and be comfortable enough to play it in front of billions of people watching on TV!'

'Well, just come up with us then.'

'I don't like heights. I can't!'

'You play on stage then and I'll play up there!'

'I'd never learn it in time!'

Thank goodness I said no to that. But Brian was brave enough to do it.

Backstage before the gig I stood outside talking to Paul McCartney and some other people. It was great, but there were all these signs saying 'No Drinking', 'No Swearing', no this, no that. That terrified Ozzy more than anything, because with him everything is fucking this and fucking that, so he was practising not swearing. He walked up and down in the dressing room going: 'Raise your hands, come on, raise your hands . . .' instead of his normal: 'Raise your fucking hand, you fuckers!'

I thought, no way he's going to keep that up! But he did.

We went on, and Ozzy went on too soon. He was excited and was already walking on as they announced us. We did the gig and it went really good. We came off and I had a chat with a few others, Tom Jones and the rest of them.

A great day.

Afterwards we were invited to the Palace for a drink. I was standing there in this fantastic, huge, lovely room talking to Phil Collins when Tony Blair spotted me and came over: 'Tony! Tony!'

'Eh?'

I'd never met him in my life. It was unreal to have the prime minister come over to me like he'd known me for years. He said: 'I'm a big fan. I've got all the early albums!'

Then his wife came over and he introduced me to her. While I was talking to them, I saw Ozzy walking over to me. He asked me something and I went: 'Oz, meet Tony Blair.'

He went: 'Oh, eh . . . hello.'

And that was it. Tony Blair put his hand out and it was like . . . nothing. Ozzy didn't even acknowledge him and just walked off. I said to Tony: 'He's always like that, you know.'

Because I didn't know what to say.

Tony said: 'It's okay.'

Then I saw Prince Charles walk over to talk to Ozzy. I thought, oh hell, there's no way Ozzy is going to be able to talk to him without swearing. The whole thing, it was just unreal.

I ended up meeting the Queen, Prince Charles, Princess Anne and all the gang, and they were really nice. When you see them on

TV it's all very serious, but they were down to earth. I was quite surprised. The Queen didn't really say anything and I didn't say anything to her. She just comes by and smiles and you nod and that's it really. She talked to hardly anybody. But the two young princes, William and Harry, came over and said to me: 'Why didn't you play "Black Sabbath"?'

I said: 'I don't think that would have gone down that well.'

It was a great night. The original idea was to stay there for only fifteen minutes and clear off, but I'd been there half an hour, forty minutes, and I was the first to leave. Maria and me went back to the hotel, the Lanesborough, overlooking the back of Buckingham Palace, a real flash place. We went up to our room, got into bed and about two and a half hours later the fire alarm went off: 'Would you please leave the rooms, please leave the rooms.'

We got dressed and, as we walked out into the hallway, I saw the Fire Brigade going into Ozzy's room.

Somebody had set the alarm off and they assumed it was coming from his room. But it wasn't him; he was in bed with Sharon. The Fire Brigade burst in and Ozzy had a fit.

We had to evacuate and stand around outside. I couldn't believe it: twice in one day, in the afternoon at Buckingham Palace and then at our hotel. So everybody thought, that's strange, it happened over there and now here as well . . . it must be them!

82

Hats off to Rob Halford

On 9 December 2003, people from several British television shows got in touch with me to see if I would do an interview about Ozzy's accident. I didn't know what the hell they were on about, but I soon learned that he had crashed his quad bike and broken his collarbone and lots of other things. He was in hospital for quite a while where he had metal bars put in his shoulder and his collarbone. He was very lucky to be alive.

I spoke to him, of course – I wouldn't just leave him like that – and Sharon let us know how he was doing as well. Apart from him nearly dying, he was doing very well actually. Ozzy had just released the old Black Sabbath song 'Changes' as a duet with his daughter Kelly. I never knew he was going to be doing that and I was quite surprised, but it was great. And after his crash it went straight to No. 1.

It took Ozzy quite a while to heal, but in June he was well enough to do the Ozzfest again, with Black Sabbath headlining once more. We kicked off in Hartford, Connecticut. While we were playing 'War Pigs', they projected a film behind us showing George Bush sporting a clown's nose, together with Adolf Hitler. One of the problems with these Ozzfests was that all this stuff was done without us knowing about it. Either that, or they would show it to us at such a late stage that it would be a case of use it or scrap it altogether. The Hitler thing caused a bit of an uproar, but, then again, there's been uproar about everything we've bloody done.

Judas Priest was on the bill as well. Towards the end of the tour, Rob Halford had to step in for Ozzy. In the afternoon of the Camden, New Jersey, show, the tour manager and the production manager said to me: 'We've got a problem.'

I thought, oh, here we go.

They said: 'Ozzy is not going to make the gig tonight.'

'Ah . . .'

'How would you feel about somebody else doing the gig, like Rob Halford?'

'Has anybody asked Rob? If he'd be interested in doing it?'

'No, we thought we'd ask you first.'

I said: 'As long as you let the kids know that Ozzy is not doing the gig before they're coming in, or let them know well in advance that Rob is going to do it, fine. We will do it if Rob can do it.'

Rob quickly learned our stuff in his bus. He'd seen our show umpteen times so he just had to watch the DVD a bit and run over the things that he didn't know so much.

We were due to go on stage and I said to the tour manager: 'You did tell the kids, right?'

'No, we haven't said anything.'

'You're kidding. You have to let the kids know that Ozzy is not going to be doing it!'

They asked me if I would go on and announce it and I said: 'You left it this late, I'm certainly not going to walk out and say Ozzy's not showing up!'

Eventually Bill told the crowd Ozzy couldn't do it, but that Rob was kind enough to stand in, and so on. Black Sabbath followed Judas Priest, so Rob came off the stage, changed his clothes, and he had like a half an hour before he had to go on again. It went great. It was tremendous how he did his set and then ours as well. My hat off to him, he's such a great performer.

The tour went on until 4 September, when we were going to do a show in West Palm Beach. You could say we went down a storm without even playing, because it was cancelled due to Hurricane Frances. We were staying at this hotel there and I had some friends who flew out from England to watch the show. As soon as they arrived it was cancelled.

The band had a private jet so we got out before the storm came in big time, and I let my friends stay in my hotel room. They survived it. They must have been all right, because when I received the bill later I saw they drank my minibar dry.

83

Fused with Glenn again

Late in 2004 I started working on my next solo album. First we tried a singer called Jørn Lande from the German band Masterplan. He was a nice lad with a great voice who sounded very much like Ronnie James Dio. But then it turned out Glenn Hughes was free to work on a record with me again. Glenn is really talented, he is good to work with and we get on really well, so it seemed good for us to have another go at making an album.

We went into a rehearsal room in Birmingham to work on the songs of what was to become *Fused*. The first day we got together we met Mike Exeter there, who is the engineer in my own studio at home. Mike said: 'Do you want a cup of coffee, Glenn?'

'Yes, please.'

It was fatal to give Glenn a cup of coffee, because as soon as he had it, he went into overdrive. Bang! It was just like he'd had three lines of coke again. He drove us up the wall getting all excited like that.

'Well, Tone, is it all right, Tone, let's go, Tone!'

He couldn't sit still for five seconds.

I said: 'Glenn!'

He was fidgeting and talking away: 'Yeah, well, I'm sorry, I don't drink coffee! And I . . . I . . . I shouldn't drink it really!'

He wouldn't shut up. Mike came in and I said: 'No more coffee for him!'

Just like I'd done for the DEP sessions, I played Glenn some riffs. He is the sort of bloke who will sing on anything you play him.

'Oh, I like that one. And I like that one. And that one!'

'Which one do you want to do then?'

We'd pick one and build it into a song.

We had a bash for a couple of days and then we brought Bob Marlette in to work on some more songs and produce the record. I said to Bob: 'Let's put a few tracks down, let's have a little bash', and we came up with four or five tracks in no time at all. We recorded them at my house and most of those tapes were actually used for the final tracks.

Since working with Kenny Aronoff on the *Iommi* album I just thought he was a really good drummer, so we brought him over. The four of us worked on the songs, we did rough takes of all the tracks and we took it to the Monnow Valley Studios in Monmouth to record it properly there. It was all very quick: got together, wrote it and recorded it.

Fused was released in July 2005 on Sanctuary Records. We did a promotional tour for that, with quite a lot of radio stuff, but we didn't support the album with a concert tour, because I was out with Black Sabbath doing Ozzfest at the time. It was good to see that it was received very well by the critics and the audience alike. After having been met with terrible reviews and negative articles for most of my career, it shouldn't have mattered to me that much any more, but it was nice to see so many people appreciating our music that much.

84

Entering the Halls of Fame

We were up for it probably seven or eight times, and on 13 March 2006 we were finally inducted into the American Rock and Roll Hall of Fame. And a couple of months before that we'd already been inducted in the UK Music Hall of Fame.

When it rains, it pours.

We were inducted into the UK one in November 2005 at Alexandra Palace in north London. We played 'Paranoid' at that ceremony and that went great. Brian May inducted us. There was a bit of a commotion about that, because Sharon wanted Angus Young of AC/DC to do it. I wanted Brian. Then she wanted Angus and Brian to do it together, but Brian just didn't want to do it that way. I'm glad he stuck to his guns. He wasn't going to do it and I had to phone him up and said: 'Please do it. Do it for me.'

He came and made a great speech, absolutely fantastic. I was really proud of him.

Ozzy was playing there as well with his band and Angus Young said about three words about that. Well, his first few words were: 'Hello, can you hear me? Can you hear me?' He's probably as good a talker as I am on those bloody occasions.

We went into this TV station to do an interview right after the presentation, and the bloke said: 'Last year we had Michael Jackson in here. He came in with his award and when he walked out again he forgot it. I've got it in my bathroom at home now.'

I said: 'Oh, really? Fancy him doing that!'

And, blimey, if I didn't do exactly the same thing. In fact, he probably had mine sitting in his bathroom for a while next to Michael Jackson's. But I've got it back now, so everything is good.

When we collected our award for the American Hall of Fame, we stayed at the Waldorf Astoria in New York. The event was held in the hotel ballroom. It was great; you could just go downstairs, go to the presentation, collect your award and clear off. Well, supposedly, but you don't do that, because from then on you go into the different TV stations that are hooked up at the back there to do interviews. In doing so I held on to my award like it was glued to me, because I didn't want to lose it like I had at the UK Music Hall of Fame.

When we finally got it after all those years of being nominated, I was really pleased. Ozzy had said some stuff in the past, like: 'I don't give a fuck about being inducted.'

I thought it was a great honour and I am very proud of it.

They wanted us to play there, but there was some problem so Metallica played instead of us. They did 'Hole In The Sky' and 'Iron Man'. They were really good and they inducted us as well, which was really nice of them. Lars Ulrich and James Hetfield said some wonderful things about us. They are genuine blokes and they do love what we've done. In fact, James came along to a few Heaven & Hell gigs later, so he's a big fan. And in turn I think they are really good. I like them a lot.

The Rock and Roll Hall of Fame is a funny old do, really, because it gets a bit stuffy. Fortunately we could loosen up a bit with the guys we knew there. And, of course, I loosened up a lot later, when I sat in the bar with Geezer Butler until God knows what time. The next day I felt bloody awful.

When I left New York about four days after the event, I put my award in my hand baggage, just to make sure I didn't lose it. It's a big thing, maybe a foot long, and when I passed security at the airport they said: 'You can't take this through.'

'What do you mean? It's an award!'

'I know, but you could use it as a weapon.'

I thought, oh no, it's taken me thirty-eight bloody years to get it, and now they are going to confiscate it. But everything was sorted out and I managed to get it home safe and sound.

85

This is for peace

Towards the end of 2006 I was invited to work with Zemlyane, this Russian band that played the Kremlin. It was their anniversary and they wanted to do 'Heaven And Hell' and 'Paranoid'. I said: 'I'll just do "Paranoid".'

I just wanted to do something short because I didn't know who the bloody hell they were, but they're quite big in Russia and they offered me a fee I couldn't refuse. Actually, they offered an initial fee and I said to Ralph: 'I don't particularly want to do it. Just double it.'

He doubled it and they said: 'Okay.'

So I flew out there. Tony Martin and Glenn Hughes were on as well, and so were Rick Wakeman and his son, Adam, and Bonnie Tyler. The night I got in, the promoter took me out to eat and the amount of drink was lethal. It was all, have another shot of this and a shot of that and fill up and another salute to whoever. After just a few of them I thought, fucking hell, if I did this for a couple of days I wouldn't survive. I was absolutely legless. I said: 'I've just got to go to bed. I'm playing tomorrow! I'm going.'

They said: 'That's an insult, you know!'

Oh shit, here we go. And normally I don't drink shots at all.

'No, no. Have another one!'

I did. And I didn't feel all that stunning the next day.

Before the show I was sitting on my own in the dressing room; there was a knock on the door and this army walked in. About twenty people, with lots of photographers and cameramen and bodyguards – it was absolutely mad. Somebody pinned a medal on me and said: 'This is for peace.'

He shook my hand for the cameras and left.

Shoof – as soon as they'd come in, they'd gone.

And that was it.

What happened?

I never found out who it was. For all I know it was Putin himself.

Then I did the gig. There were only very wealthy people there, obviously all connected with the government, and they were all dressed up. It was in a small theatre that probably only held 200 people, right there in the Kremlin. To play a gig like that was ever so weird.

I saw Tony Martin there for the first time since the end of the Forbidden tour, back in 1995. He went on and sang 'Headless Cross'. It was all right seeing him there, first at the show and then later at the restaurant.

That restaurant was another matter. They had closed it for regular customers, so it became a private thing for the people connected to the show. We went for lunch there, me, my guitar tech, my assistant and one of the people from the promoter's office. Apart from us, the place was completely empty. I asked for the wine list and I picked this expensive wine. They brought a bottle of it, poured it, I had a sip and I said to the bloke: 'This wine is off.'

The head waiter came up and said: 'What's the problem with the wine?'

'It's off.'

The look on his face, he was so pissed off!

'It's not off. It can't be off!'

But it was. They probably weren't used to people spending that sort of money on a bottle of wine. Then they brought another one.

That was off as well.

I said to the promoter bloke: 'I can't believe it. But don't say anything. Just leave it. Because the look they gave me the first time!'

And the waiters probably thought, he's only had one sip of it . . . extravagant!

86

Heaven and Hell, tour and band

In the autumn of 2006 Ralph told me that the record company wanted to put a package together of stuff from the Dio era. I'd seen Ronnie not long before that at a gig in Birmingham. It had been fifteen years and it was good to see him again. So I said to Ralph: 'Why don't we ask Ronnie if he'd be interested in doing two songs especially for this album, just a couple of one-offs?'

Ronnie was interested and flew over from California. We sat down in my kitchen, having coffee, and another coffee, trying to get to know each other again. We didn't want to actually start yet, we were a bit like, oh, yeah, what are we going to do?

Finally I said: 'Well, shall we have a go then?'

'Oh. All right.'

We went into my studio and it just jelled again like it used to. Instead of the two songs the record company wanted, we wrote three. We were in good spirits and feeling productive so we thought, why don't we do a fast one, a slow one and a mid-tempo one? Something for everybody. The first song we wrote was 'Shadow Of The Wind', the slow one. Ronnie came up with the riff and then we added more to it and built it into a song. I came up with the riff for 'The Devil Cried'. Ronnie had to go back home to LA for a few days and I sent him a rough take of it. He really liked that. And we wrote the fast one, 'Ear In The Wall', after he'd come back again. Geezer came over and we demoed the three tracks in the studio at my house.

I'd always been in contact with Bill and I said to him: 'Would you be interested in doing these tracks with us?'

He went: 'That sounds really good. I'd love to do that!'

I got him over to England a week before the others came, so that we could run through the ideas and he could get used to playing these songs. I had sent Bill a track about three weeks earlier as well, so he could start working on that. But he obviously hadn't. Then Ronnie and Geezer arrived. Everybody was getting a bit impatient, because Bill was taking his time. He wanted to analyse everything and try out different things, which is the way he is. It was a bit difficult, because I was being asked: 'How long is it going to be?'

All I could say was: 'I don't know!'

Unfortunately we were working to a strict deadline and Ronnie in particular was keen to get going and return home. We talked to Bill about it and suggested a couple of ideas, but he wasn't happy to play the sort of thing that we were hearing on the tracks. It just didn't work out. Bill wasn't going to be the one to play on it. We thought about putting the band back together and touring as well, but Bill said: 'I don't particularly want to be doing a lot of shows.'

It would have been funny for Bill anyway, because a lot of the music we were going to be playing would've been new to him, as he'd played on the *Heaven and Hell* album but Vinny had done *Mob Rules* and *Dehumanizer*. Because of all this, we got Vinny in to play on these three tracks instead. And that was it. Ronnie and Geezer went back home and the tracks were added to the album. It came out and the interest was great.

As soon as promoters heard that we had written three new tracks together, they went: 'When are you going to tour?'

We talked about it among ourselves and decided to take it stage by stage. We didn't want to commit ourselves for years to come. We thought, okay, let's do a tour and see what happens.

They booked a tour and we went and did it. By the time *The Dio Years* came out in April 2007, we were on the road in Canada and the States. It was great and it really went down well. It was the first time in nearly forty years that I was touring under a different name. We didn't want to call it Black Sabbath, as we had been touring with the Ozzy line-up again as well and we didn't want to confuse people. We weren't playing the old stuff either; we stuck to the songs we'd recorded with Ronnie. At first we weren't going to call ourselves anything and just use our own names, while calling this tour the Heaven and Hell tour. But soon people were calling the band Heaven & Hell and we stuck with that.

We started with Megadeth and Down with Phil Anselmo, whose spot was taken by Machine Head mid-tour. It went really well. We played more than thirty dates all over America and in May we went over to Europe for summer festivals and arenas. And then we welcomed Down back for two weeks in Australia and New Zealand. Throughout September we toured America again, this time with Alice Cooper and Queensrÿche. We'd known Alice for quite a while and he's a nice guy. Eric Singer was his drummer at the time. During that tour I saw Alice a couple of times in the lobby of the hotel.

'You're going out for a bit?'

'Yeah, going to play a round of golf.'

Finishing in Japan, we were a bit sad that that might be the end. I said to Ronnie: 'Would you be interested in doing another album?'

'Yeah, I'd love to do that. What about Geezer?'

'We'll ask.'

Geezer joined us in this Japanese restaurant and he didn't last five minutes because he's a vegan. Of all the places to go with us that was the wrong one, because we were eating raw fish and everything. He only came in for a drink, saw them put all the live shrimps on the grill, got really angry and buggered off.

But he was up for it, and so was Vinny.

That settled it: we were going to make another album!

87

The Devil You Know

We didn't write while we were on the road. I did have an amp in the dressing room and fiddled about a bit and sometimes I'd come up with a couple of riffs, which I then recorded on a little digital machine. I just kept them so that I could go back to them at some point, but it never worked trying to write a proper song while on tour. We never sat down together to do it, simply because we weren't in each other's company all that much. Me and Geezer travelled on one bus together and Vinny and Ronnie on another, and we both left at different times. After a gig Geezer and myself would have a shower, get on the bus and go. Ronnie usually stayed behind for a couple of hours because he liked to relax, have a drink and see a few people. Meanwhile, Geezer and me were asleep and on the road. I'm an early riser, but Ronnie would sleep in late. With two different schedules like that, to write a track together was very difficult.

So after the tour we had writing sessions. I did a lot at home, where I put many riffs down and a lot of the structures of the songs, which I then put on a CD. Ronnie, Geezer and Vinny were at home in California, so I went over there with more than twenty song ideas on this CD. Ronnie had also put his ideas on a CD and so had Geezer. Vinny was very much involved; he sat there tapping away, but he didn't write as such. We all got together in Ronnie's house, sat down in his studio and just played the different CDs. We had a drink, casually went through them all and picked out the ideas we instantly liked, no matter whose they were. We put all those on one CD, made a copy of that for everybody, and then we decided which ones we wanted to work on first over the next few days.

We used one of Ronnie's ideas in its entirety, which was 'Atom And Evil', the first track on the album. And we used bits of each other idea. Some of Geezer's riffs would come halfway through, or some of mine. We just swapped them around, building songs. It was a great way of working. Instead of having to come up with everything myself, everybody was completely involved in it from day one, and that helped me immensely. We wrote about six songs this way.

Then we had a break to do an American tour in August 2008, after which we were all fresh and raring to go again for the next batch of songs. We did the same as before: each of us had a writing session on his own. We put our ideas on a CD again, got back together and played the CDs to each other and picked some more tracks to work on.

When we decided to record 'Atom And Evil' because we all liked it so much, Ronnie was quite honoured. He had written the words and the music, but he was very humble. He said: 'We don't have to do it.' And then he added: 'But if you like it . . .'

I said: 'It's wonderful. It would be a great song to do!'

When we were in LA putting the songs together, I had a little studio set up in the basement of the house I rented. My engineer, Mike Exeter, was staying at the house as well. We'd put the ideas together at Ronnie's, and afterwards I'd go back home. The next morning I might tinkle around with it and change the riff. And then later in the day, back at Ronnie's, I'd say: 'What about this idea?' On 'Bible Black' I had started off with a riff I'd come up with back home in England, and then Ronnie had changed this and that around. Then one morning in my little basement studio I changed the riff completely. It worked good and in the end 'Bible Black' turned into a great song.

Not all the songs came from the ideas we already had on our CDs. We came up with 'The Turn Of The Screw', 'Neverwhere' and 'Eating The Cannibals' at Ronnie's; they were done from scratch right then and there. We didn't just sit around listening; we had our instruments there and did a fair amount of writing together on the spot. Most of the songs were group efforts. Even the ones that were almost completed when presented to the other band members were changed. We'd move stuff around and put new bits in and add little twists that would make them more interesting. Ronnie might say: 'What about trying that bit there? And that bit?'

And we'd try it. It was good because we pushed each other. Instead of going: 'Eh, all right, that'll do', it was: 'Oh yeah, we can make that better!'

We got along really well and we became very close, and that helped us while writing the songs. We really homed in on the whole thing.

Recording *The Devil You Know* didn't take long at all. We'd already gone into pre-production in LA. Once we had finished the writing, we rehearsed the songs. We played them and taped them and got them fairly tight. We had a little time off and then everybody came over to the Rockfield Studios in Monmouth, in Wales, where we just played the songs live in the studio. We put them all down in three weeks instead of the five we'd originally planned. I was thrilled. To be able to write like that and get the pre-production done and then go in to play it live, it was absolutely great.

It wouldn't be right to be in the studio with no hi-jinks and this time the drummer on the receiving end was Vinny. It was cold, being November, but Vinny was as usual working up a right sweat and at every take his hair was soaked so he'd have a hairdryer next to his kit to dry it whenever there was a break. The thing packed up and he got my Tech, Mike, to repair it and was really pleased when it came back and tested it, no problem. We took a break and while he was gone I couldn't resist filling it up with talcum powder. Back to work and sure enough, Vinny picks up the dryer, but this time 'poof', instead of a black-haired drummer dressed in a black T-shirt there was now a white apparition! Being Vinny he took it in good spirit.

I find when you're coming up with the riffs and you've got the right people around you to put them together, it can go very quickly. There's actually no reason why we couldn't have played everything in one day, because we were doing that at rehearsal. It's just that you get into that thing where you think, we'll do a track a day. And then you'd want to do a guitar overdub, or Ronnie would want to do an extra vocal, and a track would take a couple of days. I could have saved an absolute fortune working this fast in the past, but you can't work that way with everybody. It takes a certain combination of people to be able to do it.

The Devil You Know was released in April 2009. Listening to it, you can hear we were really inspired and had a great time making it, and therefore it was nice to see that it was received incredibly well. The critics were raving, some calling it the best metal album of the year. In America it debuted at No. 8 in the *Billboard* album charts. I'd been at it for forty years and it hadn't always been smooth sailing, but *The Devil You Know* was another high point. I couldn't wait to tour the album and take the show on the road once again.

We started off in South America, playing big crowds that were always wild. The European summer festivals were really good and

Wacken was especially great. The crowd was fantastic and it was very well organised. We filmed it for the *Neon Nights – Live at Wacken* DVD that came out in November 2010. I was very pleased with the way that turned out and I'm really glad we did it because it was Ronnie's last filmed show.

The Sonisphere Festival in Knebworth was the last gig we played on this side of the Atlantic. It just pissed down with rain when we walked on and it stopped when we came off. Bloody marvellous that was. But even so, that was a good gig as well.

We spent August in America, with Coheed and Cambria supporting us. On the 29th we had our last show at the House of Blues in Atlantic City, New Jersey. I was thinking, why are we playing there? It's such a small place! But it was looked on as a nice little gig to finish up with, and it was all right. It had been such a great tour that we didn't want it to end.

But it did.

The House of Blues turned out to be our last gig ever.

88

Farewell to a dear friend

While we were on that last tour, Ronnie was suffering quietly. He did say to me a few times: 'I've got a problem with my stomach. I keep going to the loo and I'm taking this ant-acid stuff.'

I said to him many times: 'You want to go and get a check-up.'

He'd go: 'Yeah, when we finish I'll sort myself out.'

He battled through it. He really did give it all until the end. He wasn't well, but he still went on and did the shows, and he performed as usual. After he finally went in to have a check-up, somebody told Ralph Baker what was going on and he in turn called me to tell me Ronnie had stomach cancer. It was awful to hear that. I called Ronnie and we stayed in touch. After a while things were looking up. He said: 'I'm coping with it. I'm doing a bit better.'

He was very positive towards it all, he had a great attitude. He went into hospital and after a while they said: 'We think we've cleared it.'

Things looked great, so we arranged to do another tour of Europe, something like twenty gigs from mid-June through to mid-August 2010. But then we got the terrible news that the cancer had spread to Ronnie's liver. And that was it; once that happens it's very difficult.

I was talking to him one day and I said: 'I'm looking forward to doing this tour.'

But Ronnie said: 'Well, I don't know how I'm going to be. I don't know if I'm going to make it.'

He went downhill very quickly. Thank goodness Geezer and Gloria were in Los Angeles. They really stood close to Ronnie and his wife, Wendy, and went to see him in hospital a lot. Geezer was there right till the end.

I really didn't get to say a proper goodbye to Ronnie. I'd had the phone call saying he didn't have long and I said to Ralph: 'We had better go out. Let's book a flight.'

But the next call was: 'It's too late.'

It was that quick. I think the last thing I got off him was a text. He did stay in touch texting me, because sometimes he couldn't call. Talking was tiring him out a lot, because he was very ill. And he braved right through it.

A couple of days before the funeral me and Maria went to see him in the chapel of rest. He was lying in the coffin and when I saw him I broke down. To see him like that was very hard. It really hit me then that he was gone.

When somebody close to you dies, you always look for a reason. With Ronnie I think it was a bit of everything, really. I don't think he got himself checked out early enough. He would put things off and go: 'Oh, I'll do it next time.'

And his eating habits weren't very good. He'd often drink instead of eating and some days he wouldn't eat at all. I don't know how he did that. He'd also eat at peculiar hours, because he had a really different lifestyle from anyone else in the band. We'd be in bed after the gig and Ronnie would stay up and have a few drinks for a couple of hours and then he'd stop off at a truck stop and eat at four in the morning or whatever time it would be. When he did eat, he never ate vegetables or anything; he just didn't eat any healthy stuff. As long as I've known him, he was always very thin.

When he was ill he lost weight, and he really didn't have the body to lose weight. But when I saw him for that very last time, the way they had done him up, he looked fine. He looked as if he was asleep, but seeing him there, it broke my heart.

We were going to do the High Voltage Festival in London with Ronnie. Of course we cancelled the whole tour, but the people organising that festival told us that they'd like to do a tribute show to Ronnie. We thought, that's great. We had thought of doing that anyway, so this was the ideal opportunity.

But who were we going to get to sing? Glenn Hughes came to mind, because he had known us for a long time and he was friends with Ronnie as well. As a matter of fact, there was a private memorial for Ronnie's close friends and Glenn sang 'Catch The Rainbow' there in the chapel, one of the songs by Ronnie's old band, Rainbow. There was a memorial again the following day for the fans in a big venue, and Glenn sang there as well. So we thought it was appropriate to have him on the show. We also invited Jørn Lande, who could sing the stuff we did with Dio really good.

Doing that show was very emotional. To go on stage with two different people, and with Wendy Dio on the side of the stage crying, it was difficult for all of us. But we wanted to do it for him.

We did it for Ronnie.

89

Not a right-hand man

Throughout the years I have been very unlucky with my right hand. First of all I had my fingers chopped off of it, but that was only the beginning of a whole series of bad things that happened to it. In 1995 I had an operation on my right wrist for carpal tunnel. And when we did the Ozzfest in 2005 my arm really hurt. I did get cortisone injections for it, but the effects didn't last long. I thought, what the bloody hell is this? I had X-rays and they said: 'You've broken three tendons in your right shoulder. Three ligaments.'

They put them back together and it was fine until about three years later. I was in New York, we were doing a gig on the night and I did some exercises with weights. You're supposed to exercise to strengthen your arms, but I probably did it a bit too much and I heard this sound, like the snapping of an elastic band. I had broken another one in the same shoulder. My arm was shaking, I couldn't control it and I thought, oh, no, it's gone again!

They gave me a cortisone shot and some painkillers to go on stage and I played the gig that night, but it was bloody painful. Fortunately it was the last gig of the tour. I had it checked out back in England and the surgeon said: 'To be honest it was in a state when I repaired it last time. They were frayed really badly and we were lucky to be able to repair it, but I don't think we can do it again. And also it's wrong now. The tendon has shortened too much to reconnect.'

Maybe a top specialist would've been able to repair it, but I just left it. It does affect me when I'm lifting stuff above my head. If I have to put a suitcase in the overhead locker in a plane, for instance, that's when I notice it.

I've also been bitten badly by Rottweilers on my right hand and arm. I had four Rottweilers the first time this happened. About five years earlier we had ten pups and I gave a friend of mine one of them. When he went through a divorce he said: 'Could you look after the dog for a while?'

We had the dog back, a big bitch, but my dogs didn't get on with her. They started attacking her, which was pretty brutal. I had to pull one of my dogs off her. His collar just came off in my hand and he dived back on her again.

Blimey!

I couldn't get him off and he was ripping the dog apart, so I got one of my big coats and jumped on top of the bitch, covering her up with it. My dog stopped then and Maria managed to get him inside, but the bitch was in shock and as I had her covered she turned around and 'maw-maw-maw': in a matter of just a few seconds she bit two fingers, the side of my hand and my thumb. She obviously didn't know where she was; she was just in total shock after my dog had set on her.

I thought, oh, fuck! Blood squirted all over the place and Maria shouted at me: 'You shouldn't have done that, you shouldn't have risked it!'

I just went: 'Quick, get somebody to bandage my hand up!'

Both of us shouting at each other, it was completely silly. I had to go to bloody hospital, off to surgery again, to get it checked and have rabies shots. They bandaged it all up but they couldn't stitch it, because they said you can't do that with bites. So I had to leave it, just cover it, put stuff on it, and that was it.

Bloody hell!

I got bitten on that arm again on another occasion. Maria was doing some work for the RSPCA, finding a home for animals. We had a big dog pen in one of our fields at the house and she brought a dog back to keep for a few days, while we looked for a new owner. It was a lovely Rottweiler that had been mistreated. Maria said: 'Don't go by the dog. Leave him alone for a bit.'

Of course I took no notice.

'All right, all right.'

I went to dog: 'Hello, hello . . .'

I reached out to stroke it and 'wraauw', he caught my arm. Then he looked at me . . . and bit me again more or less in the same place.

Fuck!

They are so bloody quick! The dog just grabbed my arm and it was only a warning as well. If he had wanted to, he could have ripped the bloody thing off. But he was frightened and he didn't know me from Adam. It was my own fault. I shouldn't have bent over. You're not supposed to do that. And he probably smelled my other dogs on me as well.

It immobilised my arm, so it was off to the surgery again, to the same doctor. He must've thought, what the hell is going on there? And once again it couldn't be stitched. We had a tour coming up and I thought, oh, for Christ's sake, just typical, that is. My arm bothered me for a good few weeks, but it healed eventually.

Maria had a go at me: 'You're a silly bugger for doing that. I told you not to!'

But I did go down to see the dog again the next day in the pen, just to face my problem. You can't be terrified forever. I was a bit overpowering with him the first time, so now I went to introduce myself properly. I opened the pen and went in there with a couple of biscuits. He stood there looking and I thought, don't go for me again, please. But he was all right, he was great after that. We had him for about a week, until we found him a home.

He's probably killed the new owner by now.

The worst thing that happened to my hand is the cartilage disintegrating in the thumb joint. I had already had problems with that joint for a couple of years. I had steroid injections, but they were just sticking the needle in roundabouts and some of it didn't hit the right spot. Eventually I heard of this place in Birmingham called The Joint Clinic. This doctor called Anna Moon is a specialist in hands. She injected me under X-ray, so that she could see exactly where the needle went in, which was brilliant. I had steroids first, and then I tried this new stuff, like a jell that they use on knee joints. It looked like glue and I had to have three injections in between my joints over the course of a week. It basically buffered the joint like an artificial cartilage and stopped the bones from rubbing against each other. It was all right but it still didn't work properly. My hand swelled up from all the playing and I had to put ice on it and take anti-inflammatories and painkillers all the time.

Eddie Van Halen had problems with the joints in his hand as well and he saw this doctor in Germany, Dr Peter Wehling from Düsseldorf, who does stem cell treatment. It's the only place that does this kind of treatment. Eddie told me it really helped him, so I went to see this chap. I did four hours of all different sorts of X-rays. They checked everything because they can't treat you if you have any other kind of problem. On the X-ray they found a white mark in my joint and they said: 'I don't think we are going to be able to do this. If that's what we think it is, you are going to be on antibiotics for six months.'

I thought, oh, for Christ's sake, and said: 'What do you think it is?'

'We think it's fluid in the joint.'

They checked again and found a hole in my joint where one of the doctors had at some point injected a steroid right into the bone. That's why I was getting a swelling in my hand. They said: 'Now that we know what it is we can actually go ahead with the procedure.'

They took blood from my arm, sent that to the lab overnight and grew new cartilage from it. Then, a day or two later, they injected it back into me wherever it was needed. The doctor changed his surgical gloves about three times in the course of the five minutes it took to give me the injections: that's how clean they were. I had to be there at the clinic for a week. Go in the morning, have the injections, and then back to the hotel. They took quite a few big files of blood in case I needed a top-up later, which I did. They grew the cells and I went in every day for that week and the difference was amazing. It really, really helped. I wasn't getting any pain any more.

I did have to go back to see Dr Wehling again a couple of months later, because the next joint up and also my left hand were playing up. I had a full body scan as well to see if there were any problems anywhere else. There was just a little bit at the base of my spine and at the top of my neck, in between the neck joints, but that was just normal wear and tear.

All these guitar players, like Jimmy Page and Pete Townshend, used to jump up and down and roll on the floor on their knees. Years later you really feel that. Like footballers, they get these joint problems because of all the abuse. I just stood there with the guitar for forty years, but you're standing funny when you're playing guitar, so all that gradual wear and tear and putting more weight on one leg and all that caused back problems for me. Dr Wehling gave me injections in my back as well and after about four days of those I never had another problem there again. All the pain disappeared. It's great.

The last time I saw him, he said: 'It should be growing all right now.'

They didn't even X-ray it to check it; he just knows that it's growing now. He said to keep him updated about what's going on. It does hurt a bit in certain places now, but it's nothing at all like it was. When I'm playing for a bit, I forget about it. Since I've had this stem cell treatment I haven't felt the need to take any painkillers or anything. It's just been brilliant.

Until something else goes . . .

90

Good news and bad

One thing that was a lot of fun to do was the 'Out Of My Mind' charity single with Ian Gillan, Jon Lord, Jason Newsted, Linde Lindström and Nicko McBrain. It was a quarter of a century ago that we recorded our first charity single in aid of the Armenian earthquake victims, 'Smoke On The Water'. It was a big thing with just about everybody involved, like Brian May, Bryan Adams, Ritchie Blackmore and David Gilmour. We did a video for it and raised a lot of money. And then, in 2009, twenty-five years later, President Serzh Sargssian of Armenia got in touch. He wanted to give an award for what we'd done back then to Ian Gillan, myself and keyboard player Geoff Downes.

We went to Armenia and they showed us what they had built with the money from 'Smoke On The Water'. We had dinner with Prime Minister Tigran Sargsian and the British Ambassador Charles Lonsdale. We were there for a few days and did a couple of press conferences. At one of those we started talking about maybe doing something else to raise more money, because, when they showed us around, we saw this music school, which was just awful. It was like a tin shed, all cold and damp, so we thought, we've got to do something about this. The first thing we did when we got back home was send them a lot of guitars and drums and whatever. We also wrote and released a couple of songs to help build a new school, that's what 'Out Of My Mind' was all about.

First, Ian and myself got together at my house. I wrote the music and he did the lyrics. We wanted some other people to play on it, and Ian mentioned Jon Lord. I said, 'Yeah, that would be great!'

I suggested Nicko McBrain, and then we also got Jason Newsted on the bass and Linde Lindström on guitar. It worked out great, and we had a fantastic time recording it. The song turned out really well and we did raise a fair amount of money once again. Since then we've put out *Who Cares*, an album with tracks that were never used before, or only used as bonus tracks in some countries. I put in tracks from the album I did with Glenn Hughes, and Ian Gillan put some tracks on there, either from his solo albums or from Deep Purple. And of course it's got 'Out Of My Mind'. So it's a little bit of a mixed bag really. We had such a good time doing this that we actually talked about making ourselves into a proper band.

Whatever I do, Black Sabbath will always be there one way or another. On the day of Ronnie's funeral Maria and I had dinner with Eddie Van Halen and his wife. The phone rang. I picked it up to answer it without looking at the display first, and it was Sharon Osbourne.

Blimey!

I hadn't spoken to her for over a year. She said: 'Oh, I've got the wrong number. I thought it was another Tony.'

When she realized it was me, she said she was sorry to hear about Ronnie. Then she went: 'Will you call Ozzy? You must speak to Ozzy!'

I called him a few days later. He said: 'I'd like to get together and have a chat.'

I said: 'Well, I'll be back in England in a couple of days.'

'Good. I'm coming over to England as well, let's see each other then.'

We stayed in touch, Geezer came round to have a listen to some of my ideas and over the Christmas break Ozzy and Sharon came up to the house and slowly the concept of getting back together again, making music again, became more real.

In January 2011, we decided properly to get together and have a play. I went to LA and things got serious when all four original members of Black Sabbath got together in the studio under the Sunset Marquee hotel in Los Angeles, to listen to about forty ideas for tracks I had come up with. That was the germ of it all. We made a list of the ideas we all liked best and then tried them at Ozzy's house. He has a studio in the basement, which made it really easy to work without having the world peering in at us.

It was really inspiring, ideas came up and it all sort of gelled.

It was the same way of working as I had done before with Heaven & Hell. My initial idea might spark the guys off and they, for instance, would pull it apart and use the original riff of one song, add some other bits, and then we might take it into another direction and make a new song out of that.

We then started learning the new songs. Bill hadn't played for a while so he was a bit rusty at first, but it was going well. The quality of the music was already good before we started and, certainly, when Geezer got involved, it turned into the old sound again. My initial ideas turned into Black Sabbath songs.

When we talked about us getting back together, we thought it would be good to have somebody else to take the reins and work at getting the best out of each of us. The record company liked the idea of us working with Rick Rubin. We had met him before of course, back in 2001 or 2002, when we thought about doing a new album. We went to his house to see him, just like we had all those years ago. Back then it was like we were visiting Buddha himself, but this time we were on a more even level.

It wasn't a long meeting at all; most of the time was taken up by Rick playing us the original Black Sabbath album, the one we recorded in one day back in 1969. He was on about the vibe from that album and was into us doing more stuff as a jam-type of thing, just as loose as we did in the early days.

I thought a producer would be there when you're writing the songs, getting involved and going: 'What about trying that bit there?' or whatever. But Rick hasn't been so far. He's left it to us. I guess that's good, we've done enough writing over the years to know how to do it. When we worked at Ozzy's studio, I was in touch with Rick and he'd just say: 'Let me know when you've got something for me to hear.'

So whenever we had one or two new songs, I'd phone him and he'd come down. This happened four or five times, and that's really as far as we've got with him. We'd play him stuff, and he'll say: 'I like that, I don't like that, I like that . . .'

Of course we in turn will go: 'Why don't you like it? How do you see it then?'

And that's it. That's what he does.

Rick joined us at the Whisky A Go Go in Los Angeles, where we got together on 11 November 2011 to announce our new album and tour. Henry Rollins hosted this press gathering and said some very nice things about us, after which we told the whole world about our plans. It was special, certainly because the four original members of Black Sabbath announced they would make a new studio album, the first one since *Never Say Die!* in 1978.

When we were at Ozzy's house, in early December 2011, Sharon came down to the studio and she mentioned some dates for us to perform. There was the Coachella Festival in April 2012 in California, followed by a European tour. We all wanted to get on with the album and not tour yet, but the reaction to our re-union was so great it seemed like a good idea. We thought, we'd go out and play for a while and then go back in and do the album. However, back in October 2011, I was in New York for a few days promoting the first edition of this book, on my way to Los Angeles, and that's where I got a pain in the left side of my groin. I noticed a lump, about an inch wide. I got a doctor over and he gave me some antibiotics. He said: 'It looks like an infection. Take these for two weeks and when you get to LA see another doctor if it's still there.'

I saw Ozzy in LA and he said: 'You don't look very well.'

I said: 'No, I'm a bit uncomfortable.'

'You ought to get that checked out,' he said.

'Well, I will.'

I took his advice and did see another doctor who gave me some more antibiotics, which at least cleared up the infection. I didn't think much more of it. I'd had a prostate examination about a year before and it turned out the lump was the size of an orange. It had caused a bladder infection, which I thought then in turn caused the lump.

I came back home to England and had an operation on my prostate. The surgeon, Mr Manu Nair, said: 'While we are doing that we might as well take that lump out and check it.'

The operation was painless, but afterwards I needed a catheter, so over Christmas I had this bloody pipe hanging down with a bag attached to it. I couldn't get up from the bed and move about, so Maria was changing the bag and everything. All the stuff she's had to do, she's been like a nurse really. Talk about 'for better or for worse': she really got the worse side of it there.

When the catheter came out, I went to see the surgeon and he said: 'Good news on the prostate. Its cut down to a sensible size now and everything is good there. But on the lump we took out, we found lymphoma.'

I thought, what's that?

He said: 'It's not bad, we can cure this. It is treatable. It is follicular lymphoma grade I, which is at an early stage.'

I went: 'Oh, right.'

But I was still gutted when he told me what it was. I went home depressed, thinking, Christ, that's it, I've had it! I didn't know anything about it, cancer was death to me. I started writing myself off. I would lie awake at night, thinking about selling this and getting rid of that and preparing everything: who should speak at my funeral and where I'd want to be buried. Really grim stuff. But I also kept thinking, I'm not ready to go yet. I've got too much to do and I like being here.

About three days later, my GP, Dr Michael Abdou, phoned me up and said: 'They've done more tests and we found it's not grade I, but grade III A.'

I think that it's out of four, it might even go to five, so grade III was bad news. I went: 'Oh, no!'

Dr Abdou knew a local specialist and friend, Professor Donald Milligan, and got me an appointment to see him. He said: 'We'll treat it. We'll do chemo and all the things necessary to try and contain it.'

I went for numerous scans to see if it had spread to anywhere else. It hadn't, it was all in the left side of my groin. I was still suffering from the aftereffects of my prostate operation. All the antibiotics and other medication involved had knocked me about a lot and I was really weak and tired, but once I got over that they got me in to start the chemo. They told me I needed six courses of chemo, one every three weeks. It takes about six or seven hours to give it to you, intravenously, on a drip. The chemo for lymphoma is similar to what they use with other cancers, but they put this fourth ingredient in and that's an antibody. You can have an allergic reaction to it, so they had to do it slowly at first. But the treatment went well.

I had the first one and they said: 'You're going to lose your hair.'

Initially nothing much happened and I thought, oh, I might be all right. I had the second chemo three weeks later. I then started to feel tired and sick, and when I brushed my hair it all came out. Within two or three days the lot had gone. When I'd get up in the night to go to the toilet and I'd look in the mirror, it was, Oh, God! The hair on my head went first, and some on my chest. My beard and my moustache went thin but nothing drastic happened to my eyebrows. I've always had long hair, whether it was the sixties when they said, 'Oh, get your hair cut', or more recently, when it was short compared to back then but longer still than most anybody else's. So the hair on my head gone, that was a terrible shock.

Of course, the skin underneath was white. It was like an egg. It was so sudden that it was really hard to get used to. I showed it to Ozzy and Geezer and their first reaction was: 'You look like your dad!'

Being bald, bloody hell, it's freezing cold. I started wearing a beanie, but I felt funny in that. I never wear hats normally. But having chemo you have to watch your temperature. Mine went dangerously low. It was 35 degrees, so we had to try to build that up. My nutritionist, Bev de Pons, recommended a Russian healing blanket. It's made from the same stuff that astronauts wear, a silver type of fibre. It's bloody warm. So I'd sit there with this blanket around me and my beanie on my head. Bloody sad really.

Seeing myself with no hair, I thought, I can't have that. I don't want to shock people. They go by how you look and you can either look ill or look good. If people see me with no hair, they'll go: 'Oh, blimey, he looks terrible.'

So I got in touch with this company called Optima in Birmingham that do hair replacement as well as wigs for cancer patients and they did one for me. They were really good and replicated the way my hair had been before. My own hair is growing back now, but it's growing back in the back and on top, and a salt and pepper grey on the sides. I actually like it. In a way.

After going through three rounds of chemo treatment, the Professor felt that instead of going for the full six, a switch to radiotherapy would be better for me. They gave me a month off, after which I had radiotherapy every day for three weeks.

It takes a lot out of you, and the staff at the hospital were tremendously helpful. However, they don't put you on a special diet or anything, they don't say: 'Take this or avoid that.' That's why, from the start of my treatment all the way up to now, I have been seeing nutritionists. My nutritionist, Bev de Pons, had lymphoma herself ten years ago, so she has first-hand knowledge of what a patient needs. She is a naturopath and body-energy therapist and uses a treatment where she puts vacuum cups on you that suck on to your skin, which gets your energy going. That really helped me. She gave me advice on my diet, and she introduced me to John Stirling.

John is a biochemist who owned a vitamin company called Biocare. Although he sold that and retired he continues to do research. He also went through cancer: melanoma. He told me what to eat and what I should leave off and prescribed certain vitamins, saying: 'You can't just take any vitamins, because it might affect the chemo. It has to be a certain cocktail of vitamins that work *with* the chemo.'

It helped me keep my energy levels and my immune system up. John had the key to that. He wouldn't accept anything, either, saying: 'I don't need the money, I'm doing it because I want to help.'

John and Bev have been a fantastic help.

With the old radiotherapy, they just blasted the whole general cancer area. It would make you very ill. But with the latest technology, they can focus on the exact area with pinpoint accuracy, which is great. Having radiotherapy every day often burns away your skin. Thanks to all of Bev's and John's nutritional advice and a cream that they gave me, that didn't happen in my case. It got painful, it still is and the after effects can go on for a year or so, but I didn't get any blisters or anything.

The last radiotherapy session was in April 2012. I am writing this a couple of months later, at the start of the summer. I've just had a check-up, including another scan, and they said: 'It looks quite good.'

When I found out I had lymphoma back in December 2011, Coachella was blown out. I spoke to my doctors, saying: 'Look, I've got this European tour coming up. Will I be able to do it?'

They said: 'We don't know. Too early to tell.'

I really tried to get myself together to do that tour. But the promoters wanted me to guarantee that I would be able to do it. If I gave them such a guarantee, I'd get sued if I then couldn't perform. So Ralph said: 'You're not doing that.'

In hindsight, I wouldn't have been able to tour: I wasn't allowed on planes because of the risk of infection and I was too tired some days, other days just too sick. Ozzy and Geezer went out on the road, billed as 'Ozzy and Friends', and sometimes I thought, oh, I could have been out there now! But I had an e-mail off Geezer, saying they weren't on stage until 11 p.m. one night, 11:30 the next. I wouldn't have been able to do that. It would've been much too tiring. I mean, nowadays, by 9:30 p.m. I've had it!

I have to recuperate. John Stirling said: 'You've got to be selfish, because it's your life you're talking about now. You can't just carry on where you left off; you've got to rethink the whole thing. Plan and get yourself in a proper state of mind and get healthy to a point of being able to handle all that. I've got friends who have cancer who've taken a year off altogether, and have done nothing, just to get themselves better.'

But I've been trying to work through it, with the rehearsals and writing. After finding out I had lymphoma, we decided to work from my house in Birmingham. Ozzy and Geezer came over to England and we were writing all through the chemo period. Some days I couldn't do it because I didn't feel well, but they understood, they were great. Ozzy would then probably have a go at a vocal or something. We worked five days a week, wrote quite a few songs, and at the time of me writing this we're still at it. I am eager to start recording. I asked Rick Rubin: 'When are you planning on this being done?'

He said: 'Well, when we have the songs.'

When Ozzy and Geezer get back from the tour, we might just knock a couple of more songs out. We'll go through the stuff we've got, make changes or not, use this or that one or the other, make a decision, and then the next thing will be to start recording. I can't wait. I really have got that urge to get stuff done now, before I can't do it any more.

I didn't tour but I did do two UK shows. The first one was a charity gig at the O2 Academy in Birmingham on 19 May 2012. We did that because we needed to have a play together at a gig, and we needed to do it for me, to see if I could last for two hours.

It was nice to do a hometown gig and give some money to a charity. We did it for Help for Heroes, for people who come back from the war injured, whether it's mental or physical. The only thing that disturbed me was a lot of the tickets were being bought up by scalpers and sold for up to £1,000 per ticket. It would be one thing if they would have given it to charity, but to make money on it like that was sad. And some of the true fans had to pay a lot for tickets, which is a shame.

We also wanted to do a full set to see how long it would be. This was done in preparation for the second show we did, at the Download Festival in Donington on 10 June 2012. There we would only be allowed to play one hour and forty-five minutes and that was it, because they had a curfew. At the O2, we had ended up playing a little under two hours, so Download would be about the same.

The last few times we've been together, we played roughly the same set. Now we wanted to do other songs we hadn't done for a long time.

When we planned to do the O2, I was really concerned about doing a two-hour set. That for me was a big challenge. I was thinking, I've got to deal with it, and I've got to get a bit of rest before I go on. Of course that didn't happen, because before we went on, I was in the dressing room talking to Ralph and Mike Exeter about this and that and the other. But on stage I was fine. The adrenaline kicked in and I felt great even after we came off. It actually perked me up.

I worried about Donington as well. Since I've been ill I usually go to bed about 9:30 p.m., watch the TV for half an hour to an hour, and then go to sleep. And I'm normally awake anything from 5–6 a.m., and I get up at 6:30, 7 a.m. at the latest. But Download was due to finish at 11 p.m. I thought, blimey, I'm normally in bed by then! Pretty sad really.

On the day of the show I tried to stay in bed, to get as much rest as possible. Of course, I couldn't. I was wide-awake real early in the morning, thinking of stuff, and I finally just had to get up. I thought, I've got to leave for the gig early, be there and prepare. But the same thing happened again: people talking. I did start to feel tired before the gig, but I went on and I was all right. And again, when I came offstage, I felt great.

I really enjoyed both gigs. To be able to do them was a great achievement for me. Just being able to be back on stage again, I think we were all emotional. And the crowds were as well. If the audience can give that back to you, it pushes each of you more. The atmosphere was fabulous. And the great thing with us, is that we've known each other for so long. It's not Ozzy and his band, or me and my band, it's all of us and we can rely on each other. So I'd really like to do the tour we didn't do this time as soon as I can.

91

Coming out the other side

The problem with this disease is that it can come back at any time. The surgeon said: 'It's not going to go away. You've got 30% chance that it may, but it could more than likely come back, at any time. But it's manageable. You won't die from this, you are more liable to die from something else.'

So I thought, that's nice, then, I'll probably die from something else that the radiation has caused. Bone disease or something. I have started a new course of treatment now. It's another drip that I'll get every two months for two years, with an antibody that'll keep the lymphoma in check. It sort of coats it and kills the cancer cells, stops it from going anywhere else. You want to be strong about it, but at the same time there's this little doubt in your mind that keeps nagging: What about if this pops back next week? Every day I'm feeling around for fresh lumps. If it comes back it would be the same again: chemo and radiation.

It's very scary and because of it, I look at life differently. I could be here another ten years or just one, I don't know. I get really dismal about it, lying awake at night, thinking: Am I still going to be here this time next year? If I go, what about my daughter, Toni, and Maria? Maybe we should get a smaller house, because the big place we have now would be too much for Maria to manage on her own. Maybe it's time to scale down anyway and try to live more of a peaceful life.

But then I think, Well, I really don't want to let the illness take over. I want to almost try to forget about it and just carry on. I've always fought through any adversity in my life, I can't do it any other way. And with cancer I have no option but to fight. I've got to do what I have to do and try to beat it.

I can go out for walks again now, which I love to do, often with my old pal and collaborator Geoff Nicholls, but I still get tired. I have days when I wake up and I feel as tired as I did before I went to bed, but I do feel a definite improvement.

The music has really helped me, being able to play and write stuff. Musically, my illness certainly inspired some new songs. I think the songs actually got better. More, for lack of a better word, 'doom'. I didn't feel well enough to play and write music on certain days. On the days when I could, studio engineer Mike Exeter would drop in and I came up with lots of ideas. Making music has always been my passion, but now it's even more meaningful to me. I'm definitely not thinking about retiring.

When something terrible happens to you, it brings out the best in people. I've had loads of support from all around the world. It's been great, all the e-mails and texts I received from friends, fellow musicians, fans, plus so many people I didn't know.

Lance Armstrong, who has had cancer himself, sent me a book and some T-shirts, and a letter that said: 'We're here to help in any way, stay positive and live strong ... you're not alone I'm in this with you.'

Really great.

Jon Lord, who suffered from pancreatic cancer, said: 'I learned a lot since having it. If I can be of any help, let me know.' Sadly, I've just heard he lost his final battle.

Brian May has constantly stayed in touch, and came up to visit me at my house. When you are very ill, often you actually don't feel like having even the best of friends visit you. It is too tiring, but you don't want to say that to them. Brian, he really understood. He's been great.

It seems like nearly everybody in the music business sent wonderful messages. I couldn't believe it, it was such a great thing that people would take the time to do that. It really does help to know that people are thinking about you. It just encourages you.

I couldn't have coped with my illness without the support of the people around me.

My GP, Dr Michael Abdou, has been brilliant all the way through. He was always there when I needed him, answering my many questions and giving me advice, choosing the surgeons and generally steering me through these difficult times. Dr Manu Nair operated on my prostate at The Priory Hospital in Edgbaston and got the lymph node out. Professor Donald Milligan at Spire Parkway was in charge of my cancer treatment. Nurses Claire and Sandra gave me the chemotherapy, and after that Dr Zarkar oversaw the radiotherapy at Spire Little Aston Centre. These wonderful people and everybody else that helped me during my treatment have just been brilliant. I'm indebted to them all.

Ozzy and Geezer have just been great. When you have problems they come and back you up. Ozzy of course, if you say: 'I've got lymphoma,' he's the sort of guy who'll go: 'Oh, yeah? So and so died of that, didn't he?'

'Oh, thanks!'

He doesn't even realise it. It's just funny, it's just him. Ozzy is always coming up with some funny line or other. Having a good laugh like that really helps me. He has phoned every day, checking on me. He's been absolutely fantastic, and Geezer as well. I think the three of us have grown closer than ever.

*

Bev Bevan and I go way back of course and still live near each other. He's been round a lot to support me, and he's also recording the audio version of this book at my studio!

I'd like to thank Pat and Dave who've been a real 'golden couple' and look after our house and garden when I'm away working and Maria's with me. They have my two boisterous Rottweilers for company so it's quite a task, knowing things are okay at home is a huge help.

Ralph really stuck by me and took a lot of the strain and pressure away from me and Maria. He really has been the backbone of it all. And also Ernest has been such a great help. I couldn't wish for better managers and, even more important, better friends.

And of course, Maria . . . All the work she's had to do since I've had this, how she's done it, I don't know. I got to a stage where I was almost useless and she basically had to babysit me. We tried a few times to go out for a walk, but I got so tired I couldn't breathe. I sound like an invalid now, but I felt like I was 95 years old. It was difficult to accept, but when I was down she boosted me up. She was waiting on me hand and foot. And she never complained, I've not heard a moan about anything. God, she's been like an angel.

Well . . . she *is* an angel.

92

Reflections

Writing all of this, my story, has obviously given me a lot of time to reflect on my life. It has been a bit like everybody else's I suppose: up and down. Apart from the lymphoma, I've got no real complaints, although it would have been nice to have had less hassles in the past with the business side of things. You've got to have those as well, I suppose. These things are meant to try us. But when I look around the world now and see all the things that are happening to people, I've had a good life in comparison to most everybody out there.

I'm really proud of what we've achieved. Our music has helped inspire a whole new generation of music. You can even say that our music has saved a few lives. Judging by the letters we've had from people writing: 'Without you . . .', people who might have wanted to commit suicide, or do whatever, were it not for the music, there's always somebody you've helped out there. It's very rewarding.

There was a time when all of the Brummie bands felt the city didn't really care much about us so it was great when all of a sudden the people that run Broad Street decided to honour the city's famous residents. So it came to be that in November 2008, while recording 'The Devil You Know', we all took time out so I could receive my star on the city's Walk of Fame. It was bitterly cold, snowing, but even so a great crowd turned up and Mike Olley and his team did a great job, with bands playing and Kerrang Radio hosting the event. It was good to join Ozzy and other famous friends like Jasper Carrott, and recently I got involved in Bev Bevan's induction as well. The latest event in this change of heart from the establishment is the Home of Metal exhibition, specifically honouring all of the heavy-metal bands that came from the West Midlands, including Judas Priest and Led Zeppelin. I never thought that would happen!

And now I don't have to go out to prove anything any more, to anybody. Years ago I was trying to prove to people that I could do this and do that, but nowadays I really enjoy what I do, and only need to prove to myself that I can do things.

Of course I have regrets – a lot of them. But I think without that I wouldn't have learned anything. You can't have it all your own way all the time; you've got to have the bad side of life as well, the bad things that happen to you. But you deal with them.

I have probably upset some people along the way, what with all the marriages and all the things that have happened over the years. It's all part of life. Hopefully, the people I've upset have gone on to better things.

My daughter Toni amazes me. After what she's been through, she's so out front now! Toni lives in Finland. She moved in with her boyfriend, Linde. He's the guitar player in a band called HIM.

All I'm hoping for these days is that I'm still here in a few years. I enjoy where I'm at now, I really do. It's a good place. I've got a good home life and a good family, great friends and support. And I'm fortunate because I'm still able to create and to go out and play music.

At the O2 Academy gig in Birmingham, Ozzy called me the

strongest man he knows. It was very nice of him to say that, but since my illness clearly I am not. However, I have some of the best friends on the planet, and a family I adore.

If you measure the strength of a man by the amount of love he gets, I must be the strongest man ever.

Acknowledgements

TJ Lammers, for the endless amount of listening and patience.

My managers Ernest Chapman and Ralph Baker, for their hard work, friendship, dedication and loyalty.

Ozzy, Geezer and Bill; there wouldn't be a book without you. Through all the ups and downs, we've managed to stay friends, and, hopefully, we'll have many more good times together.

My fans and supporters: thanks so much for being there.

Brian May, Eddie Van Halen and James Hetfield, for the kind words.

The two Mike's, Clement and Exeter, and endless amounts of crew members over the years.

My closest friends (you know who you are).

Love you all!

Tony

Index

Born in the midlands, Tony Iommi is the co-founding member of Black Sabbath, and creator of the sound that came to be known as Heavy Metal, one of the most enduring and important British contributions to popular music.